GhostWest

LITERATURE OF THE AMERICAN WEST
William Kittredge, General Editor

Other Books by Ann Ronald

Zane Grey (Boise, 1975)

Functions of Setting in the Novel (New York, 1980)

The New West of Edward Abbey (Albuquerque, 1982; Reno, 1988, 2000)

Words for the Wild (ed.) (San Francisco, 1987)

Earthtones: A Nevada Album (Reno, 1995)

GhostWest

REFLECTIONS PAST AND PRESENT

Ann Ronald

UNIVERSITY OF OKLAHOMA PRESS • Norman

GhostWest
REFLECTIONS PAST AND PRESENT
is Volume 7 in the Literature of the American West series.

Library of Congress Cataloging-in-Publication Data

Ronald, Ann, 1939–
GhostWest: reflections past and present / Ann Ronald
p. cm. — (Literature of the American West; v. 7)
Includes bibliographical references.
ISBN 978-0-8061-3694-3 (paper)

1. Historic sites—West (U.S.) 2. Haunted places—West (U.S.) 3. West (U.S.)—History, Local. 4. West (U.S.)—Folklore. 5. West (U.S.)—In literature. 6. Natural history—West (U.S.) I. Title. II. Series.

F590.7 R66 2002
978—dc21
         2001046312

The paper in this book meets the guidelines for permanence and durability of the Committee on Production Guidelines for Book Longevity of the Council on Library Resources, Inc. ∞

Copyright © 2002 by the University of Oklahoma Press, Norman, Publishing Division of the University. All rights reserved.
Manufactured in the U.S.A.

To the

L & E Tribe

CONTENTS

	Introduction SHADOWED PLACES	3
1	Montana BATTLE STATIONS	11
2	Kansas BUFFALO GROUNDS	27
3	Texas COWBOY COUNTRY	33
4	Wyoming A RENDEZVOUS	53
5	Colorado SAVAGE BASINS	59
6	Oregon SAND AND SEA	81
7	North Dakota TRAIN TIME	87
8	Nevada BURIED BONES	109
9	California SAND CASTLES	113

CONTENTS

10 Arizona
THE OLD PUEBLO   131

11 Nebraska
CATHERLAND   135

12 New Mexico
LAND OF ENCHANTMENT   153

13 South Dakota
SCULPTURED STONE   159

14 Oklahoma
SHADES OF THE PAST   171

15 Utah
GLEN CANYON RESERVOIR   177

16 Idaho
LAVA LAND   197

17 Washington
ANCIENT FORESTS   203

Sources and Suggestions for
Further Reading   227

GhostWest

INTRODUCTION
SHADOWED PLACES

Resting in the September shade of Truckee River cottonwoods, a weary gathering of men and women sheltered between two ordeals. Behind them, the long trek across a hostile Nevada desert; ahead, a difficult climb over the rocky Sierra crest. Even as the travelers celebrated their successful journey to date, they were planning their next assault, and vowing to reach Sacramento before the winter snows. These '49ers well understood their continuing danger, for the frightening story of the Donner party's grim 1846–47 failure—the isolation, the starvation, the supposed cannibalism—had shadowed them across the plains. Although they didn't think about it at the time, their own ghosts were taking shape, too; were already beginning to shade the trail.

After they left the Truckee Meadows—where Reno suburbs today eradicate their tracks—the pioneers turned northwest through Dog Valley, southwest toward newly named Donner Lake, and finally due west again, approaching steep granite cliffs ahead. In the trees above Cold Stream Canyon, I still can see where they winched their wagons heavily up the creekside. Trees bear the marks of their ropes, rocks remain shiny from the friction of their wheels. If I follow their tracks, I can't help but imagine them.

A gaunt woman pulls at the frayed waist of a sun-stained calico dress, her eyes dark and distant. Two men, one straw-haired and sunburned, the other heavily bearded, wrestle a boulder aside. A boy and a girl, six and eight perhaps, kick at aspen leaves already golden and gray. A baby cries. Three more men push and heave and curse the bony oxen chained to the Conestoga. Higher still, a teen-age girl thrusts back her ragged bonnet while surveying last night's campsite far below—tiny inset Donner Lake, where history reached out with casual indifference. Its deep blue water, sunlit and calm and so very peaceful, belies its gruesome past. "Keep movin', Ann," her mother urges. Behind the ridge line, thick white storm clouds slowly build.

I cannot hike here without picturing a line of ghosts beside me, men and their families struggling toward a promise of gold. Nor can I snowshoe above this high Sierra lake without recalling the horror of those who suffered here. Even though summer cabins and glass-fronted winter retreats now largely line the shores, the foolish Donners and their forgotten companions still haunt this terrain. So, too, other pioneer phantoms—the gaunt woman, her pallid husband, their tired children, and thousands more like them—somehow still are here. I've read about them in books, imagined their terrifying trials. Each year, as the first blizzard of the season descends on the basin, I feel their ghostly presence lowering, too.

The '49ers themselves didn't think much about ghosts, however. For the most part, they believed they headed into a pristine landscape. They saw before them a territory with a future, not a past. And because Manifest Destiny and promise of California lured them forward so quickly, the pioneers wasted little time on introspection. It didn't matter that the American West already had spawned rich geological and indigenous stories. That the settlers were writing themselves into history rarely occurred to them either.

A hundred and fifty years later, I look at the West somewhat differently. Western storytellers and western historians have helped me understand the complex fabric of life in the goldfields, on the range, and even in the kitchen. With books as my maps and the landscape as my guide, I, unlike my pioneer forebears, have become cognizant of ghosts. I especially enjoy following their footsteps. Fascinated by the stretch of continent annexed to the United States in the nineteenth and early-twentieth centuries, I love to read tales of its settlement, listen to its regional differences, heed its cultural climates, hear its nostalgic revelations of what really happened and what came to be exaggerated.

There's something special, I think, about places haunted by history. On grassy hills above the Little Bighorn, I found myself counting the paces between white crosses. In Oregon, I stepped from a beach into a maritime museum to gaze at shipwreck pictures and the broken shells of old boats. I climbed precipitous canyon ledges to Anasazi cliff dwellings and tried to imagine raising children there. I jeeped past abandoned mining camps, even paid ten dollars to tour an empty shaft, twenty to go inside a lifeless mill. Whenever I stand alongside a dam, I always wonder what lies beneath all that water. And wherever I wander, I never tire of hearing stories from the past, or of dreaming about what's missing—massive herds of buffalo, for example, or continuous stands of old-growth forests. What makes historic sites and stories so compelling? That question has never stopped puzzling me.

Born and raised in the West, I've spent my adult life either reading about westerners or exploring new parts of western terrain. Geology, ecology, archaeology, history, literature—all these interests pull me from one place to another. But when I visit such pilgrimage sites as the Willa Cather Pioneer Memorial or Mount Rushmore in South Dakota, I find myself not only looking at the memorabilia, enjoying the scenery, and re-envisioning those who made history there, but also eyeing the other visitors. What are they thinking, and why? What draws them in the first place, and what intangibles do they take away? What is so special about a locale that defines itself in terms of a past that no longer is present?

Inside California's Donner State Park headquarters, display cases show pieces of clothing, cooking pots, letters, a diary, a fragile doll, and other keepsakes. Outside, a larger-than-life statue stands on a pedestal eighteen feet high—the snow depth in the winter of 1846–47. A plaque invites tourists to imagine the plight of the cast-iron family, eternally and optimistically looking west. Tens of thousands of visitors annually do just that—gaze at the statue, stroll a few hundred yards to a one-time cabin site, speculate about a hunger that apparently led human beings to cannibalism, then picnic placidly nearby.

A popular stopping place along a very busy interstate highway, this shrine defines itself in terms of a past that has vanished almost entirely. Other than the few museum artifacts and an archeologist's outline of a shelter, no physical remainder of the Donners exists there any more. In fact, the Donners themselves actually camped two miles away and never directly participated in the distasteful events linked so sensationally to their family name. The rush of traffic and the constant rumble of visitors' voices make it very difficult to reconstruct imaginatively the desolation of the tragic events that occurred beside the lake. Nonetheless, people flock to this notorious scene and pretend to access its legendary past. Somehow, its artifacts and its ambience feed a hunger for a personal connection between history and sense of place. Such passion for historic sites absolutely intrigues me.

The new settlers acknowledged few ghosts but, in truth, ghosts preceded them everywhere—ancestors of the American Indians, the dinosaurs that vanished, the glaciers that gave way to valleys filled with ancient trees. Ghosts pursued the pioneers, too, for the miners and ranchers and shopkeepers and homemakers themselves were giving birth to their own ghosts with every footstep. I myself, in fact, am becoming my own ghost, even as I write this page. An ongoing process, this creation of ghosts, one that has made the West a haunted land as much as one of promise, a land of pasts and futures intertwined.

What follows is a book of ghosts. *GhostWest* travels to places where something once happened, locales where people and events from the past still define and determine the aura of the present. These are sites informed by western history and western lore. Some might be characterized as tourist destination points; others are far more obscure, often deserted and forlorn. Each location reveals something about the way ghosts from the past overlay a twentieth- or twenty-first-century sense of place. Each site, in effect, is haunted. These particular settings

INTRODUCTION

and their phantoms answer some historic questions about why ambience and artifacts are so inherently appealing.

I chose these special places for reasons difficult to pin down precisely. Because I wanted to illustrate the variousness of western scenery and stories, I decided to isolate a different locale in every state west of the Missouri River. But my individual choices are idiosyncratic. Any single focus might be different—Denver instead of Tucson, Lake Mead instead of Lake Powell, John Steinbeck instead of Willa Cather, mammoth bones instead of desert aborigines. Taken all together, however, the chapters represent my personal sense of the breadth and depth of what comprises the American West, present and past, mythic and modern. Thematically, temperamentally, these sites seemed to me especially characteristic.

I discovered the title for this book in my imagination. No dictionary combines *GhostWest* into a single word, so I borrowed a conception from those indigenous peoples my imagined pioneers ignored. Although my '49ers traveled through land that had been inhabited by the Paiute people for thousands of years, they would have been rather indifferent to the tribe. Aside from an occasional brief encounter—a possible trade, perhaps an uneasy moment or two—most wagon trains would have skirted the native presence in Nevada. Later, however, as ranchers settled in the valleys and foothills just east of the Sierra, they found the Paiute tribe useful to help run cattle, raise alfalfa and hay, and perform domestic chores. One such spread was the Wilson ranch in fertile Mason Valley, where an ordinary Paiute field hand gave new energy and credence to the Ghost Dance, an aboriginal ceremony that had been practiced quietly for nearly a quarter of a century.

On January 1, 1889, Wovoka was chopping wood on the flank of Mount Grant when an eclipse of the sun occurred. A man given to cataleptic fits and recovering, that winter, from scarlet fever, he apparently went into a trance of some sort. When revived, he said that he had "gone up to heaven when the sun died." Wovoka's vision, widely rumored and variously reported, coincided with an impressive natural phenomenon, a total solar eclipse. At the same time it pulled together a skein of native American myths, conjectures, and aspirations. Not only did his out-of-body experience remind everyone of the importance of ghosts and ancestors in tribal memory, but the ensuing Ghost Dance religion gave promise of a better world.

Wovoka articulated a Utopian future where all dead Indians from the past would return to earth and where large herds of game animals would be restored. Whites would disappear. The old Native American way of life would prosper. In fact, the new way of life would be better than the old, for tribal distinctions would be erased and a kind of pan-Indian identity would result. This resuscitated Ghost Dance religion answered many prayers. Combining pacifist aspects of Christianity — Wovoka had been well indoctrinated in boarding school — with aboriginal wishes to be rid of white interference, projecting the reunification of ancestors with those Indians still living, and hypothesizing a reconstituted landscape of plenty, it was the right liturgical message at the right time. American Indians from all over the West flocked to Mason Valley to greet the self-proclaimed new messiah and to participate in the appropriate rituals. Wovoka didn't disappoint his visitors.

A tall, muscular Paiute sits cross-legged on the ground. Balanced on his knee, a five-gallon Stetson; hanging from his shirtsleeves and collar, eagle and magpie and crow feathers. On the blanket before him, more magical feathers and the locally made red ochre paint so prized by Indian visitors from the Great Plains. An expression of melancholy and grief settles across Wovoka's face. The dancers, faces and bodies painted with bars and dots of red and white mineral pigment, begin. For five days and four nights, their rhythmic circles move slowly right to left. Shuffling clockwise around Wovoka at their center, swaying, chanting as they go. The prophet stiffens, his body rigid and his expression fixed. The dancers never waver, their steps never falter, their eyes never close. Above the cataleptic figure, a gray-brown hawk riding the thermals of the thin blue sky. Wovoka sits motionless. The plaintive chant continues. Nuva' ka ro'rani'! The snow lies there — ro'rani'! The drums, the dancers, never pause.

Each Ghost Dance culminated in a shaking of blankets and a dip in the nearby Walker River. The finale, while cleansing the participants of evil and sickness and disease, also highlighted Wovoka's sacred Utopian vision. Not only the Paiute people, but the Shoshone, Cheyenne, Arapaho, Kiowa and Sioux were enchanted by the ceremony and convinced by its message of deliverance. Leaving gifts for the messiah piled high alongside his blanket, and taking sacred feathers and the special red paint away with them, the visitors then returned to their own tribes to share the ecstasy and fervor. As the Ghost Dance religion flourished, however, so the apostles misinterpreted its potency. Less than two years after Wovoka's first trance, the massacre at Wounded Knee effectively put an end to Ghost Dance optimism. Just as ghost shirts failed to protect those trusting Sioux from the white man's gunfire, so the Ghost Dance could no longer be trusted.

Although isolated ceremonies continued to be held in distant Nevada, the essential enthusiasm had dissipated. GhostWest—my term, not Wovoka's—had replaced the Ghost Dance. A "Song of the Ancient People" mourns such passing:

> For the fires grow cold and the dances fail,
> And the songs in their echoes die;
> And what have we left but the graves beneath,
> And, above, the waiting sky?

The West bears so many ghosts now, it's difficult to isolate them. Not only the tribal ancestors of the Paiute and other indigenous peoples but the haunting phantoms of my ancestors, too. Mountain men and miners, ranchers and farmers, cowboys and cavalrymen, schoolmarms and barflies, mothers and children, uncles and aunts—their spirits inform the western landscape; their memoirs and their stories inscribe for me an historic sense of place.

They're not alone, either. Who is to say that grizzlies don't haunt Donner Lake alongside the ghosts of those ill-fated pioneers? Or that the shadows of wolves don't lope beside the neighborhood coyotes? In a previous book, I described some extensive mineral explorations in the new West, and wondered if the landscape itself was becoming its own ghost. What, indeed, happens to the spirit of a mountain that becomes an open copper pit, is denuded by a clearcut, or carved into a sculpture? A Glen Canyon that becomes a Lake Powell? Such lost landscapes, I believe, are part of *GhostWest*, too.

The following pages explore such twilight terrain. One dusky October evening, for example, I stopped by the edge of the meadow where Tamsen and George Donner actually camped in 1846. Suffused in alpenglow, the grasses were orange and umber, the trees a green counterpoint to the warm fall colors. No snow, no ice, no sign of premature winter. No other human, either. A lone coyote loped silently from west to east, paused for a moment to sniff the wind, then continued on her way to somewhere. *I thought I saw her shadow, ruffling the rye-grass meadow. I thought I saw a second silent shape, just ahead. I thought I heard a Ghost Dance drum, though the sound was probably only the wind brushing the pines. I thought I heard a rhythmic chant, soft and slow and sad.*

A *GhostWest* landscape, this quiet lonely place. Enchanted, haunted, the scene compelled me to write the following pages, to create my own panorama of shadowed places.

MONTANA
BATTLE STATIONS

"One must have a mind of winter," Wallace Stevens wrote, "To regard the frost and the boughs / Of the pine-trees crusted with snow." I must have a mind of autumn. When I think about *GhostWest* images, I regard golden aspen, a harvest moon, and wheat fields blanched by the sun. Ghosts I regard as autumnal, the last vestiges of a season's close. This intuition first came to me one September, when I experienced the oppressive melancholy of the Little Bighorn. There, in the long shadows of an afternoon, I apprehended the powerful connection between a battlefield and its stories crusted with memories. That day, the spirits were haunting.

I had gone to Montana to participate in a series of gatherings hosted by the Western Heritage Center in Billings. For a week of almost perfect Indian summer weather, Mary Clearman Blew and I crisscrossed eastern Montana, talked about our writing, and watched panoramic Big Sky scenery unfold. This prelude to winter was unconditionally beautiful. For a few free hours before an evening session at Crow Agency, we took time to explore the infamous Custer battlefield, renamed Little Bighorn Battlefield National Monument in 1991.

Our first stop was Custer Hill, where the general, his brother, and more than forty of their men met their deaths, and where an imposing marble obelisk marks the location. The area was nearly deserted. The sun, slanting through the iron fence, lined shades of gray up and down the column and across the smaller white marble stones. George Armstrong Custer's own marker, painted black to stand out from the others, and dozens more all sprawled down the hillside. Dried grasses ruffled in a fading breeze. Only a handful of tourists wandered respectfully nearby, gaping at the spots where individual cavalrymen had fallen. Almost no one spoke.

Leaving the climactically fatal scene, we drove along the ridge line southeast to the Reno-Benteen battle site, where the troops who might have helped Custer were themselves trapped by Indian fire. The far parking lot was empty. No one else in our car seemed very interested in the walking tour, so I spent an hour by myself, strolling from one interpretive spot to another, learning about the difficulties faced by the rest of the Seventh Cavalry. Normally I'm impatient with guided walks, but the atmosphere of a dying season perfectly shadowed the entrenchment path.

A Park Service trail guide opens with a soldier's recollection that "everybody now lay down and spread himself out as thin as possible. After lying there a few minutes I was horrified to find myself wondering if a small sagebrush, about as thick as my finger, would turn a bullet." I wondered the same thing. The booklet describes shallow trenches dug by some of the men. "Only three or four shovels were available, and much of the digging was done with knives, hatchets and mess gear. Dead horses and mules were dragged up and laid on the parapet as added cover." Interpretive signs pointed to several niches hardly big enough to notice. Some "trenches" were L-shaped; others, more circular and womblike. National Monument regulations forbid stepping off the walkway or lying down in a trench, so I could only imagine myself curled into the grass—listening to the spin of bullets and arrows, smelling the putrid odor of dead flesh, crowding my face into the dirt—heedless of anything but the sheer terror of the moment.

"The sun beat down on us and we became so thirsty that it was almost impossible to swallow." Under sharpshooter protection, fifteen volunteers finally braved a way down to the river, filled kettles and canteens, then dashed back to the wounded. I eyed the distance between the site of the makeshift field hospital and the gently flowing water, measured the lack of cover, calculated the necessary bravery. Under those circumstances, how fast could a man run?

> U. S. Soldier
> 7th Cav.
> Killed
> June 25 or 26, 1876

Although separate markers indicate where certain corpses were found, they offer few details. Occasionally a specific soldier might be identified—Pvt. Thomas E. Meador or Pvt. Julian D. Jones, for example—but most of them remain anonymous, some marked without even an exact date of death.

Since I couldn't quite imagine myself as a cavalryman, flattening my body into the prairie, or cowering behind my horse's carcass, or sprinting recklessly toward the river, I tried to picture how a woman might relate to the scene. A mother, a sister, a sweetheart, or wife would read the headlines—Custer's Cavalry Doomed—then wait for further news. If her loved one rode with Custer, that news would be grim. If her loved one had paused instead with Major Reno or Captain Benteen, he might have been spared, though certainly traumatized, even badly wounded. Meanwhile, the woman would be isolated, uncertain, fearful, wholly unable to conceive of her son or lover interred as:

> U S. Soldier
> 7th Cav.
> Fell Here
> June 25, 1876

Such markers, which now scatter more than four miles of landscape, knell a visual dirge of death.

I personally dislike war, and I am not in the habit of visiting battle sites. What I knew of Custer was less than impressive, and I had little sympathy with cavalry tactics during the Indian wars. Given my disinterest, this particular place should have affected me very little. Yet it chilled me both emotionally and intellectually. Perhaps the sound of the wind swaying the sun-bleached grasses, perhaps the long shadows of a September afternoon, perhaps the secret gullies and pockets of the rolling terrain, perhaps the random marble markers with their casual anonymity—whatever the causes, an entire cavalry of ghosts cantered through the Little Bighorn monument that day.

And the place has continued to haunt my imagination. To describe the scene of Custer's Last Stand, however, I needed more than romantic autumnal memories. I wanted to witness the landscape as the cavalrymen must have seen it that early summer day in 1876, in June, the hillsides not brown and dying but redolent with green grasses and flowers. I wondered if a place teeming with the energy and life of spring would still seem haunted by the ghosts of battle. Would morning, in fact, be less melancholy than afternoon? I also suspected that tourists crowding over Custer Hill might change my response, that incessant conversations about military strategy and the ensuing political machinations would shadow my initial, more visceral and vernal, reactions.

So one year I joined the June crowds, and entered a landscape more like a garden than a mausoleum. I tried to persuade myself that the prairie flowers were funereal, that the massive pink thistles, the white yarrow, the yellow mustard were appropriate remembrances for empty graves. Maybe the cluster of rosebuds growing against the wrought-iron fence looked as if a mourner had strategically placed wild rose bushes there? Maybe the sprays of color really belonged in a cemetery? My own argument was unconvincing. Because the monument has been closed to grazing for nearly a century, its wildflowers and native grasses grow more abundantly than in any of the surrounding coulees and draws. The springtime prairie feels more cheerful than depressing, more hopeful than hopeless.

Other writers have noted the resemblance between cavalry swords and the yellow yucca that everywhere thrusts above the grasses in late June. I thought the analogy ironic—the Seventh Cavalry didn't carry sabers—and disquieting, especially when I retraced my steps on the Reno-Benteen entrenchment walking tour. There the wildflowers were even more dominant, with orange globe mallow, yellow blazing star, and a five-petal blue blossom I'd never seen before. Next to the yellow yucca, more spiny-soft wild roses grew, as if a woman's shawl were gently wrapped around a scabbard. Strolling the paved pathway, I listened to the meadowlarks and I confess I opened my flower book more often than my battlefield brochure.

Artifacts from the 1876 encounter—bullets and bullet casings, arrowheads, buttons, scraps of leather, even undiscovered corpses— still lie buried throughout the monument. Archaeologists some day hope to examine other unexcavated areas, so most of the preserve's hillsides and coulees remain off-limits to the casual walker. Below Custer Hill, however, a short trail opens for summer visitors. The route down Deep Ravine, where Sgt. Daniel Kanipe later said he "counted 28 bodies in the gulch," literally folds into the prairie, as if the walker were entering a grassy tomb. From a distance this landscape may look deceivingly rounded, but closer inspection reveals pockets and depressions and undulations that might hide a cavalryman or an Indian warrior or a corpse.

"In 1983 visitors discovered a human skull fragment at markers 33 and 34. Formal archeological investigation in 1984 recovered a .50/70 bullet, bullet fragment, lead shot, rubber and mother of pearl buttons, cervical vertebra, wrist and hand bones and a coccyx," reports the trail guide. More white markers bury themselves among the grasses of Deep Ravine. Historians now reconstruct the battle's progress in a way that makes this particular cut the scene of some of the fiercest fighting. Once again I tried to imagine myself huddled in a curve of earth, with the clash of war all around me. Swallowed here in Deep Ravine, a soldier would have been unable to see the panorama playing on the hillsides above him. He would have fallen among the late spring flowers without knowing Custer's fate. And even today, he might still lie beneath the roots! As the monument brochure tantalizes: "a Rapid

Geophysical Surveyor Investigation in this area indicated magnetic and metal detector anomalies scattered throughout the ravine, with target density higher in the upper two-thirds of the area. Future investigations may someday reveal the missing 28 soldiers."

No one knows exactly what happened to those men. One of the romantic—or grisly—qualities about the Battle of the Little Bighorn is the fact that no cavalryman survived the Last Stand. Only the bodies could attest to the soldiers' fates, and even their corpses provided sometimes misleading evidence. A certain amount of corporeal degradation took place, first from Indian clubs and knives and then from the excessive heat. By the time a burial party could attend to the remains, decomposition was so advanced that the ensuing burials were made as hastily as possible. Expedience superseded forensic science, and a certain amount of tact kept the observers from describing too many of the details.

One man wrote to his wife, "It was a horrible sight and one never to be forgotten." Trooper William C. Slaper, from M Company, remembered the repellent chore fifty years later:

> Here, with a few spades, we were set to work to bury them. We had but a few implements of any sort. All that we could possibly do was to remove a little dirt in a low place, roll in a body and cover it with dirt. Some, I can well remember, were not altogether covered, but the stench was so strong from the disfigured, decaying bodies, which had been exposed to an extremely hot sun for two days, that it was impossible to make as decent a job of interring them as we could otherwise have done. There were also great numbers of dead horses lying about, which added to the horror of the situation.

Slaper notes, too, that most of the bodies had been stripped naked and robbed of their valuables. He says nothing, however, about the bodies' locations, and little about the battle's sequence of events.

Despite the initial paucity of information, and despite the acquisitiveness of early souvenir hunters, twentieth-century historians finally have managed to detail most of the battle tactics. No soldiers with Custer survived, but Indian participants could provide first-hand accounts of what happened. Chief Two Moons reported, "The whole valley was filled with smoke and the bullets flew all about us, making a noise like bees. We could hardly hear anything for the noise of the guns. When the guns were firing, the Sioux and Cheyennes and soldiers, one falling one way and one falling another, together with the noise of the guns, I shall never forget." Thomas B. Marquis interviewed Kate Bighead exactly fifty years after the event. She remembered a startling sequence of events:

> On all sides of this band of soldiers the Indians jumped up. There were hundreds of warriors, many more than one might have thought could hide themselves in those small gullies. I think there were about twenty Indians to every soldier there. The soldier horses got scared, and all of them broke loose and ran away toward the river. Then I saw a soldier shoot himself by holding his revolver at his head. Then another one did the same, and another. Right away, all of them began shooting themselves or shooting each other. I saw several different pairs of them fire their guns at the same time and shoot one another in the breast. For a short time the Indians just stayed where they were and looked. Then they rushed forward. But not many of them got to strike coup blows on living enemies. Before they could get to them, all of the white men were dead.

Avid Custerphiles thoroughly discount her recollection, but it may well be accurate.

Archaeological findings have been the most helpful in pinpointing the actual course of the fighting. When fires swept the monument hillsides in 1983 and again in 1991, previously undiscovered artifacts were revealed. Now computers can examine the field patterns of bullets found and trace the firearms used, following the progress of a single rifle or revolver up and down the coulees. Osteobiographies have been developed, too. The body found at sites 33 and 34 in Deep Ravine, for example, turned out to be that of Mitch Boyer, the trail guide explains. "Analysis indicate[d] a male individual 35–45 years of age, who suffered massive blunt trauma to the head, and was of mixed racial parentage, part white and part Indian, and a pipe smoker (commensurate with teeth wear)." Boyer, a pipe smoker whose father was French Canadian and mother Santee Sioux, fit the description exactly. Further computer modelings have helped assess Custer's decisions and movements during the battle. Whereas earlier tacticians assumed the general stayed on the ridges, scholars now understand his troops dropped toward the river two or three times before withdrawing to Last Stand Hill.

A visitor to the monument learns the tactics in excruciating detail. Just as the countless Custer battle books endlessly reexamine every option, so the rangers, the brochures, and the marked sites themselves focus on who was where and why. At the Reno-Benteen site, for example, I could walk from one fixed post to another, and spot Major Reno's exact movements—at ten- and thirty-minute intervals—on June 25, 1876. The overall dynamics, I must admit, became almost mechanical to me, like those of a computer game both violent and oddly impersonal. As described, the precise tactics were much less terrifying than the shallow simulated foxholes and the bemused question about a sagebrush's ability to turn a bullet.

Back on the self-guiding tour road, I passed Calhoun Hill and the Keogh Sector, where Companies I, C, and L met their demise, then continued on to Last Stand Hill, where the rest of the soldiers died. How many cavalrymen rode down to the Medicine Tail Ford and back? How many scouted down to the river beyond the present-day national cemetery? How many penetrated Deep Ravine? Altogether, two hundred and sixty-three soldiers died on these hillsides. Where, exactly, were they? And why? Some historians have spent their careers calculating the answers. Some regard such shrines as this as sacred space.

When I look at a landscape, I tend to see it pictorially. My father, an amateur photographer whose heroes were Ansel Adams and Eliot Porter, taught me to see scenery framed. So did college art classes. But a visitor simply cannot experience the Little Bighorn terrain that way. This is a narrative landscape, a place where the story dictates the vision of the land.

The empty rolling hills fill imaginatively with Indians and soldiers, a ghostly diorama in motion. The white marble markers blur together as fallen enemies, blood and bones. Tactics replace texture; stories replace style. Even the shapes and colors of the land fade into the background, play a secondary role to the events that made this place so famous. History overpowers the terrain. If a viewer tries to look at narrative landscape in a pictorial way, the result is off kilter, the flowers a funereal counterpoint to the disaster, the call of the meadowlark an inappropriate tune. A narrative landscape forces the viewer to heed the stories more than the scenery, to listen more than look. Visitors come to this monument to relive the narrative, not to aesthetically examine the spacious rolling hills. They come to a theater-in-the-round rather than a gallery of pictures.

Thirty-five miles to the southeast of the Little Bighorn battle site, preservationists, with the help of coal tax dollars and rancher Slim Kobold, have saved another piece of prairie, another battlefield, another set of stories. Some would say the narratives of General Crook on the Rosebud are less compelling than those of General Custer on the Little Bighorn. Only nine soldiers were killed, after all, and twenty-three wounded. But the battle assumes prominence as a prelude to the Custer disaster a week later.

On June 17, 1876, General Crook's forces paused for breakfast at a picturesque spot. "Rosebud stream, indicated by the thick growth of wild roses or sweet brier, from which its name is derived, flowed sluggishly" through the valley, reported John Finerty, an editorial staff member of the *Chicago Times* who accompanied the Second and Third Cavalry. "The hills seemed to rise on every side, and we were within easy musket shot of those most remote." That morning, Indians charged the inattentive soldiers, who quickly took defensive positions and fought back. Six hours later the Indians retreated, leaving a frustrated army behind. Suddenly low on supplies, burdened with wounded men who needed medical care, cognizant that any hope of surprising the Indians had ended, and unsure of the exact whereabouts of their enemies, General Crook chose to withdraw. His decision proved fatal for Custer, though strategists quarrel when interpreting his options.

The site of Crook's encounter with the Lakota and the Cheyenne, while not nearly as well known to tourists as the Little Bighorn, interests scholars for important historical reasons. It was the second engagement of the Great Sioux War, the first Indian success of any magnitude. The state of Montana acquired the Rosebud property—a stretch of land larger than the Little Bighorn Battlefield National Monument —in 1981. A park was established to commemorate the place; an interpretive brochure establishes the narrative with precisely marked increments. So a guided visit to the Rosebud resembles a tour of the Little Bighorn. Post #4: Where Chief Comes-In-Sight Was Rescued. Post #5: Van Vliet's Hill. Post #6: Crook's Hill. Post #7: Conical Hill. Post #8: Packers Rocks. Post # 9: Packers Ridge. Post #10: Andrews' Point. Post #11: Foster's Ridge. Post #12: Royall's First Position. Post #13: Royall's Second Position. Post #14: Royall's Third Position. Post #14: The Wounding of Captain Guy V. Henry. Post #15: Limpy's Rescue.

As I sit at my desk and reread the brochure, however, my memory reconstitutes the pictorial rather than the narrative. I re-envision the first baby badgers I've ever seen in my life, and the lone antelope that followed me across the hillside, and the slender brown snake that blocked my way. I'm surrounded by purple lupine and sawsepal penstemon, chokecherries in blossom, pink rosebuds clotting the creek. I remember the hot damp feral smell when I curled down in the grass and pretended I couldn't be seen. I hear the silence of a park without visitors that day. I can frame my own personal satisfaction at the Rosebud, my thorough enjoyment of a pleasurable day, but my imagination refuses to reconstruct the battle tactics. Even when I try, the visual landscape gets in the way, and spins new stories of its own.

On Crook's Hill I watched a kestrel diving and swooping in the wind. The smallest of American falcons, a kestrel hovers over its prey before plunging. This one, hanging in midair, was hunting for its midmorning meal, an Indian warrior waiting for the kill. Crook's men, unwary field mice or gophers perhaps. The Lakota, the Cheyenne, the feathered falcon taunting. The inevitable clash.

Not enough soldiers died at the Rosebud, however, not enough to capture the public's imagination. So the battle remains an historical footnote, deserving a book or two but not hundreds, attracting occasional visitors but not four hundred thousand each year. I had the place to myself, sharing it only with raptors, badgers, snakes, and my pictorial reveries.

The American public, with its Titanic insatiability for tragedy writ large, prefers tragedies of epic proportions. Of all the travelers who pioneered the California Trail, we remember the Donners. Of all the Indian skirmishes and battles, we're most enamored with Custer's Last Stand. In the case of George Armstrong Custer, several reasons account for the enduring legend. A reckless man, the "Boy General" boasted uncommon bravery—and good fortune—during the Civil War. That he was probably foolhardy at the Little Bighorn mattered little to his idolaters. His wife deified him, and devoted the rest of her life to illuminating his reputation. She chose a gifted biographer, Frederick Whittaker, who rushed the story of Custer's life into print. She herself wrote three memoirs about her hero's feats, embroidering his accomplishments and downplaying his foibles. Even the timing of the notorious battle proved fortuitous. Word reached the newspapers just as the nation was celebrating its hundredth anniversary, and the debacle instantly became a symbolic reminder of the country's precarious youth. Scholar Richard S. Slotkin comments ironically: "The events of the Sioux War of 1876, culminating in Custer's Last Stand, were treated as a paradigm of the disaster that might overtake 'civilization as we know it' if moral authority and political power were conceded to a class of people whose natural gifts were like those of 'redskin savages.'"

Thanks to Custerphiles, the general and his men became an emblem for the mythic struggle of good and evil in the Old West. Revisionist history has corrected this black and white interpretation of events, but many visitors to the monument still honor the fable of the soldiers' heroics, still embrace the romanticized legend. When I chatted with Kitty Belle Deernose, museum curator at the Little Bighorn Battlefield National Monument, she was gathering materials for a pop culture Custer exhibit. "The general public hasn't been here at the battlefield," she explained. "Most of their perceptions are based on movies, the media, comic books and westerns." She showed me German, Italian, Spanish, and French versions of the Custer myth, a poster from the 1912 film *Custer's Last Fight*, a Custer Battlefield bumper sticker, a T-shirt with the words "Custer Got Siouxed." She even handed me a nineteenth-century lithograph, a copy of which decorates the paperback cover of Thomas Berger's 1964 *Little Big Man*, with the figure of movie star Dustin Hoffman substituted for one of the original cavalrymen. She was planning an exhibit that would reveal the paucity of naïve interpretations and help explain reasons for the creation of the myth.

From Kitty, I also learned more of the cultural complexities of the centennial Sioux wars. What I had read in books suddenly made more sense. According to the Crow people, the Sioux were interlopers, invaders who had pushed onto land that didn't belong to them. The Crow had sided with the cavalry, served as scouts, helped round up the hated Lakota and Cheyenne. Stories from the diverse tribes were tangled, much less clear-cut than western movies would have audiences believe, much more intricate than I had understood when I first visited this battle site. Perversely, I had always despised Custer and cheered the Sioux. Now I wasn't sure. Who were the good guys? And the bad?

I asked Kitty what she thought of the Rosebud site, how its relative isolation compared with the present-day Little Bighorn attraction, and whether or not the Crow were interested in its story. "Never been there," admitted the woman who had grown up just a few miles away. "There's nothing there," she shrugged. She did tell me about another battle memorial, though. In nearby Lame Deer, a wooden sign spells out the following:

> SQUAWHILL
> DIRECTLY NORTH TWO CHEYENNES
> HEAD CHIEF & YOUNG MULE RODE
> DOWN & FOUGHT 1ST U. S. CAVALRY
> SEPT. 13, 1890. THEY CHOSE TO DIE
> FIGHTING FOR THE DEATH OF
> HUGH BOYLE

The word *squaw* is disfigured; the word *death* a euphemism for a word that's clearly been excised—*murder*. Thousands of tourists must drive past every summer, but they don't stop at the marker buried in thigh-deep grasses and surrounded by old Styrofoam boxes and plastic Coke bottles. I don't even know the story.

But the obscure marker is a telling counterpoint to its neighboring battle sites—the Titanic Little Bighorn and the sequestered Rosebud. The one, larger than life but overcrowded and overhyped; the other, less pretentious but more viscerally appealing in its isolation. The third, simply forgotten by almost everyone. Wallace Stevens ends his poem about "a mind of winter" with a phrase that reminds me of all these embattled scenes—his listener "beholds / Nothing that is not there and the nothing that is." Those ambiguous lines have always puzzled me. How can someone simultaneously behold both an absence and a presence? But after experiencing the milieu of big battlefields enshrined and lesser sites deserted and forlorn, I think I understand at least one level of Stevens's meaning. All the historic participants have long since vanished but, in our imaginations, they nonetheless will always be fighting in these rolling hills. Their stories repeat themselves over and over again, dictating the "nothing that is" and that will always be there. Even the two Cheyenne, Head Chief and Young Mule, obscurely righting the death of the long-forgotten Hugh Boyle.

Even tangential events will somehow always be there, too. While the Little Bighorn tragedy was developing, General Crook's forces were recovering from their Rosebud encounter by relaxing near "a delightfully romantic spot, nothing more beautiful, at least at that season, this side of Paradise." Finerty later realizes that at the very moment of the battle at the Little Bighorn, "we reveled in the crystal water, and slept beneath the grateful shade of the trees that fringed the emerald banks of those beautiful tributaries of Tongue River, that winding Daughter of the Snows." John Bourke, General Crook's aide-de-camp, found the Tongue just as picturesque. "Rapids and deep pools of icy-cold water, shaded by a heavy growth of willow trees, give home to a multitude of mountain trout which have been heavily assessed all day to give the officers and men a delicate meal," he wrote on the evening before the Bighorn confrontation. "Bright and clear. Day rather warm. Camp is about equally divided in occupation: one fourth reading, one fishing, one hunting and one on picket," he noted four days later, innocently unaware of what had just occurred fifty miles away.

Traveling toward Crow Agency for the 1995 gathering, our touring discussion group had paused along the Tongue, too. At the time I imagined camping there, even though I hadn't yet read either Finerty's or Bourke's descriptions. We stopped farther downstream than where the cavalry had halted, but I still found the locale idyllic. Part of a ranch, the pastoral spot is off-limits to overnighters. That fall, the river gurgled past rocks and riffles, and through autumnal fields of brown. At the time, I actually thought about a group of Cheyenne or Sioux taking September refuge there.

The setting felt less spectral when I revisited in early summer, but it still was lovely. I wandered through June grasses as high as fence posts, leaned over to admire thick heavy clusters of wild roses. Although occasional pickups sped noisily by on the dirt road, I heard an enormity of bird song, mostly barn swallows flitting in cloudy masses. Close to the river, I found what is called "Creeping Jenny," a field bindwood from Europe that has invaded the high plains. With white flowers tinged in lavender and shapely arrow leaves, it's perniciously attractive. But the tightly woven vine uses the native grasses as climbing stakes, and the weed effectively is throttling the native species, just as the soldiers finally conquered the Indians who tried to defend their land, their families, their way of life.

At the Little Bighorn and in the surrounding landscape, I meant to recapture the autumnal aura of the past, and to puzzle over the ways in which Titanic tragedies remain with us for so many years. Instead, I found an eastern Montana June to be green—almost lush—filled with flowers, young wildlife, and immense vitality. Encountering a masked mother badger with two kits was much more exhilarating than figuring out why Captain Royall merited three separate stations at the Rosebud memorial. Nothing, not even a regimental cemetery, could make me depressed. Watching hawks soar, smelling the roses—I just couldn't reincarnate those storied spirits from the past when the present was so deliciously seductive.

MONTANA: BATTLE STATIONS 25

Kitty Belle Deernose shared with me a translation of an 1825 incantation by Arapooish, a Crow chief. "The Crow country is a good country," Arapooish begins. "The Great Spirit has put it exactly in the right place; when you are in it you fare well; whenever you go out of it, whichever way you travel, you fare worse." The United States Seventh Cavalry found the opposite to be true, but I think Arapooish was correct. "The Crow country is exactly in the right place. It has snowy mountains and sunny plains; all kinds of climates, and good things for every season." In spring, the fertile land bursts green with life; in autumn, it glows golden with chiaroscuro and change; in winter, it bides its time. Away from the legendary battlegrounds, June is spirited; September, serene. And whether interpreting this particular landscape as pictorial or narrative, I have to agree with Arapooish. "There is no country like the Crow country." On the other hand, that some would honor it solely in the name of Custer's failure suggests the limitations, I think, of a strictly storied point of view.

KANSAS BUFFALO GROUNDS

Next day, oh, there they were, thousands and thousands of them! Far as the eye could reach the prairie was literally covered, and not only covered but crowded with them. . . . a vast expanse of moving, plunging, rolling, rushing life—a literal sea of dark forms, with still pools, sweeping currents, and heaving billows, and all the grades of movement from calm repose to wild agitation. The air was filled with dust and bellowings, the prairie was alive with animation.

Across the highway from old Fort Hays, a tiny herd of eight buffalo and one calf pace restlessly along a fence. Their pasture, hardly more than an acre or two, shows the wear and tear of overgrazing. The month-old calf seems to enjoy showing off for tourists, though. He gallops left and right, circles his mother, pauses when she makes a low guttural sound, grunts back with a higher pitch, then returns to her side. Meanwhile, she and the rest of the herd pull at the meager grass, their tails flicking with indifference. A sign on the fence reads:

DANGER BUFFALO
PRIVATE GAME REFUGE
NO TRESPASSING

Not far from here, "Buffalo Bill" Cody earned his nickname by felling eleven buffalo with twelve shots while a group of army officers watched with astonishment. When Billy Comstock, another buffalo hunter, challenged Cody's right to that nickname, the two men held a contest.

> Referees were appointed, the field was chosen, and the big show was on. Buffalo were plentiful near the railroad. On the first run Cody out-scored Comstock quite easily. Then they had lunch and made two shorter runs in the afternoon. For the third run Cody . . . rode out bareback. To wind up his day he chased a huge buffalo bull toward the crowd of spectators and, the women screaming in excitement and alarm, dropped it with one shot almost at their feet. Then the kills were totaled and Cody was declared the winner, with sixty-nine to Comstock's fifty-seven. The Kansas and Pacific had the 126 buffalo heads mounted and distributed them throughout the country for their advertising value.

Across the highway from the tiny captive herd, where historic Fort Hays now neighbors the trim fairways of a local golf course, a life-sized buffalo sculpture—called "Monarch of the Plains"—stands on a pedestal. Below the tail of the statue, a plaque explains that "Herds of 60 million buffalo once roamed the prairie until reduced to 300 and near extinction. They were the basis of Indian economy; food for the emigrant, railroad worker and soldier." Etched panels appear on the remaining sides of the statue—one shows a small herd, the railroad, and a rabbit; another, a single buffalo and a lone Indian hunter; the third, a buffalo and her calf. Just as the sign's rhetoric implies no particular responsibility for the buffaloes' attrition, so these pictures tell only a part of the story, too.

> Five miles west of Fort Ellsworth we were fairly in the buffalo range, and for miles in every direction as far as the eye could see, the hills were black with these shaggy monsters of the prairie, grazing quietly upon the richest pasture in the world.

Cultivated farmland spreads out between Hays and Dodge City. The landscape looks as if someone had crumpled a newspaper and then tried to flatten it again. The back roads follow carefully plotted lines, like rectangular columns across the earth. Cattle, grazing haphazardly or else placidly chewing their cuds, alternate squares with corduroy fields of corn. The fences are well-kept, taut, and functional.

... as far as the eye could reach the broad valley was literally blackened by a compact mass of buffalo, and not only this; the massive bluffs on both sides were covered by thousands and thousands that were still pouring down into the already crowded valley, and as far as the eye could reach, the living dark masses covered the ground completely as a carpet covers the floor. It looked as if not another buffalo could have found room to squeeze in, and if a man might have walked across the valley on their huddled backs as on a floor.

Due south of Dodge City, on the Big Basin Prairie Preserve, a massive bull rests atop a buffalo wallow. He rolls periodically in the dry dirt, sending a cloud of dust into the wind. His coat is summer-sleek, his chest thickly ruffed, his head hung with a heavy beard. He rubs his hump, though he never rolls all the way over, then lifts his head and calculates his domain. He could have modeled for the buffalo nickel, I think, or for the monarch statue outside Fort Hays. Separated in springtime from the cows and calves, he gathers his strength for the summer rut.

"We found the buffaloes very thick south of Grinnell state [Kansas]. We made a camp on the Smoky [Hill River] and I went to killing just for hides. When Charlie came up I had killed 1900 buffaloes and hauled the hides to Grinnell station." A "remarkably good" hunter could bring down between seventy-five and a hundred bison a day. "One man does the hunting, sometimes for six teams, two men to the team. One or two men are left in camp to make pegs, to cook and to peg the hides down to dry. . . . Nixon, when hunting was at it's [sic] best, killed forty eight hundred in a little over three months." Tom Nixon once set an unbelievable record, downing a hundred and twenty bison in just forty minutes. With such relentlessness, an estimated three million hides were taken, and shipped east from Dodge City in 1872 and 1873.

The Finney Game Refuge, west of Dodge and just south of Garden City, Kansas, has protected buffalo since 1916. Karen Tanner, a tour guide who knows more about prairie wildflowers than anyone I've ever met, maneuvers the four-wheel drive Suburban along a sandy track until we are almost in the middle of a cow/calf herd. Indifferent to the familiar vehicle, some thirty-five mothers and their thirty-some offspring work their way up a grassy hill. One pauses to scratch her head on a natural gas pump, and makes a grunting sound that resembles a belch, an odd counterpoint to the clicking of the machinery. The whole group pauses for a moment by a big wallow, larger than normal, with perhaps room enough for six in what I take to be a buffalo version of a hot tub. One young calf wallows once, twice, and then slumps over half-asleep. Then the herd scatters up the hillside away from us, wandering hungrily and purposefully.

> We went north about thirty miles and made camp for about forty days. We killed 2400 buffaloes and a number of antelope. Then we went northwest . . . Camped there about thirty days and killed about 800 buffaloes.

At the Garden City Zoo, a sign explains that most bison today live in captive herds. Across the compound, a single cow and her yearling slouch in the shade of a dilapidated shed. They're too far away for me to see them clearly. The sign also tells me that bulls can weigh two thousand pounds, but are quick, and extremely agile. These two are lethargic, as if drugged by captivity, their sluggish bodies motionless and still.

"Five years ago the plains were white" with bones, the *Hutchinson News* reported on June 19, 1879. "Look wherever you would, in valley, on hillside or plain, they were sure to meet the eye." After the wind and the weather had scoured the carcasses, a new industry thrived briefly—bison bones for fertilizer, for sugar refineries, for bone china. Buyers would pay anywhere from $4 to $12 a ton. In 1873, the Santa Fe Railroad handled over seven million pounds of bones. "J. E. Woodruff, of St. Louis, shipped twenty-one car loads, two hundred and fifty tons, or five hundred and four thousand pounds of buffalo bones from Kinsley this week."

Dodge City, once the shipping center for the hide and bone trade, boasts of its violent past and its prominence as a way-stop for longhorn cattle and cowboys. Wyatt Earp Boulevard separates downtown from the railroad tracks. The quaint lampposts, the brick storefronts, and a sidewalk promenade remind me of a *Gunsmoke* stage set, as I'm sure is the intent. On this day in May, a Cowboy Heritage Festival touts the Fort Riley Mounted Guard, a reenacted Boot Hill Gunfight, Cowboy Poets and Balladeers, and a gen-u-ine Chuckwagon Lunch. The literature I pick up from the Chamber of Commerce makes no mention of the buffalo holocaust. Sitting on a street-side bench, watching a Wyatt Earp look-alike stride by, I try to imagine the overpowering bloody stench of the hides.

"People living in this vicinity, who have never seen any buffalo should ride out a few miles west," suggested the *Ellsworth Reporter* as early as 1873, "and they will find small detachments of the former immense army of buffalos that used to roam over our prairies." Five years later, the *Hays City Sentinel* sounded more pessimistic. "Messers. Orrill and McCoy, ran across a herd of seven buffalo near the southwest corner of the county, last Monday, but did not succeed in killing even one. Probably these are the last buffalo that will cross the line of Ellis county in their native state of wildness."

Across the highway from the Fort Hays "Monarch of the Plains" statue, the tiny bison herd has wandered away from the fence to the back of their pasture. One, hock-deep in a shallow water tank, methodically splashes the flies; two more stand in their feeding trough; the rest mill together aimlessly. I park in the shade, looking up now and then as I trace the day's route on my map. One cow is particularly restless, lying down, pacing, lying down, pacing. Are those hoofs emerging from beneath her tail, those tiny castanets of color? I climb out of the truck. In the thirty seconds or so while I have my back turned, a fully formed buffalo calf oozes onto the ground. Motionless for another half-minute, the mother then hoists herself to her feet and immediately begins licking away the placenta. Within moments, the tawny calf shakes its head, breaks out of the fetal sac, and peers at the world. Twenty minutes later, the surprising fifty-pound creature is trying to stand, kicking first its hind feet and then its front, awkwardly rocking fore and aft. Soon it's successful, wobbly, but upright and ready to nurse. The remainder of the herd, no longer necessary for protection, disperses across their enclosure, while the new mother gently nudges her calf into the shade.

> Jove but it was glorious! and the next day too, the dense masses pressed on in such vast numbers, that we were compelled to halt, and let them pass to avoid being overrun by them in a literal sense. On the following day also, the number seemed if possible more countless than before. . . . On, on, still on, the black masses come and thicken — an ebbless deluge of life is moving and swelling around us!

3
TEXAS COWBOY COUNTRY

More than a thousand cattle roil in the dusty pens and alleys adjoining the Ranger Livestock Auction sale barn. Standing on the narrow planks of a catwalk, looking down at the seething cows, I smell the sweet stench of a west Texas summer, of dust and drought and manure and sweat. I also hear a jazz ensemble gone berserk, clarinet and tenor sax, alto sax and bass, all squawking out of tune. Calves separated from their mothers, cows searching for their calves, bulls irate, steers just bawling on general principles, their off-key pitches riffing up and down in half-step dissonance. Gates slam like cymbals, whips snap an emphatic beat, percussion hooves drum the powdered dirt, as the unhappy animals mill in their enclosures.

A pen empties, its livestock diverted along a narrow alley toward the enclosed auction arena. Some cows move apace; others, more recalcitrant, stutter step or try to turn back, mooing and moaning in clashing sonorous tones. Finally, into the ring they go, sometimes alone, sometimes in pairs, more often in groups of eight or ten. Out of my sight for only a minute or two, these same cattle emerge from the other side of the sale barn. Sold to the highest bidder! Now, their fates determined, they're separated or herded together according to plan. A slender denim-clad woman, her gray hair plaited in a single braid, orchestrates their movements by hissing at the cows just released. She rarely raises her voice, wields neither whip nor cattle prod, moves lightly in her sneakers when one angry steer hooks his head at her knees. Like a conductor, she waves the livestock past her in a rhythmic sequence as mysterious to me as a musical score. A sweat-stained redhead with freckles teases her about being fast afoot. Obviously he admires her prowess, as do I (standing safely on that catwalk above the swarming herds).

This is as close as I care to get. A cattlewoman I am not. Most of my knowledge of ranching and cowboying comes from books and from film. Though I'm an avid reader of Western American literature, I tend to choose books without livestock. Though I've hiked thousands of miles of western trails, I've only been on horseback once. I have no inclination to ride a second time. Even my first-hand Texas experience has been limited to the DFW airport, a couple of conferences in nearby Denton and Fort Worth, and a single hasty drive across the panhandle on Interstate 40. Omitting Texas cattlemen from *GhostWest*, however, would be the equivalent of leaving the clarinet out of Benny Goodman's band. So here I am, watching, smelling, listening to the variations playing out below, and imagining myself riding herd on the noisy bunch.

The cowboy myth has overstated and romanticized cowboy life, sanitizing the dust and dirt. In reality, nineteenth-century trail driving was hard work. Frequent stampedes, dangerous river crossings, long stretches of prairie without water, hostile Indians, and unpredictable weather combined to make every hour a test of courage and endurance. "The day turned out to be one of torrid heat," explains Andy Adams in *The Log of a Cowboy*, "and before the middle of the forenoon, the cattle lolled their tongues in despair, while their sullen lowing surged through from rear to lead and back again in piteous yet ominous appeal." Adams punctuates the episode with a quote from his foreman, who said that "if he owned hell and Texas, he'd rent Texas and live in hell." Another chronicler of this distant past, Frank Collinson, describes a phenomenon just as dangerous and life-threatening, when thunder and lightning and rain drenched the men and stampeded the cattle. "Finally when they were herded there was water standing everywhere, and it was difficult or impossible to bed them again. Then the cowboys, cold and miserable, and often wet to the skin, stood guard the remainder of the night."

Adams and Collinson describe the Western Trail of the 1880s, which superseded the more famous Chisholm Trail after the railroad in Kansas was extended farther west. Both trails began in south Texas but, where the old Chisholm Trail bent east to follow roughly what today is called the I-35 corridor, the Western Trail bent west to trace a route that eventually led to Dodge City. Along the way it passed Fort Griffin, which squatted on a hilltop above the Clear Fork of the Brazos River. Fort Griffin was one in a series of forts established to protect settlers from Comanche and Kiowa raids, but its particular history was colored by its location as an important way-stop on the Western Trail and by its later prominence as the Texas hub for buffalo hide hunters and bone gatherers. Its history also was colored by a reputation for prostitution and continual violence, and by the reality of its vigilante justice. "I was out on the buffalo range," reports Frank Collinson,

> but every time we had news from Griffin we learned that someone had been found hanging from a tree along the Clear Fork. One day in 1875 a teamster and I went to Fort Griffin for supplies. The next morning we were looking for our horses in the river bottom when we came upon two men hanging from a pecan limb. A printed notice was penned [sic] to the clothes of one—'Anyone moving these men will fill their places'—so we let them hang.

Such is the material of Hollywood, but such was the earned reputation of the real Fort Griffin, "among the toughest spots on a tough frontier." So disgusted were the local ranchers that, when it came time to establish a county seat, they platted an entirely new location in the center of Shackelford County, avoiding Fort Griffin altogether and removing themselves from the very past they had helped create. The abandoned site, now a state park where Longhorn cattle graze the old parade grounds, is marked "in honor of the true western spirit" by a plaque commemorating the "seat of west Texas civilization."

Long before Fort Griffin's appearance in 1867, frontiersmen had been ranging cattle up and down the Clear Fork of the Brazos, where the western Cross Timbers give way to the southern edge of the Rolling Plains. Here was some of the best grazing available in west Texas. No one owned the land, exactly, so the newcomers sought to control it. When the Butterfield Stage came through the region in 1857, the ranchers even had a convenient market for their steers. Troop protection waned during the Civil War, however. The men and their families, running into a full measure of Indian trouble, "forted up" for themselves, and survived the trying times. After the war, after the days of the long cattle drives and after the demise of the buffalo, after Fort Griffin gave way to Albany as Shackelford County's hub, after the railroad came to this part of the country, after barbed wire closed the frontier to further speculation, those earliest settlers continued to thrive. Consolidating their herds and legitimizing their land holdings, they became, I think, archetypal. Their children and grandchildren and great-grandchildren still ranch along the Clear Fork, their family stories embodying the realities of cowboy life. Neither Zane Gray heroes nor John Wayne look-alikes, the Clear Fork cattlemen are not only the ghost riders of the past but present-day ranchers dedicated to the future.

Of the handful of Anglos who first settled on the Clear Fork, two of the best known were the Reynolds and the Matthews families. Arriving in the late 1850s, they forted up at Fort Davis during the Civil War years, then began accumulating property and building their cattle herds. Since suitable mates were scarce on the Texas frontier, they also began marrying each other. By my count, twelve intermarriages between 1867 and 1883. One especially fortuitous one occurred on December 25, 1876, when Sallie Ann Reynolds, age fifteen, wed John Alexander (Bud) Matthews, age twenty-three, fortuitous not only because the couple and their offspring went on to become prominent Shackelford citizens but also because Sallie wrote down her reminiscences.

Published in 1936, *Interwoven: A Pioneer Chronicle* tells the story of ranching "on the outside border of civilization. The country just northwest of us was occupied solely by Indians and wild animals for hundreds of miles; great herds of buffaloes, deer, antelopes and wild horses roamed the plains. The nearest ranch, Camp Cooper, was five miles east." Because it was written from a woman's point of view, *Interwoven*—the name reflects the numerous intermarriages—focuses on the domestic side of life, but it includes some tantalizing glimpses of early cowboying, too. Like Adams and Collinson, she describes storms, stampedes, dry trails and wet. She recounts one instance when six herds drifted together in a snowstorm—"fifteen thousand head of cattle of different brands all mixed in one bunch and strayed thirty miles south of the road." The incident gives her an opportunity to boast. The two Reynolds herds, one with a Matthews boss, lost only eight head, while the remaining four herds lost three hundred. Those other cattle "had been driven too hard and were jaded. These trail herds had to move slowly, and not every man put in charge of one knew how to handle it." By implication, the Reynolds and Matthews men were much more capable.

In the early days of Clear Fork trailing, the herd owners worked as hard as their cowboys. The *Virginian* or the *Shane* myth tells me that cattlemen owned the range and that cowboys trailed the herds. Real-life chronicles, such as *Interwoven*, suggest less precise distinctions. Reading first-hand accounts, I discover that the terminology begins to blur. Cowboy, cowman, cattleman, cattlewoman. Many of the earliest Texas cattlemen were themselves cowboys of real prowess. *The Historical and Biographical Record of the Cattle Industry and the Cattlemen of Texas and Adjacent Territory*, published in 1894, voices annoyance with the mythic definitions. A chapter entitled "The Cowboy, As He Was, And Is, And Is Supposed To Have Been," opens with a standalone paragraph: "It is doubtful whether any human being in any age or generation has ever been so absurdly characterized and misrepresented as the cowboy." After setting the historical record straight, describing the cowboy's actual tasks and accomplishments, the tome then presents biographical records of prominent Texas stockmen, in effect putting the cattleman and the cowboy in a synchronous relationship.

The second volume, for example, includes a biography of J. A. Matthews, now called "the Judge." In *Interwoven*, Sallie says that when she asked her husband why he wanted to run for the county judgeship, he replied that he was tired of being called "Bud," perhaps articulating a subtle linguistic transition from cowboy to cattleman. Although the cattleman and his wife had long since moved to Albany, the biographical entry highlights the cowboy excellence of their headquarters, Lambshead Ranch, and the cowman talents of the Judge.

> Mr. Matthews' location in Shackelford is an ideal one. The Clear Fork of the Brazos, running through the ranch, furnishes an abundant supply of water at all times, and this, with a never-failing supply of nutritious grass, and the shelter which the river bluffs afford to the cattle in winter, renders it one of the most thoroughly desirable locations for stockraising in the State. The ranch is stocked with about 6,000 head of cattle, and though Mr. Matthews is continually selling and restocking, he rarely allows the number of his cattle to fall below the figures given. He also farms to some extent, and owns some 4,000 head of sheep, though sheep raising receives but little of his attention.

The last line of the paragraph reminds me of an Elmer Kelton novel, *The Time It Never Rained*, where the author explains how economic necessity had driven most west Texas cowmen to run sheep on their ranches, too. "Now they raised cattle for respectability," Kelton mocks, "and sheep for a living." Apparently the purist view of cowboys dealing only with cattle is a mythic relic rather than a modern truth, though no one likes to admit it.

The Judge and Sallie's son, Watkins "Watt" Reynolds Matthews, born in 1899, managed Lambshead Ranch from the 1940s until his death in 1997. He honored the old traditions while running the ranch for twentieth-century profitability. Called the Dean of Cattlemen in the Southwest, distinguished by the National Cowboy Hall of Fame, Watt Matthews personally epitomized the complexities and overlaps of real-life cowboy culture. He had a degree from Princeton, but he always slept in the Lambshead bunkhouse. The ranch ran mostly Herefords, but he kept a small herd of Longhorns in deference to the old days and to lend "an aura of frontier mystique to the setting." A helicopter helped with the roundups after 1981 but, as long as he was physically able, Watt branded every Lambshead calf himself. He preserved historic buildings on the ranch, including the Reynolds House where his parents were married and the old Stone Ranch House where his mother lived as a young girl. Known for his conservation efforts, Watt made Lambshead Ranch into a haven for quail, turkey, deer, and feral hogs. Because he and his men grubbed out much of the invasive mesquite and prickly pear cactus, the range remains in good condition—so attractive, in fact, that many of the old Marlboro cigarette commercials were filmed on Lambshead property.

Lawrence Clayton has devoted his professional career to writing articles and books about the rich complexities of cowboy life, including a recently revised edition of *Cowboys: Ranch Life along the Clear Fork of the Brazos River* and a 1990 biography of Watt Matthews. Both books contain dozens of anecdotes that characterize this old-time Texan's code. Matthews emphatically believed, for example, that it was a rancher's responsibility to leave the range in better condition than when he inherited it. This was the way to honor one's parents. He also believed in a cowboy's innate abilities. A good one "can handle cattle without upsetting them; a bad one can't," he said. He insisted, too, that he kept sheep only to keep down the grass and weeds that might provide cover for snakes and rats. Like his father, he never admitted their economic value.

Cowboys includes a description of Watt Matthews's 1997 funeral, a gathering that in effect synthesized the cowboy and the cattleman. Cowboy pallbearers, dressed in denim jeans and white shirts, laid his casket on bales of hay decorated with Clear Fork wildflowers. After the ceremony, the pallbearers loaded the casket onto a buckboard driven by two of Lambshead's old-time ranch hands. A bagpiper preceded the mourners, who followed on foot, while another cowboy led a horse carrying Watt's saddle. Then, placing the casket to rest near the river's bluff, the cowboys themselves shoveled Lambshead soil into the grave. Watt had wanted to have a party, "just like he was present," so a sit-down dinner of prime rib and all the "fixin's" took place late that afternoon. Lawrence Clayton concludes, "The spring carpet of green grass and flowers represented what Watt Matthews always said of the season: 'The land has its Sunday clothes on.' Thus ended an era in ranch life in the Southwest."

I'm not sure I agree that an era ended that day. Although Watt Matthews was surely a link to the Clear Fork's past, he was just as much a connection with its future, a transition between the old ways and whatever lies ahead. By improving the land itself, he enabled ranching to continue at Lambshead into the twenty-first century. By honoring the traditions of the past, he kept them alive for those who would follow his lead. By serving as a role model, he showed others the importance of leadership and community service. I never met him, I've only read what others have written about him, but for me Watt Matthews is a Texas cowman model who far surpasses the trite cowboy of myth.

In fact, Clayton's *Cowboys* goes on to describe more than two dozen men whose real lives give the lie to Hollywood's invention. The Peacock brothers, for example, third-generation Clear Fork cowboys. George, the oldest, manages the Nail Ranch; Benny, the youngest, is foreman of the T. R. Green Land and Cattle Company; Troy, foreman of the Mitchell Ranch. George's profile—horse wrangler, then foreman, now manager, with a wife, four children, and eight grandchildren—doesn't match John Wayne's. Neither does Benny's personal story, nor Troy's. They're all family men who learned their ranching skills from their father and their grandfathers. *Cowboys* also includes profiles of the son of a sheriff, the son of a veterinarian, a graduate of the ranch management program at Tyler Junior College, a man with a degree in agricultural economics from Texas A&M University, a man with a degree in animal husbandry, and the vice-president and trust officer of a Fort Worth bank. Clayton doesn't mention his own background, either, or how his job as dean of liberal arts at Hardin-Simmons University fits with his own cowboy-cowman profile. His picture on the back cover, however, resembles all the others—Stetson hat, arms akimbo, eyes narrowed against the sun.

Another Clayton book, *Ranch Rodeos in West Texas*, repeats an old-timer's comment about cowboys' photographs: "I can tell the real ones—they have pain in their eyes." Technicolor versions of cowboy confrontations mistake gratuitous bloodshed and violence for the sorts of ills, and pain, that actually accompany life on the range. While rounding up and branding cattle can still be excruciating work, can lead to tumbles and dislocations and broken bones, outwitting market fluctuations or outlasting unpredictable wet spells and drought can, in a different way, be even more stressful. But few genuine cowboys would change their lives. Clayton quotes one man who says, "It is something that has been in my blood for as long as I can remember." Another expresses the thoughts of thousands: "I love it, and I wouldn't do anything else."

The life of a cowman is a precarious one, however. Sometimes drought holds west Texas hostage. In 1849, Captain Randolph B. Marcy pronounced that "no place in the universe is better suited to stock raising," words which drew the first ranching families to Clear Fork country. Frances Mayhugh Holden, who wrote *Lambshead before Interwoven* as a "prequel" to Sallie Reynolds Matthews's book, agrees. Holden describes how a clear pure stream "flowed rapidly over dazzling white limestone and gravel. The precipitous banks were lined with giant trees, pecan, hackberry, black walnut." And the hills bore the "best varieties of grama and mesquite grasses." Her words remind me of the Matthews entry in the *Cattle Industry* biography: the "ideal" Shackelford location, the "abundant supply" of water, the "never-ending supply of nutritious grass." Benny Peacock fondly calls Lambshead "the prettiest ranch I ever worked on."

The drought of 2000 has sucked the shrunken Clear Fork nearly dry. Cattle could cross easily between its red parched banks. I'm told that, in May, this land should be as green as Watt Matthews's description of spring, with "its Sunday clothes on." Instead I saw acres of parched brown dirt, a river of pooled green puddles, and underfed cattle bawling in the heat. Across the river, six or seven nuzzled at the ground, their tails twitching at the flies. When I stopped for lunch in Throckmorton, north of the Fort Griffin–Clear Fork crossing, I listened to the conversations. "How are ya?" one Stetsoned man asked another. "Nothing that four inches of rain couldn't help," was the reply. "Just too darned dry," drawled a third.

At the Ranger cattle auction, I watched another cowman shrug his shoulders. "I sit in front of my television set for hours, just watching radar on the Weather Channel," he shook his head. "Every cloud, every blip, I cross my fingers." Alongside the sale barn, I saw too many bony cows, their haunches narrow, their brisket bones protruding. When to sell livestock, when to hang on, is an intricate dance with destiny. Elmer Kelton's *The Time It Never Rained* documents well the precariousness of staying solvent through sequential years of drought. In the nineteenth century, cattlemen could move herds from range to range when the grass got too dry; in the twenty-first century, especially on small spreads, such mobility is impossible.

One of the co-owners of the Ranger Livestock Auction echoed Kelton's characterization of the inherent problems. "Normally we auction between 900 and 950 animals each week," she explained. "Today we're handling 1534." Why? "They're shipping 'em to Oklahoma, where it's not so dry. Not much grass around here this year." Hanging onto a herd too long is costly. The cows can turn skeletal, the expense of feed may bankrupt a ranch.

"It is the standard rule that about every twenty-five or thirty years about half of the farmers and ranchers go broke," Watt Matthews once observed. He didn't mention what I think is a truism of western life, that average annual rainfall is a misleading term. Sometimes it rains a lot; sometimes it doesn't rain at all. To average the two extremes is to compute a meaningless statistic that has little to do with the actual day-to-day presence or absence of rain. Drought seems to be a condition of life in west Texas, recurring more often than seasons of heavy rain. It can, however, rain hard in this dry country, as trail-driver Frank Collinson described. Abilene's 1881 birthday celebration, for example, took place in "a sea of cold, thick, chocolate-colored mud."

Watt Matthews kept personal track of the Clear Fork's climactic vagaries for more than half a century. Almost every entry in his diary records the daily weather. Some days, like June 18, 1963, were benign: "61°–86° Cool (chilly side) foggy morning. We have had as much muggy humid weather so far this June as I can remember." Other days were more dramatic. On September 19, 1956: "The hot dry weather continues with no let up. A new all time record . . . .90 [inch] of rain since May 28 & 92 days of 100° or above. . . . Hit 106° which is pretty high for this late in year." On August 4, 1978, the extreme opposite: "Poured rain all night & is still doing it. . . . By 10 we had over 19 inches from around 6 yesterday. Total since 12 A. M. yesterday 24.86 inches. Other gauges wouldn't hold enough. Phones out and hemmed in by creeks. . . . Stuck in mud a good part of the day. We checked on river late. A sad, sickening sight. About 5 ft deep in Reynolds house." The river "looked like an ocean."

I myself saw a gully-washer darken a noon sky almost black, but, because the earth was so parched, the run-off that day did more harm than good. My west Texas friends report that the storm I enjoyed was the last appreciable precipitation all year. The next winter, however, I slipped and slogged through snow, ice, and viscous Clear Fork mud. Now the locals are crossing their fingers, hoping the nine-year drought finally has broken.

Riding point, Lawrence steers his aging Jeep down a dusty track. Riding drag, his wife Sonja, their daughter, their granddaughter, and I follow in a battered Chevy Suburban. Hearing the motorized sounds, some thirty or forty cows and calves emerge from the mesquite thickets and herd between the vehicles. When Lawrence pulls a string attached to a feed box secured to the back of the Jeep, protein pellets fall to the ground. The cattle jostle to be first in line. Texana, a Texas Longhorn who was Lawrence and Sonja's seed cow, a family pet almost, shakes her horns and wins the battle of the buffet, though there's plenty for all. This is a twenty-first-century version of riding the range, I guess, cowboys on jeep-back and cattle in need of protein supplements when their drought-stricken grass dries out in the blistering sun.

"All this was Irwin, all the way to the river." Sonja Irwin Clayton waves her arm in a broad gesture of pride. "Fifty years ago the fields were all cleared." Now they're a tangle of mesquite and prickly pear cactus, the peach orchard "long gone." Sonja's great grandfather, John G. Irwin, showed up at Fort Chadburne and soon became the first sergeant of the Second U.S. Dragoons. He married in 1852 and fathered Sonja's grandfather in 1854. Then he resigned from the army. The *Throckmorton County History* explains that he "secured a contract [signed by Robert E. Lee] to furnish Camp Cooper with beef and moved his family there in September 1859, establishing a ranch at the Comanche Indian Agency about two miles below the Fort, and which was at the time the furtherest ranch west on the Clear Fork and also in northwestern Texas." Later killed on a cattle drive to Santa Fe, John G. was buried near Fort Sumner. His wife raised their five children alone.

This particular property, located north and just east of Lambshead, has been in Sonja's family for more than a hundred years. The governor of Texas signed the original land grant for 160 acres. Her grandfather, John Chadbourne Irwin, ranched here until he died, as did her father, J. C. Irwin, Jr. But "daddy and his brother didn't get along," Sonja reports. "My uncle was a mean man." The two brothers built double fences and double gates, then blocked the roads to each other's acreage. They ran the surveyor off with guns, until the sheriff intervened. Sonja recalls a fist fight at a nearby mudhole, when the brothers were in their seventies. "The fighting Irwins," they were called. Because they disagreed so violently, they divided their resources into small spreads all too susceptible to the vagaries of the marketplace.

Across Highway 283 lies another piece of family land once ranched by Sonja's cousin, Morris. These 850 acres belong to the Claytons now. The old Ledbetter property stretches right along the Clear Fork of the Brazos—God's embrace—where live oak and pecan trees give welcome shelter from the hot sun. In fact, the river runs deeper here than at the upstream crossing near Fort Griffin's empty shell, and this water looks more like its name. Lawrence is still riding point, but the cattle on the river section are less tame than those nearer home. He toots his horn and guns his motor, waiting for the cow/calf combos to wander out of thick mesquite before he triggers the pellet-dropping apparatus. Sonja continues with her stories.

She points to the house where she lived until she was six. "We could see clear to the highway, then. Hardly any mesquite trees at all." Now the thickets grow so close together that they're "too tight for horseback." Lawrence remembers "backing his horse" out of a thick tangle when rounding up the cattle last year. The Irwins, the Ledbetters, and the Claytons haven't grubbed out the invasive species for decades, so year by year the undesirable trees and cactus crowd the forage. One cow is eating the sharp-barbed prickly pear, head thrust out, chin up. "It's lousy for digestion," husband and wife lament in tandem. "Leads to blockage." When drought is most severe, some ranchers burn the barbs off the cactus and feed the pulp to their livestock. The Claytons hate to think about this possibility.

Three young steers gawk at the vehicles and paw at the ground. "Like sixth-grade boys," Sonja snorts. Watt Matthews once made a similar comment, comparing bulls to teen-aged boys, saying that they fight just for fun and to show off their prowess. Sonja and I turn to laugh at a tiny calf, perhaps two weeks old, that totters alongside the Suburban. "The littler ones bawl the loudest," she speaks from experience. These cows, mostly longhorn/shorthorn crosses, don't fatten well. Cousin Morris, who died when he was eighty, "got lax. He liked 'em wild." If the Claytons, who live and work in Abilene but spend as much time as possible at the ranch, want to make their spread profitable, they'll need to breed for fattening ability. They'll need to outlast the drought, too.

"Even if he didn't pay much attention to the cattle, though, Morris built things." Sonja interrupts my thoughts to point out some intricate constructs made with discarded pipe. An oil pipe corral, full-sized and fully functional, with oil pipe pens and oil pipe alleys, the pieces fitted together like a giant rust-red erector set. A pipe hitching post, itself hitched to more pipe. A water pump and a shower. A shaded bench crafted from a drill core. Morris created almost every one of his ranch necessities from oil drilling detritus. "He never let anything go to waste," so he utilized whatever the drillers left behind, and he built everything to last forever. "I only mean to do it once," Morris used to say, so he left behind a stage set of ghostly props.

While Sonja admires her cousin's innovations, she is not as sanguine about the drilling itself. That afternoon, she drove me to the oil well on the old Irwin ranch. She's been nagging the small operator who leases the drilling rights, and she wants to see if he's cleaned up an unfortunate leak. He has, kind of, but Sonja is still unhappy about the spill and the subsequent pollution. As I look at the oil and water oozing underneath the tanks, I wonder aloud if the royalties are worth the mess. The operator takes $\frac{7}{8}$ths of the profit; Sonja's family splits the remaining profit eight ways. In effect, she and Lawrence get $\frac{1}{64}$th of the money, though they have 100 percent of the contamination. "Not worth it," the Claytons agree.

The intricacies of drilling leases and mineral rights, the necessity for family trusts and the unhappiness of family feuds, the complexities of ranch land inheritance—all these are very real ingredients of Texas ranching today. Of the Claytons' sixteen hundred acres, for example, half were inherited from cousin Morris. Another quarter were purchased in Morris's name so that Sonja's aunt, who had suffered a stroke, wouldn't know Sonja and Lawrence were the new owners. "I'd never been in this house until we bought it," Sonja remarks of the ranch home that looks as if she's lived there forever. Sonja also manages her father's twenty-one-year trust, of which the oil well lease is a part. She tries not to think about the future, when the trust dissolves and the Irwin heirs must settle up. Meanwhile, every heir gets an oil check annually, dollars the Claytons might use for grubbing the mesquite, refitting the buildings, and improving the stock.

Disagreements about land use and ranch land dispersal seem to be characteristic of Texas families. Some offspring, like Watt Reynolds, eagerly carry on the tradition, but many others are willing to break up the property and divide up the assets. Before I visited the Claytons' ranch, I spent a day with Mary Batchler Gaggino, whose great grandfather also had successfully settled in this part of the country. Initially, James Monroe Batchler had done very well. Once, at the turn of the twentieth century, he made a million-dollar deposit from a single cattle sale. Now Mary and her husband, who live in the house her parents built, run no cattle at all, but lease their pastures to another rancher. "Because of the drought, we had him take the cattle off early this year. Nobody's getting rich in these times."

Driving from Throckmorton to the old Batchler place, I had noticed an abandoned ranch house to the south of the highway. After Mary's brother died, his widow and children moved away. Mary, estranged from her sister-in-law and her nephews, doesn't speak to them any more. The empty yellow house looks forlornly across fields rapidly filling with yellow prickly pear. The bump gate near the entrance sways shut with weeds and blown brush. Nearby, an idle oil pump stands silhouetted against the bright Texas sky. "Conoco seismographed this area. There's still a lot of oil here," Mary reported. "Oil keeps ranches alive, the income carries them along. The 1980s were almost obscene. But the oil eventually will play out. It can't go on forever."

An oil pump, kicking up and down, looks like a tired bucking bronco to me. First the head dips and the backbone stiffens. Then the hind legs pivot up, red hooves higher, lower, higher, lower, higher. The older pumps kick more slowly, their haunches tired, their energy almost all played out. The beat, though, is rhythmic, constant, just slow. Sometimes in Texas, this bronc has been an eighty-point ride; sometimes, though, it's been a twister or a stargazer or a dud, unseating its riders right and left. Today, at the Batchler-now-Gaggino ranch, the motionless oil pump seems as fallow as the pastures around it. Mary's daughters probably agree. They live in Michigan; they're not interested in Texas.

Mary's stories weren't fallow, however. Settling back in a black leather chair, she spun yarns as cattle-proud as Sonja's. Mary's grandfather, an inveterate tinkerer, invented the gooseneck trailer that revolutionized the way cattle are moved to market, though he never profited personally. Mary's mother drew the logo—a half sphere with the bent head of a goose. "Gooseneck is like Kleenex in Texas," Mary mused, perhaps dreaming about what might have happened to the family fortunes had her grandfather been patent-savvy. "He invented the bump gate, too." Her grandfather raised her father in the ranching tradition, but, like so many Texas scions, Mary's father didn't get along with his dad. He left the ranch, and didn't return for years, so Mary grew up in California. "At least he didn't go to east Texas," Mary said, tossing her head to one side. "It's not good to go beyond the Brazos. The cattle's heads are smaller," she teased parochially. While Mary joked, I thought about her family feuds, and the way the Batchler ranch had grown smaller with each generation.

Even the biggest ranches are shrinking now. Mary gossiped about the nearby Swenson property which had just been sold the week before. First established in the 1880s, the Swenson ranches once totaled more than 225,000 acres in west Texas. Then, beginning in the 1970s, the heirs began dividing and selling the properties. Most recently, the 106,000 acres of the Throckmorton operation had been put on the market. A local speculator bought part of the acreage for the oil rights; the Mormons purchased the rest. I went out to look at the rolling pastures of the erstwhile spread, where the huge white SMS brand is still visibly etched on a hillside. The fences were tight, the fields devoid of mesquite, the cattle fat. Such land dispersal is typical of Texas today, though, where the heirs want their checks and where boutique ranching is more and more in vogue. In the old days, the most extensive ranches, like the Matador and the XIT, boasted three million acres apiece, though that might be an exaggeration. Now the King Ranch is probably Texas's largest, at 825,000 acres; the Four Sixes in the Panhandle, half a million. "To have a legitimate ranch takes 10,000 acres now," Lawrence says. "With 64,000 acres, that would keep three cowboys and a manager busy. A hundred and fifty cows per pasture—that's about all that can be worked in a day." That's what modern ranchers can handle, using helicopters, four-wheelers and pickup trucks, squeeze chutes and branding tables, gooseneck trailers and cell phones to make their tasks more manageable.

Lawrence filled my head with modern ranching data. Raising cattle is a complicated genetic process now, with some cattlemen choosing pure breeding and others opting to crossbreed. The long-legged trail-savvy Texas Longhorns were unsuccessful in the pasture. Like Morris Ledbetter's cows, they didn't fatten well. As trail-driving diminished, so did the Longhorns. Herefords replaced them, along with Durhams and polled Angus. For a long time, steak-and-potatoes Herefords were the most popular breed of all. A sign over Albany's main street, in fact, announces "Home of the Hereford." The town never has relinquished its affection for Longhorns, though. Each June, Albany holds what's called a "Fandangle," a musical pageant that celebrates the area's history. A 1931 poem written by Berta Hart Nance always opens the festivities: "Other states were carved or born, / Texas grew from hide or horn," the poem proudly begins.

On the range today, however, crossbreeding is in favor. The R. A. Brown Ranch in Throckmorton, for example, breeds composites, as Rob Brown explained in a 1998 interview. "Senepol bred to Red Angus (Senegus) and Simmental bred to Brahman (Simbrah). Then, we crossed those two hybrids (Senegus bred to Simbrah) to come up with the Hotlander. They are moderate-sized cows that are highly reproductive and efficient." Best of all, they're heat-tolerant, bred especially to survive south of Interstate 40 and west of Interstate 35, even in times of drought. Nothing is left to chance. Computers keep track of genetic predictors, called Expected Progeny Differences; a spread sheet calculates the best EPDs for each cow and bull combination. Then the registered cows are plan-mated, using artificial insemination.

All this is expensive, too expensive for the Claytons' J Lazy C, which runs only eighty cow/calf pairs on 1662 acres. Even that is risky, with the drought parching the pastures and the increasingly high cost of feed. Fuel is expensive, too, as is the purchase of new machinery when the old can no longer be wired together. Lawrence, like many other Clear Fork ranchers, brings in extra dollars by leasing his hunting rights to three men from Abilene, who hunt turkey, quail, deer, the occasional antelope, and feral hogs whenever they're in season. "One year, the Nail Ranch made as much—or maybe more—money from hunters as they earned in the cattle business!" Some ranchers have even tried to make the incursive mesquite profitable, turning the water-sucking trees into barbecue chips for city consumers. To Lawrence, that idea didn't sound appealing. "Not really ranching," he scoffed.

Lawrence prefers to ranch in the old ways. He'd rather be on horseback than do almost anything, I think. But I couldn't see the J Lazy C from horseback, so I excused myself from the Clayton stories, and took a walk. Like true cowboys, Lawrence and Sonja looked at me as if I'd lost my mind. In the 94-degree heat, I wandered from outbuilding to outbuilding, and then on into the nearest pastures. Most of the buildings had been moved from elsewhere. "We're into recycling junk," Lawrence laughed at himself. The centerpiece was an old schoolhouse, which served the Irwin kids and other area students for decades and then housed three schoolteachers for several years more. Sonja's aunt and uncle bought it, moved it to the ranch, and used it as a barn. Then Sonja and Lawrence mucked it out, moved it again, and restored it to its original splendor, with vintage wooden desks lined up inside and an old bell to ring when guests arrive.

The mint condition of the red-top schoolhouse contrasted sharply with Sonja's father's house, which stands as empty as Mary's brother's, its white frame structure beginning to sag. "Daddy's house," Sonja had gestured on our Suburban ride. "There's a rattlesnake den underneath it. We killed fourteen the last year he was alive." On the farm-to-market roads, I saw many such abandoned places—their roofs sunken in, windows broken, porches leaning sideways, doorways collapsed. In contrast, the old Irwin place is in good condition, but I wonder how long it can withstand its abandonment. Here was a sight too common in west Texas, where the ghostly dreams of one generation have given way to the realities of another.

On our way to feed the cattle, Sonja and I had passed the squared-off foundations of an even older house, where her grandparents once lived. Mesquite and prickly pear grew where her father and his siblings once had stretched upward instead. I walked back to it by myself, sifting the Irwin stories through my imagination. Children playing together; brothers and sisters no longer speaking. Thousands of cattle herded along a Western Trail that seemed to run forever; eighty cows and their calves on 1662 acres. "Abundant water" and "a never-failing supply of nutritious grass"; drought and dirt, mesquite and prickly pear. Then I remembered the lilt in Sonja's voice when she narrated her stories, and the light in Lawrence's eyes when he talked about the roundup next week. I thought about their house, filled with generations of treasures—spurs and hackamores, bits and bridles, tiny moccasins and boots, barbed wire turned into art. "We never throw anything away."

Opening the pasture gate, I walked back toward the corral to check on the sprawl-legged foal born yesterday morning. The Claytons' eight-year-old granddaughter leaned against the fence, gently talking to the colt, so I tiptoed quietly away. A trailing wind blew smells and sounds from the field beyond. Unseen cattle lowed a soft clarinet chorus in the hot afternoon sun, while the sounds of grasshoppers and bees hummed in the air. "It was a comforting sight, this country," Elmer Kelton wrote of west Texas. "It was an ageless land where the past was still a living thing and old voices still whispered, where the freshness of the pioneer time had not yet all faded, where a few of the old dreams were not yet dark with tarnish." I thought about the proud way Sonja looked across these hills. "All this was Irwin, all the way down to the river." I remembered how Lawrence had smiled at her words. It's Clayton now, of course, but in ancestral memory the home place will always be Irwin, "an ageless land where the past *is* still a living thing and old voices still whisper."

Some months after my Texas visit, I went to a video cattle auction in a Nevada casino. The buyers, sellers, and I watched cattle chest-deep in Technicolor grass parade across five giant screens. They did so soundlessly. I missed the snapping whips and clatter of the gates; even more, I missed the bawling dissonance of noisy heifers and steers. Inside that air-conditioned hall, I missed the hot smell of the sun and the sharper smells of manure and the powdered dust that inevitably billows from a thousand hooves. Up front, the auctioneer and the clerk looked and acted much like the auctioneer and the clerk at the Ranger sale barn, the one trolling his soft seductive sounds, the other marking tickets as each batch of cows was sold. Even the computers seemed the same. The bidders, mostly wearing straw hats, western shirts, and denim jeans, resembled their Texas counterparts, too.

But without actual cows, the energy was absent. Spotters, waving their hands, tried to bring life to the mechanical process. Failing that, the auctioneer broke his cadence to speak directly to the crowd. "From a grand gentleman, these cows have been living right." "It's not what you spend but what you get." "A good family of cattlemen, been buying good bulls." "On that mineral plan, not implanted." "These are dolls." "You boys want to get your trucks in here right away." "No rat tails here." The soundless cattle drove themselves endlessly across the huge screens, trailing in a way no nineteenth-century cowboy could have imagined. "Those are big ol' cows, aren't they?" a man across the table remarked to his wife. The auctioneer's patter drowned out her reply, but she nodded her head in agreement. To me, the cows just looked like one-dimensional specters of their bloodlines. For almost five hours I watched them. On screen, I never saw a man on a horse moving the cows along. If I closed my eyes, though, I could picture Watt Reynolds, his mother, Sallie, and his father, the Judge. I could imagine James Batchler in his prime. I could picture Irwins of five generations. And I could see Lawrence and Sonja riding the range on the Clear Fork of the Brazos, God's embrace.

WYOMING
A RENDEZVOUS

When I was a student at Whitman College, Narcissa Prentiss Whitman served as a surrogate housemother. Her painting hung hugely in the virginal living room of the women's residence hall that bears her maiden name—Narcissa Prentiss Hall. She glowered inhospitably at us every evening when we gathered for dinner, every weekend when we greeted our dates. We could go nowhere without passing beneath Narcissa's disapproving glare. I still groan at the memory of that room of overstuffed furniture and its portrait's stiff missionary scorn.

Hundreds of miles and dozens of years away from Whitman College, I one day found a stone marker commemorating Narcissa and Marcus Whitman's initial route west. Between July 6 and July 18, 1836, the Whitmans and their fellow travelers, the Spauldings, camped along the Green River in present-day Wyoming. There, where Horse Creek gallops into the Green, the two missionary families apparently joined an encampment of mountain men and Indians known famously as the Green River Rendezvous.

Explosive excitement greeted their arrival. A small group of Indians and trappers on horseback raced toward the newcomers, whooping and hollering and savagely firing their guns in the air. The incident lasted only a few minutes, but caused momentary consternation among the wary travelers, especially as the live ammunition flew over their heads. Joseph Meek, who described the event as "demoniac hub-bub," noted later that the missionaries failed to appreciate their welcome. Frightened and slightly panicked, they gathered their livestock and prepared for a genuine attack. When Marcus learned it was all a joke, he heartily laughed at himself, but the women were less sanguine. "What strange emotions filled the breasts of the lady missionaries," Meek mused, "when they beheld among whom their lot was cast, may now be faintly outlined by a vivid imagination, but have never been, perhaps never could be put into words."

The ladies found themselves in the middle, not only of fur-trading and business transactions and the swapping of tall tales, but of drinking and sporting and assignations and games of chance and fistfights and knifings and ribaldry and revelry and general decadence. "Saturnalia among the mountains," quipped Washington Irving. Each summer, from 1825 until 1840, the Rendezvous in the Rockies was the biggest annual party in the West. Quite frankly, I cannot imagine Narcissa joining the fun. Stepping hesitantly between one dusty tent site and another, she must have mimicked her pictured self—tightened her lips, pulled her shawl more closely around her shoulders, and frowned with disgust.

For the missionary wives, two weeks at the Green River Rendezvous brought a brief respite from the rigors of their journey, but the festivities surely made them uncomfortable. For the buckskin-clad trappers, however, this gathering was the highlight of the year. First they took care of business, swapping their pelts for fresh supplies. Then the men partied and played. Because Rendezvous prices were high and alcohol rampant, the trappers of the 1830s usually came away with no money at all. The beaver trade, already well on its way to extinction, was barely profitable for anyone by then, and most of the mountain men carelessly squandered their meager earnings. Nonetheless, they relished the joyous camaraderie—the drinking, the dicing, the decadence.

Looking across this rendezvous valley today, its hayfields fading with the coming heat of summer, I find it almost impossible to picture the chaos of ten thousand temporary inhabitants. From Trappers Point, happily out of range of the river's ever-present mosquitoes, I peer down at the sinuous twists of the Green, its sandbars and overgrazed banks clearly visible. Cattle herd together in a nearby field, where a harrier hawk stoops from the sky. I see no humans at all, though cars pass in the distance. To the west, the Wyomings, called the Bear River Mountains a century ago, uplift a roadless expanse of melting snow. In modern times, snowmobiles make them more accessible in winter than in summer, but they proved a formidable seasonal barrier for the mountain men. The more rounded Wyomings, however, are not as rugged as the mountains to the east of this gentle valley. The storm-swept Wind River Range is still almost impenetrable once winter sets in.

I personally found the Winds rather impenetrable one summer, in fact. For two weeks in 1974 I backpacked up Porcupine Creek from Green River Lakes, crossed behind Square Top (the sentinel mountain in this part of the range), hunkered down at Summit Lake in a blizzard that dropped two feet of August snow, cross-countried to Peak Lake where wind gusts upended our tent with me inside, posed with one foot on either side of the Green River (the true headwaters of the Colorado), side-hilled back around to Square Top, climbed cautiously without reaching its flattened summit, then traced the swelling Green back down to the double lakes trailhead and to the car. The trip was memorable. I wore every piece of clothing I carried, all at once, every day, and I was never warm enough. Hiking out, we met a party hiking in. "President Ford," they said in conversation; "ex-President Nixon resigned." "Til Hell freezes over," I thought, as I recalled the summer blizzard five days earlier that had coincided with Nixon's fall.

A mountain man, without benefit of freeze-dried food, down parkas, and zippered tents, and certainly without the omnipresence of modern communication, may actually have fared better than I did in the Winds. With a small ax and heavy skinning knife stuck in his belt, one or two pistols matched to the caliber of his rifle, and a small sack around his neck holding a pipe and tobacco, he would easily have survived unexpected snow. A pack animal hauled all he would need: a half-dozen heavy traps, flour, salt, a kettle, and a few trade goods for the

Indians. Prior experience, plus his own wilderness savvy would see him safely through.

At the same time, that very expertise was destroying the life he loved. A. B. Guthrie, Jr.'s classic novel, *The Big Sky*, underscores the inherent irony. "It's all spiled," Boone Caudill moans to his friend, Jim, "I reckon I spiled it all." Although Boone perhaps never comprehends the full extent of his own role in the desecration of what seemed wild and free, the reader is certainly aware that the real-life counterparts of the fictional Boone and Jim were just as guilty. I re-read Guthrie's book about the mountain man's fate alongside Green River Lakes last summer. Still somewhat wild—it's forty miles from pavement, and a moose and calf shared my campsite—the area is partially tamed, too, with peeled-log high-tech outhouses, an annoying drone of motors drowning the mosquitoes' hum, and more campers than I remembered.

Hiking around the lower lake, through fallen pines and sweet undergrowth, I imagined mountain men enjoying a layover in what once must have been prime beaver habitat. I saw them setting their traps and, later, counting their kill. I saw them sewing the pelts, the plews, to willow hoops, and lashing the catch together. I saw them sprawling close to a tiny smokeless campfire, and then trailing on up the Porcupine at dawn. Listening to the thawing stream cascade over rocks and broken trees, I recalled my own trek up the fast-falling creek, and the countless crossings back and forth. Superimposing my 1974 adventures upon theirs of the nineteenth century, and the 1974 campground upon the twenty-first century version, I mused about my own complicity in the wilderness demise.

Mountain men invaded the Rockies and stripped them of beaver. After their way of life came to an economic end, they found employment guiding pioneers and wagon trains over the best routes through the mountains. In effect, they hastened the coming settlement of the West, as did Narcissa Whitman and Eliza Spaulding, the first two white women to travel on what soon would be called the Oregon Trail. A backpacker since I was nine years old, I suppose I've done the same. Long before Gore-Tex and granola, I wandered unmarked routes traveled mostly by fishermen and hunters. I explored trailless knapsack cols, led groups to distant lakes, brought my own brand of civilization into a landscape no longer pristine. Like Narcissa, I entered what might be described as gendered space, set up camps, cooked and cleaned up. I and my friends, in effect, populated the remaining unpopulated West. The Winds. The Chiricahuas. The Kaiparowits Plateau. The Uintas. The Cascades. The Olympic Peninsula.

Today at Green River Lakes, a doe with a knee-high fawn skitters across the meadow and reminds me of other deer in other places. Heavy black clouds blow together, and apart. Last winter's snow catches in the pockets of Square Top's shoulders, then ridges down its perpendicular face. I step aside when a pack-laden group of hikers passes quickly by, but follow them with my eyes. While I watch them stride up the trail, the ghost of my younger self joins me here, and joins culpable hands with the spirits of the mountain men and the specter of Narcissa. Unlike the missionary's wife and the trappers, however, I can ascertain what I have done.

COLORADO SAVAGE BASINS

With one hand lightly resting on the steering wheel and the other holding a cellular phone, Dave Rote of Dave's Jeep Tours slouched nonchalantly in the driver's seat and maneuvered his dusty Silverado up the narrow grade. To the left, an almost perpendicular rock wall stiffened upward. To the right, a drop of perhaps two thousand feet plunged toward emptiness. Sitting in the open-air back of the truck, dust blowing in my face, I couldn't decide where to look.

Forward, I could watch red-shirted Dave finish his phone conversation, toss his black cowboy hat onto the passenger seat, then gesture toward the distant horizon. Space dropped off into space. I couldn't be sure if the front tire was holding steady in the track, if the steering wheel was steady in his hand. Reminding myself that Dave would be out of business if he bounced customers into infinity, I nonetheless shuddered with the rock ruts in the road.

Backward, I could watch the track recede, the orange summer paintbrush climb the cliff, the dust swirl in circles, the tangible earth. Occasionally I made myself glance the other way, nod at the view, survey the distant peaks, acknowledge the increasing depth of Telluride below. Mostly, though, I just hung on, past Royer's Gulch, alongside Whispering Jim's deserted shack, past the old Smuggler post office, alongside ruined foundations clinging to the cliff, and then under the profile of the Elephant.

Dave's Jeep Tours turns into Dave's Snowmobile Tours in the winter. One customer from southern California asked if he brought snowmobilers up here. "No way," Dave answered. "Too dangerous. Too many avalanches." The Silverado slid past the Elephant's buttress, the steepest avalanche chute on the Tomboy Road, now July green and cobbled black instead of January white. "Too dangerous," our driver repeated as he wedged us around a dark blue Ford Explorer coming down from the basin ahead. Explorer on the inside; Dave's Jeep Tours on the outside. I closed my eyes until I thought we were safe.

"Too dangerous." In 1906, however, more than twelve hundred people lived where we were headed on this dusty afternoon. Despite the avalanche danger, the mines in the Savage Basin operated nonstop, through summer sun and winter snow. The miners calculated the risks, took a few precautions, and went on about the business of extracting valuable ore from the earth. They cabled the Smuggler boarding house and mine offices against the side of the cliff, keeping it tightly bound beside the Elephant's chute. They erected a series of tramways to swing ore and men more quickly and easily across the steepest slopes. They dug tunnels both in the rock and through the snow.

While most of the workers lived permanently at the numerous mine sites dotting the landscape, other men traveled the precipitous route regularly. Mules brought supplies up a Tomboy Road that was narrower then, rarely wide enough for one team to pass another, never wide enough for a Silverado to pass an Explorer. Those men would have scoffed at my fear. So would their wives.

A few intrepid women made their homes in the Savage Basin, which once boasted the highest YMCA in America. Families lived there, children attended school. There Harriet Fish Backus began her married life, living nearly 11,500 feet above sea level through four stormbound winter seasons and summer reprises between 1906 and 1910. She rarely traveled the Tomboy Road back down to Telluride. "Too dangerous," perhaps.

COLORADO: SAVAGE BASINS 61

The narrative of Harriet's early years with her husband, George, starts like this chapter does, en route to the basin. Harriet's trip takes place in December, however, not July; she rides in a horse-drawn sled, not a modern four-wheel-drive vehicle. "Steeper and steeper we ascended," she writes, "and deeper plunged the gorge beside us. An occasional glimpse was all I dared take. Only a few inches separated the sled from the menacing drop below." Snow falls, softly at first and then quite heavily. Farther up the trail, the driver reports "a stroke of luck." Part of the Elephant just slid. "If we had got here a little sooner it would've been the end of us," he announces. Harriet, clutching George's hand, responds through chattering teeth. "How *can* we get through?"

On that first frightening expedition and on others described in Harriet's 1969 reminiscence, *Tomboy Bride*, they manage. Every winter trek is dangerous. One time, near the lower tunnel, her horse slips on the ice. "For one heart-rending instant Bird's hind foot pawed the air above the thousand-foot drop. Only his God-given instinct and sharp reaction saved us both," she shudders. Leaving the basin for the final time, she describes how the horses crept past the Big Elephant, how "we could feel its menace." To the end, she fears "the treacherous snow-covered trail."

Although I personally felt no menace from the Elephant, with its summer array of flowers and its shattered aspen trees, I never felt comfortable on the Tomboy Road. Because of the relentlessness of the drop-off and the ever deepening chasm just a tire-width to the right, I never relaxed. Insouciant Dave, on the other hand, casually traces the summer route to and fro every day, driving passengers from Telluride to Tomboy, the largest abandoned mine in the Savage Basin, one-time home of Harriet Fish Backus, and site of substantial gold and silver operations in the early years of the twentieth century.

Actually, the Tomboy ruins are a popular stopping place on a well-used jeep route from Telluride to Ouray, Colorado. Any summer day, dozens of vehicles navigate the steep terrain, climbing more than three thousand feet in five miles to the Tomboy, winding sixteen hundred feet in just another mile and a half up to Imogene Pass, then dropping down to a different ghost mine relic at Camp Bird, and finally arriving in Ouray. The jeep route covers seventeen miles across the San Juan Mountains. By passenger car, on circuitous pavement, it's forty-nine miles, and faster. Tourists and locals love the dangerous challenge, however, and generally make the trip without incident. I wonder what Harriet Fish Backus might think of a jeepster traffic jam?

Dave takes most of his customers up to the pass and then back down the road to Telluride, but he dropped me off on The Flats, a level area above the Tomboy mine and in between what used to be the Japan and the Argentine properties. This was the early-twentieth-century residential district. While most of the single men lived in bunkhouses, the families lived in shacks on The Flats. Little remains now. In fact, the tallest structure on The Flats today is a $15,000 solar-powered outhouse, constructed for the jeeping tourists. That's where Dave left me with my backpack, left me to see if I could imagine Harriet Fish Backus's life in the Savage Basin. I wonder what she might think of a solar-powered outhouse?

I decided to follow a single ghostly voice in Colorado, to walk in Harriet's footsteps, to see what she saw ninety years ago, to contemplate what she remembered and what has changed. What could I learn, not only from the way she conceived of her own past but also from the ways she imagined the pasts of those who preceded her? What might I perceive differently? So I began as she did, letting someone competent transport a somewhat fearful passenger up the Tomboy Road while at the same time looking eagerly to the adventures ahead.

Although Harriet arrived in December, her welcoming scene was far from dismal. She describes "the brilliantly lighted buildings of the mill," and characterizes the ongoing sound of the sixty stamps as "a dull, heavy, continuous 'thud.'" In contrast, no electricity serves the Savage Basin today. At night, it's totally dark, and almost totally silent. A major difference between then and now, I think, is the non-stop noise of a sixty stamp mill crushing thousands of tons of ore to isolate ounces of gold. Harriet's basin was never still. Mine was resonant, too, but in a different way. I heard the rush of creeks and a patter of rivulets, the crash of a rock slide off the southwest wall, the scared squeak of a pica, the rhythms of rain. I also heard the grinding of gears and an audible curse, commercial jets overhead, and the flap of the wind against the fly of my tent. Sounds of commerce, then and now.

Because a well-traveled jeep road cuts through the Savage Basin few collectible artifacts remain. The bottles, the broken dishes, the tools, the cabling must have been irresistible, for the earth has been almost picked clean by scavengers who have swept whatever was available into their four-wheel-drive vehicles. They even downed the electrical poles, felling them with saws in order to snatch the insulators, leaving twenty-foot armless stumps scattered on the ground. Unlike many ghostly mining camps in the West, where purple glass still layers and dates the dumping grounds, the Tomboy seems cleansed of itself.

I backpacked away from the outhouse and put up my tent on a bench above The Flats. From there, my view extended across the basin in three directions. Telluride was barely visible, though I could spot the new ski runs extended above the town. The weather wasn't wonderful. Squalls blew around the surrounding peaks, while clouds formed and re-formed like the billowed residue of dry ice. Harriet notes "few electric storms, none close or severe. Thunderheads were quickly blown away but often we could see lightning in the valley below, and heat-lightning far far away." I observed the same phenomena—storms that didn't settle in the basin, faint echoes of thunder with bolts of lightning striking far below my vantage point, and a great deal of precipitation that would be snow, rather than rain, between September and May.

The next morning I hiked to Imogene Pass. Though the old horse trail was regraded into a jeep route in 1965, it still zigzags steeply above the basin. Harriet and George once ventured up the trail to see Ptarmigan Lake, which was the water supply for the Tomboy operation, and to visit Camp Bird on the other side. "Trips between the mine and the lake were few," Harriet summarizes, "and rarely did anyone take the trip for pleasure." Now a county road crew plows the winding track between Telluride and Ouray as soon as is feasible. Only seven days before I was there, workers had finished cutting through thirty-foot snowbanks so that jeepsters could reach the pass easily. When Harriet rode to Imogene Pass, she imagined those who rode before her. "I was tingling with excitement," she remembers, "thinking of the challenge these formidable barriers had been to pioneers first trying to cross them." I wanted to do the same thing, to imagine Harriet and George. I was excited, too, thinking of Harriet's own challenges, her body rigid, her heart pounding, her tentative "I'm afraid to go," which she spoke as she urged her horse forward.

I've read a lot of first-person narratives and reminiscences of the American West. I've especially read a lot of women's recollections. Few are expressed with the joie de vivre of *Tomboy Bride*. Though she often admits her fears, she as readily projects curiosity about her surroundings and enthusiasm for new experiences. Harriet Fish traveled alone from San Francisco to Denver to meet George Backus, her husband-to-be. As soon as they exchanged their wedding vows—a day late because bad weather delayed the train—they set out for the Savage Basin. Once there, this remarkable woman sank to her waist in snow, laughed at herself, pushed her Tomboy Road fears away and thanked the driver for "a wonderful ride," then opened the door to her new home, a "room ten feet square which was the living-room and bedroom combined."

She learns to order food, every package and pound freighted up from Telluride. She learns to cook at high elevation. She learns that meat must thaw before roasting, and experiences the hazards of spoiled meat. She reports that their best canned fruits and vegetables would be unacceptable now, but no fresh food was available. Housekeeping turns out to be relatively easy in a shack with little furniture, or relatively difficult in a household shared with busy pack rats. One day she discovers long-missing potatoes, cheese, and chocolate stowed carefully in a box of prized photos.

When the Backuses move to another dwelling, a bigger place with two rooms and a tiny bed niche in between, Harriet and George pad the walls with newspapers, paper the padding with blue drafting paper, carpet the floor with denim. "The view was superb," Harriet enthuses. Best of all, "the important outhouse was only fifty feet" away. In a severe storm, however, the setting is not so perfect. "On one such day

COLORADO: SAVAGE BASINS 65

of gathering fury our unprotected shack shook violently and creaked." She worries if they dare stay there overnight, though of course there's nowhere else to go. "What kept the cracker box standing I'll never know," she concludes, while her "chattering teeth kept time to the rattling of the old stovepipe fastened by wires to the rafters." By the next evening the storm has abated and Harriet's point of view has brightened. "After the fury of the night before we settled down to enjoy the silence and beauty of softly falling snow." So the pattern of her prose continues, with moments of fear or discomfort immediately followed by longer passages of contentment.

A shack similar to the Backus abode still stands awkwardly on The Flats. The main room measures approximately 10' x 15'. The kitchen, nearly as big, has a lean-to alongside. All the walls are aslant now, but I could tell that someone had taken care to paper them with something green, and had painted the window sills a complementary darker shade. Two stove holes in the ceilings of the two rooms poke through a bent tin roof; underfoot, a dirt floor. I thought about living here in winter, through long nights and constant blizzards and loneliness while my husband worked twelve hours a day, seven days a week. Even as I pondered the difficulties, however, I realized "the view was superb!"

Clearly Harriet prefers summer to winter. Her summer descriptions are softer, quieter, calmer, more pictorial. "The bowl of blue sky over the cirque, sun glitter sparkling on the snow crowning the rocky heights, the velvet-green in the canyon, and far below the mesas of the San Miguel reaching for the lost horizon." Even the worrisome avalanche chute takes on a gentler mantle. "The Big Elephant, attacked by the sun," she writes, "rapidly shed his heavy coat of snow and burst forth in myriads of long-stemmed purple columbines nodding gracefully."

Certainly the wildflowers were in full blossom when I was wandering around the Savage Basin. The hillside where the Backuses lived was a nursery of colors. I camped ankle-deep in white ballhead sandwort which, as the days passed, gave way to yellow buttercups. Not only columbines but Indian paintbrush shading from white to yellow and from orange to fuchsia covered the grassy slope. Higher, where the swampy remains of snow still moistened the ground, marsh marigolds grew almost solidly side by side. I startled a ptarmigan family into a red-green cluster of king's crown. Chicks darted in four directions while the mottled hen squawked a dire warning, then skittered through the tufted grass. Harriet remarks sadly that, in her day, the chipmunks were too tiny and the marmots starving. "Cruel scarcity of vegetation took its toll," she observes. Nearly a century later, unoccupied ruins and jeeping picnickers must be more agreeable neighbors, for this summer's marmots were almost obese, and I saw healthy chipmunks everywhere.

So the basin changes and yet remains the same. Where Harriet could never escape the thunder of the stamps, I could often imagine myself distanced from civilization. Even the fallen towers, the broken cribbing, the shattered glass, the isolated brickwork, the rusted cables and pipes, the mining detritus everywhere couldn't detract from the summer serenity I found. The ongoing stream of basin visitors was easily ignored because few ventured far from their vehicles. A typical carload would pause at the mill site, read the sign, take half a dozen pictures, glance around the basin at the other remains, then hurry up the grade, low gears grinding, to the next photo opportunity or vehicular challenge. Some might stand around a little longer; some might eat lunch. No one climbed to the gardens of flowers and snow ponds exquisitely benched above the basin.

Sociability didn't permeate my tourist Tomboy world, but for Harriet things were quite different. Nearby neighbors became frequent visitors and, eventually, lifelong friends. George's fellow workers came to dinner, which Harriet graciously prepared. Tongue-in-cheek, she acknowledges that they came for the sociability, not the gourmet food, but she thoroughly enjoys their conversations. She loves George's company, too, especially delighting in their ritual evening toast and hot chocolate. And of course the mines themselves were a constant noisy presence.

A month after her arrival in the Savage Basin, the Japan mine foreman invited Harriet into the depths. She facetiously describes the episode as "pure hell," but she also contributes some fascinating firsthand observations. Up a vertical shaft, with water dripping from above and her candle sputtering, she "stepped carefully for fear of tripping on my skirt." Then she crawled through a confining cross-shaft. "In the darkness, broken only by a flicker of the nearby candle, I twisted, turned, writhed like a snake, stopped many times to rest and capture a mite of courage." Finally, the three of them—Harriet, George, and the foreman—rode the cage down to the one thousand foot level, "alone in the bowels of the mountain. Sounds of water gurgling out of crevices echoed through the vaulted caverns. Our voices resounded weirdly. I wandered around the large underground cave peering into empty stopes, drifts and storage rooms until mounting claustrophobia started my stomach to quiver." Harriet confesses her uneasiness but again confronts adventure with little hesitation.

Even pregnancy is undaunting, though she moves down to Telluride for the actual birth. There she lives in a rented house a block from the miner's hospital at the base of the Tomboy Road. Empty now, though the local historical society plans to restore it, the old hospital is a visual reminder of the mining community at the beginning of the twentieth century. So is the New Sheridan Hotel, where Harriet and George stayed during their brief sojourns to town.

Apart from Harriet's two-month stay when baby Harriet was born, the Backuses spent little time in Telluride. As I look at the town then and now, however, I see the profound differences a hundred years have made. Where George and Harriet had only the Sheridan Hotel to choose from, visitors now might opt for the Mountain Village, an immense blockish ski complex with advertised room rates beginning at $500 per night. Sitting in the lobby of The Peaks hotel, I contrast the heavy opulent appointments with the Backus "honeymoon suite," as described by Harriet. "Our cheerless hotel room contained a double bed, a dresser, one chair, and the usual stand with a water pitcher and basin. Wearily falling into bed, we found the sheets cold and damp." What might Harriet think of The Peaks? Or of the newly redecorated

Sheridan Hotel where she could order caribou, ostrich, kangaroo, or elk from the current dinner menu? How would she interpret today's Telluride?

This mountain community has escaped some of Aspen's misfortunes, although in-town properties are selling for better than $300,000 per antiquated home. A strict building code prohibits high-rises and restricts inappropriate architecture. Every structure must be three stories or less; every design, Victorian in nature. Billboards, chain stores, and strip malls are banned. On the other side of the mountain, the wealth-driven Mountain Village is invisible from downtown Telluride. A gondola, free of charge to summer tourists, connects the two halves of the resort, giving winter access to more than a thousand acres of advanced ski terrain.

As I sat snug in the swaying glass-enclosed gondola car, I compared my comfort to the discomfort of the miners who rode the trams. In open swaying ore carts, huddled beneath heavy quilts, noses and beards sheltered from the freezing snow, they managed. I shared my bubble gondola with a less venturesome Colorado commuter. She staffed the Mountain Village Spa but lived in Telluride proper. "An easy commute," she said, "just fifteen minutes over the mountain." On a warm summer evening, she wore only a thin T-shirt. Below us, the lights of Telluride twinkled together, suggesting a summer Christmas card.

With the advent of mega-ski operations, Colorado high country has changed enormously since the Backuses lived there. Aspen, losing its old mining-camp charm, became an overnight resort sensation. I remember skiing there when I was a graduate student, sleeping in an old VW bus in the parking lot and eating a single meal a day because I couldn't afford any extravagance. I skied at Vail, too, a newly minted destination in the 1960s now spreading amoeba-like down Eagle Valley. When I return to Colorado now, my Boulder days long behind me, I see the Rockies not only through memory's haze but also through some very real dust. Driving Interstate 70 in the 1990s is like passing through an ongoing construction zone, with plumbers and realtors replacing miners and geologists as extractive entrepreneurs.

COLORADO: SAVAGE BASINS 69

Perhaps George and Harriet would appreciate my incredulity. They themselves rode an economic pendulum back and forth across the West. They left the Tomboy for a brief stint in distant British Columbia, tested a rather unsuccessful mining venture in Idaho, and then made their way back to the Centennial State. George's new job was unique—to reopen, refurbish, and make profitable an idle mill. Using the flotation process successfully tested by Herbert Hoover in Australia, the Pingrey Mines Company planned to buy and treat old tailings dumps to recover additional salable minerals. George would superintend the operation. So the Backus family moved to Leadville, site of one of Colorado's grandest nineteenth-century mother lodes. The year was 1913. Harriet stepped into history.

Leadville began typically enough, with a gold strike in 1860 that boomed and busted quite rapidly. Ten years later, only a few residents remained. Then, in 1875, William Stevens and Alvinus Wood realized the black sand clogging the sluice boxes was actually full of silver. The bust was over and the boom began anew. By 1878, Leadville's population had swelled to 20,000, and the highest incorporated city in the country was one of the wealthiest.

Horace Tabor set the standard. A stone mason turned placer miner turned shopkeeper, he grubstaked two prospectors who struck the Little Pittsburg ore body. Using his profits, he bought the nearby Matchless Mine for $117,000. It went on to produce an average of $2,000 per day, with ore assaying to ten thousand ounces of silver per ton. H. A. W. Tabor—"synonymous with silver and Leadville"—went on to become one of the wealthiest men in Colorado. Even though poor business practices and the 1893 silver panic later decimated his investments, Tabor's legend lives. When he had money, he spent it flamboyantly. He paid for Leadville's elegant Tabor Opera House, for example, erected in just a hundred days. He built a business block in Denver. He befriended east coast moguls and western politicians alike. He ran for public office, and even bought himself a vacant United States senatorial seat for a single month. He loved to gamble.

Known for his roving eye, Tabor soon found a woman more glamorous than his wife. With too much fanfare, perhaps, he courted Elizabeth McCourt, a free spirit nicknamed Baby Doe. An extravagant courtship, a harshly contested divorce, and a lavish wedding headlined the social news for months. The Tabor and Baby Doe story so fascinates people that, even today, the couple and their properties are the headliners of Leadville. "Leadville is Tabor: Tabor's mine, Tabor's hotel, Tabor's Opera House, Tabor's residence," intones scholar Stephen Voynick.

I toured the Tabor Opera House. I drove to the Matchless Mine, and saw Baby Doe's cabin from a distance, declining to pay for the Matchless tour out of deference to Augusta, the first Mrs. Tabor. She did, after all, have a difficult time of it, and I found myself annoyed by the prostitution of the legend. I read Matchless realty ads, looked in the window of the Matchless Hair Salon, walked on a street named Baby Doe. I couldn't escape the Tabor aura.

Harriet Fish Backus couldn't escape the Tabor aura, either. Renting a house on Leadville's Leiter street, she soon learned that its previous tenants had been Baby Doe Tabor and her daughter, Silver Dollar. Dead broke by now, owing money for rent, the two had fled without paying, grim reminders of the cyclical nature of mining. Their story intrigued Harriet, however, and she soon immersed herself in Leadville's past. "The structures of Leadville," she writes, "are saturated with history, memories of human drama, romance, pathos, and tragedy."

Choosing a house on Leiter Street, and later buying one a block away, the Backus family lived in the most prestigious part of town. Capitol Hill once housed the community's wealthiest residents, but capitalism is transient. Harriet notes with some pride that the home they bought for five hundred dollars "probably would have sold for ten thousand dollars in the heyday of Leadville." I smiled at both prices as I browsed through the Leadville Alpaca Company, a newly opened upscale establishment that foretells trends for acquisitive tourists. Alpaca pullovers cost $200; hand-sewn vests, $100; a hand-carved table, $1400. Paintings and sculptures were in the $500 to $1200 range.

If the Leadville Alpaca Company seems pricey, however, the rest of the town so far has escaped the second-home syndrome. With no

COLORADO: SAVAGE BASINS 71

nearby ski resort and with an unforgiving climate, not as many newcomers have flocked there as elsewhere in Colorado. No high-rise hotel, no valley of condominiums, no gondola, no espresso carts, no Wal-Mart. Harrison Street, the main thoroughfare of downtown Leadville, looks very like pictures taken fifty years ago. Some buildings have been refurbished, some not, so the old and new stand side by side. Red brick sidewalks, faded red brick buildings. A sandwich board advertising Massage Therapy and the Groggy Bottoms Sports Bar. The words *Leadville Mining Company*, chiseled on one façade. The words *T-shirts 9.99* hanging alongside. Szchuan Taste II downstairs; an empty floor for rent above. A Kum & Go gas mart next to a vacant lot filled with lavender fireweed. A satellite dish. The silent steeple of an empty church.

Harriet speaks of Sunday afternoon walks. They began, of course, on Capitol Hill, which today has taken on a reconstructed elegance. Most of the old mansions look well-tended, with fresh Victorian tricolor coats of paint. The Backus rental, for example, and the neighboring home of its 1913 owner, Mrs. Brittain, mirror each other. The rental property is painted gray now, with beige and amber gingerbread, while Mrs. Brittain's old home is beige, highlighted with amber and gray. A large stained-glass window, with an inlaid miner's figure, lights the downhill side of the rental. Between the two homes, a wrought-iron fence encloses a spacious lawn. Beyond, an extraordinary view of Mt. Massive dominates the western skyline. "Majestic beyond all telling," raptures Harriet, "grand, snowy and sublime!"

While I appreciated the view, too, I was more interested in the Backus environs. Nearby houses were as attractive as the old Brittain places. Three shades of lavender for one; three shades of yellow and beige for another; three shades of blue. Not all of the homes have been recently redone, for I saw a few that leaned with age, an unpaved alley bumping unpretentiously between them, but the block as a whole was very appealing. I could well imagine Harriet and George walking with young Harriet or wheeling young George down the hill toward town. As soon as they left their sanctuary, however, the scenery would change: "the picket fences around little houses in various stages of disrepair, gutters carrying away snow-water, fringes of dreary dumps, mounds of discarded ore and waste rock, unused trestles, broken gallus frames, and old shaft houses."

Even today, the veneer deteriorates almost immediately. At the foot of Capitol Hill, the houses are one-story functional homes without gingerbread. Few have been repainted in the last twenty-five years. Purple columbine, apparently transported from a mountain meadow somewhere, filled one yard, but most of the lawns were unkempt and cluttered with weeds. A few blocks farther, the houses shrunk again. They looked so aged and frail, I fretted for the occupants when wintry blizzards blow through the cracks and crannies. "Then on through Stumptown, Bucktown, Chicken Hill, and Shanty Town to the mill" where George worked, Harriet maps the way. Nothing but the foundation of the long-deserted Pingrey mill remains. It stair-steps up a brown-stained hill, with the mottled dwellings of Stringtown pressing against its ruins.

Back uptown, but east of Harrison Street, the setting is even more depressing. Here the deserted mines and their accompanying moonscape tailings edge right into town. Fouling their own nest, nineteenth-century miners paid no attention to the niceties of a neighborhood. Fingers of unearthed soil touch every street and every yard. Red, white, black, beige, amber, gray, the oxidized earthen colors ironically image those of the Brittain houses, gaily painted in new post-Victorian dress. Here and there, twentieth-century nature seems to be overtaking the unnatural nineteenth-century leavings. A low yewlike evergreen shrub covers the draws between the mounds, and flowering yarrow, cinquefoil, and paintbrush grow everywhere. Barbed wire blocks many of the old roads, so the tracks are fading from disuse. *No Trespassing* signs mark the terrain. Overhead power poles mirror the broken hoists; power lines simulate the torn and rusted cable littering the dirt.

No matter where one walks in Leadville, one cannot forget the mines. The excavations dominate the landscape, just as the historic names lend character to the buildings and businesses. Even when I tried to return to nature's present, I couldn't quite escape the mechan-

COLORADO: SAVAGE BASINS 73

ics of the past. Climbing Mt. Massive, the 14,000-footer that looms to the west, I could see the diggings more clearly than the town itself. Turning, at tree line, to look across the valley, I could see various stages of Leadville's past carved up to the horizon. Tenting at Turquoise Lake, long the favorite retreat of Lake County residents, I could choose one of several campgrounds: the Tabor, the Baby Doe, the Silver Dollar, the Matchless. Hiking almost anywhere in the vicinity, I came upon tailings large and small. Pure lake water might lap against a Vesuvius of discolored dirt and rock, an adit might collapse along a trail.

As dominant as Massive to the west is fractured Bartlett Mountain to the east, not a part of Leadville's glamorous Tabor past but very much a part of George and Harriet Backus's Leadville years and very much a part of the community's later mining history. A prospector named Charles Senter filed and lightly worked a number of claims on Bartlett. He dug no appreciable silver or gold, but did strike what appeared to be carbon or some sort of graphite-like substance. Assays proved the find to be a sulfide of molybdenum. The unusual metal had little commercial value at the beginning of the twentieth century, but Senter managed to interest George's boss, O. A. King, in his discovery. King, in turn, interested George.

The story, as I understand it, is complicated by the biases of the tellers. Harriet's version coincides with King's, as narrated in his own reminiscence, *Gray Gold*. Briefly, George was able to utilize flotation techniques to mill molybdenum concentrates from the Bartlett ore. At the same time, the moly market grew larger when scientists learned it could be combined with steel to form a particularly strong alloy. With the onset of World War I, weapons and tanks and airplanes needed such reinforcement. So the market potential apparently was immense. But Senter, King, and the Pingrey Mining Company were not alone in their molybdenum quest. Equally interested and considerably more powerful, the American Metals Company began buying adjoining claims.

The competition turned bitter, escalating from warnings to threats to fights to lawsuits. Because a German corporation held 49 percent of

Amco's stock, it seemed imperative for the Americans to win control of what turned out to be the largest molybdenum deposit in the world. Amco was too strong to dislodge, however. With the establishment of a subsidiary, the Climax Molybdenum Company, and the institution of an aggressive leader, Max Schott, the *gesellschaft* operation at Bartlett Mountain quickly overshadowed King's smaller enterprise.

Besides, the Climax Molydenum Company wasn't playing fair. At least that was the conclusion reached by King in *Gray Gold*, by Harriet Fish Backus in *Tomboy Bride*, and by Stephen M. Voynick in *Leadville: A Miner's Epic* and his later *Climax: The History of Colorado's Climax Molybdenum Mine*. Although Voynick doesn't personalize the events, as Harriet and King do, he nonetheless argues their case. King, in fact, won all the lawsuits and countersuits filed during the turmoil. But by the time the court cases were settled, the Climax Company effectively controlled the deposits, the water rights, and the mountain itself.

What began for George as an intellectual and practical scientific experiment—to test the untested flotation process in innovative ways—ended in nightmarish repetition of the frontier West. The bully outgunned the opposition. As Harriet narrates her final Leadville chapters, her tone changes. No longer the sheltered young bride, she must grapple with menacing events. "Every night when George came home I heard of new offenses, more interference, and brawls," she writes ominously. Nothing "could dispel the shadowy forebodings always at the back of my mind. I feared for George's life." No wonder she never liked Leadville as much as she loved Tomboy.

While claim-jumpers moved survey stakes, hired thugs disrupted the workers and patrolled the trenches. Most critically, the Climax Molybdenum Company usurped the only available water, displacing the prior Senter claim. All this took place above Fremont Pass, at elevations in excess of 12,000 feet, often in blinding snow with temperatures well below zero. Without sufficient capital, King and his friends helplessly watched their remorseless rivals expand their diggings, stretch tramways from tower to tower, build a whole company town complete with post office and school, and gain total control.

COLORADO: SAVAGE BASINS 75

Bartlett Mountain isn't there any more, at least not the Bartlett of George and Harriet's time. The mine eventually consumed not only the side of the peak but finally, with a 1960 mill expansion, the company town of Climax itself. Optimistically, the operation could go on for another half century, since half the mountain remains to be mined. When the bottom fell out of the steel industry, however, moly mining ceased to be profitable. Now the Climax Molybdenum Company, like the mountain against which it rested, isn't there any more either.

Owned by AMAX, the Climax mine shut down in 1982. A skeleton crew staffs the buildings, while a few other workers deal with some of the environmental damage downstream. I'm told the entire operation could be reopened quickly, should the moly market recover, but today the site looks almost deserted. Close at hand, the entrance station needs paint and dandelions fill the parking lot cracks. The word VISITORS over one door has partially peeled away. A handful of pickups nose up against a bulky seven-story building where the walls are peeling, too, and where a tunnel marks the entrance. Three men in hardhats walk by. Otherwise, I can see no movement in the entire complex, save for two flags—USA and C for Colorado—snapping in the wind. The scene, harsh, elemental, barebones, is the unromantic side of mining, a specter of faded illusions and thwarted technology. All this machinery standing idle; all that menacing ill-will between Schott's men and King's, mostly forgotten.

Across the highway from the mine entrance, AMAX put together a mining display for tourists. A few rusted artifacts sit spaced around a fenced walk, while interpretive signs explain the molybdenum mining process and the advent of the Climax operation. No mention is made of O. A. King. Reading the signs, I learned that the past according to AMAX is very different from the past according to King and Harriet Fish Backus. Here was the site of a progressive American undertaking, where hard-working honest miners risked their lives under harsh climatic conditions to bring a necessary industrial component to the Armed Forces of the United States. The leadership of far-sighted Max Schott provided the catalyst for their enterprise. Schott merits his own sign, signaling his success. One sign praises the Climax school; another, the Boy Scout troop; still another, productivity statistics. A larger sign details the subsequent reclamation process, with more puffery for AMAX's endeavors.

I can understand why AMAX might not want to introduce the inauspicious beginnings of the Climax operation in a roadside picnic area, but I didn't expect Leadville's National Mining Hall of Fame and Museum to whitewash the early events as well. I guess I'm naïve. Devoting a full room to the molybdenum mining process, the museum shows dioramas of the extraction and milling operation from start to finish. It outlines its historic beginnings, too. No mention is made of O. A. King. Even though King began mining Charles Senter's claims in 1915, and even though George Backus supervised the new flotation process by which the mineral could be separated from the ore, and even though the Pingrey company made the first commercial moly shipment, none of their activities is credited. Max Schott, who took charge of the Climax Molybdenum Company when it was established in 1916, gets all the glory. His successor, Brainard Phillipson, gets all the press.

There in the National Mining Hall of Fame and Museum, a very fine monument to the placer and hard-rock miners of the past and a very fine testament to the importance of minerals in our contemporary lives, I saw for myself what new historians argue so eloquently. "Winners" write themselves in history; "losers" disappear. I went upstairs to the room lined with Hall of Fame plaques. No mention of O. A. King there, either. I looked for a copy of *Gray Gold* in the large museum library, but found they didn't have one. I asked in the bookstore downstairs, but the clerk hadn't heard of the title. In another Leadville bookstore, I was told *Gray Gold* is out of print. How remarkable, I thought, to trace the lives of people and then to find their very existence obliterated by corporate decree.

Given the AMAX reinterpretation of history, I distrusted their other claims, too. On Fremont Pass, for example, one of the tour signs boasts that "Tenmile Creek has been restored to a healthy and vigorous fishery by the Climax Mine." After explaining their three-prong mode of reclamation—water quality, land rehabilitation, and soil stabilization—

the sign writer insists on "the company policy to take every possible precaution to guard against stream pollution." True, perhaps, but the Tenmile visual pollution is enormous. Half of Bartlett Mountain had to go somewhere. That somewhere? Tenmile Valley.

Much of the valley is filled with tailings and debris. A Red Sea with naked shores floats birdless where old mining camps like Robinson and Kokomo used to stand. The two towns now lie buried beneath a muddy landscape artificially reconstructed and rearranged. In *Gray Gold*, O. A. King remembers the valley with "a sense of awe. Such splendor was untouched by the hand of man except where he burrowed through a few small tunnels in quest for gold," he recalls, without any sense of irony. The creek itself was awesome, too. "The water, clear as crystal, was leaping from rock to rock, forming little eddies and pools."

From a distance, the lower creek seems to run as clear today as it did a century ago. A company sign boasts of the excellent fishing downstream, but I couldn't get a close look because AMAX restricts the area to employees only. From what I could see first-hand, however, the higher basin seems deathly polluted. Dust clouds blow harshly off the tailings, while red and turquoise trickles etch the dirt. A single flatbed truck; a single worker maneuvering a heavy hose onto the bare ground, then inching it toward an isolated building. I saw no other sign of life. No transient birds, no marmot or deer prints in the dirt, no vegetation whatsoever. Just as the Fremont Pass display inadequately prepared me for the historic past, so it ill-focused on the visual realities of the present. Tenmile Valley is just plain ugly. Not even the crisp outline of the Mountain of the Holy Cross, rising in the distance, can redeem it. Tenmile's future seems problematic, too, since there's nowhere else for the rest of Bartlett Mountain to go.

I've written elsewhere that modern mining methods turn the terrain into ghosts, diminishing mountains while creating new ones, redesigning streams and lakes and entire water supplies, manipulating the landscape in whatever ways are most profitable. At the same time mining has become more invasive, however, it also has become more cognizant of environmental issues. Or so public relations materials would have me believe. At least a few companies are taking responsibility for past and current toxicity. Some people swear, in fact, that Leadville water is as pure as any in the state of Colorado. Damning with faint praise, I suppose.

Like AMAX in the Leadville area, Newmont Gold, which now owns the Tomboy property, has done some clean-up, too. In the Savage Basin I could see a series of new cement waterways snaking downward. Looking like stiltless Roman viaducts, these open conduits fast-track clean water past contaminated sites. Through the places where the old mines and mills used to be, water rushes in containment. Then it splashes freely into streams and mini-waterfalls that spill on down to Telluride's San Miguel River. I don't know if clean water actually emerges, but I'm told this process is effective. Roman viaducts, Roman civilization, I thought to myself, wondering how a few hundred yards of cement spillway can cleanse a century's worth of tailings.

Like her contemporaries, Harriet never thought much about reclamation when she lived in the Savage Basin. There's an irony about that, because she certainly discusses the detritus left behind in Leadville, its "fringes of dreary dumps" and "mounds of discarded ore." When she plays an active role, when the mines and mills are throbbing all around her, she doesn't take time to ponder scenic alterations. When she comes into a well-worked setting, however, when the oxidized leavings mound into old tailings and the shanties stand empty, she pays much closer attention to the unattractiveness of the landscape.

She pays closer attention to her sense of history, too. While she doesn't think of herself or of George as historic figures in the Tomboy story, she clearly is cognizant of the men and women who preceded them in Leadville. "Here I was," she exclaims, "avidly interested in the colorful characters who had made fascinating history of the West, teaching in a school surrounded by mines which had produced the foundations for immense fortunes." Here I am, avidly interested in the Backuses, who would hardly call themselves "colorful."

Harriet's entire conception of the Leadville portion of *Tomboy Bride* differs significantly from the Savage Basin narrative. The world

COLORADO: SAVAGE BASINS

above Telluride fills 130 pages; Leadville, only 36. Of those 36, perhaps a third retells the town's history, a third recounts the molybdenum debacle, and a third reveals personal events in the Backus family life. If I might put words in Harriet's mouth, I think she would say it was the Leadville portent and potential for tragedy that made her life there so disquieting. The boom-to-bust surroundings. World War I in the background. The flu epidemic. The molybdenum strife. A constant fear that George might be in danger.

The Backuses arrived in a Savage Basin camp bustling with energy. Even though the Japan Mine soon closed, George immediately found work at the Tomboy. Production was at its height. The two honeymooners felt, so to speak, on top of the world. Occasionally they thought of those who had gone before—when Harriet rides over Imogene Pass, for example, and thinks of the challenge posed for the pioneers—but for the most part they lived happily in the present and looked optimistically to the future.

Leadville presented a different milieu. There the wave had already crested. Rather than mine fresh lodes, George was reworking old tailings, applying unsubstantiated recovery methods and, finally, seeking an ore with no discernible value. A past filled with such ghosts as the Tabors, the Matchless, and Baby Doe portended little reason for optimism. A present fraught with claim jumpers and hired hoodlums allowed little peace. The future must have seemed uncertain at best. Although I cannot picture Harriet overtly burdening George with her worries, I know she had misgivings about life in what others affectionately called Cloud City. "As we crossed Tennessee Pass," she writes at the end of *Tomboy Bride*, "I felt a sense of relief, for during the last weeks and months 'the sorrow of others had cast their shadows over me.'" Harriet was glad to leave Leadville behind. When she did so, the Backus family stepped softly out of history.

OREGON SAND AND SEA

A curtain hangs in the heavy sky. A sheet of rain separates the shore from the sea, divides audience from actors. A January storm lashes my face and the wind bowls me sideways, as the Pacific Ocean drives massively toward me, and recedes. I'm in no danger, though. No heave of deck under my feet, no plunge, no trough, no surge, no sickening thud of rudder and hull. Dipping my head into the storm, I snug my rain jacket tighter and walk farther along the beach.

Offshore, beyond this shroud of sleet and wind, what might occur? A schooner or bark would be almost helpless today if it sailed too close to the breakers. As waves slam the sand, sea-swept ghosts sail into my imagination. I picture a ship's masts pitching violently. One snaps in two. The captain orders the rigging hacked away, thrown overboard into the surf. "Cut down the other masts," he shouts, urging the only measure left to save the ship. Two men scurry aloft. One, clinging to a crossbar, loses his footing, then his grip on a rain-slick mizzen. The other, watching his mate drop into the boiling sea, hears a cry of despair before he, too, falls from his perch with a scarcely discernible wail. Below, the captain and his remaining crew scuttle the load, try to lighten the ship so she'll float free from danger. A thump! The schooner lurches helplessly. A louder grinding crunch, accompanied by a crack of splintering wood. "Man the lifeboats!" the captain shrills too late. With an explosive force the ship snaps onto her side, buries her starboard ribs into the sand. Men flail, but the sea sweeps them helplessly away. In just fifteen minutes, only bobbing debris remains—broken boxes of cargo, the officers' mess table, some brass fittings, the shredded mainsail, the ship's masthead floating free.

The Clatsop Spit extends south from the mouth of the Columbia River, where more than two hundred major vessels have foundered and sunk, where more than two thousand smaller ships have run aground, broken apart, disappeared. "The Graveyard of the Pacific" is known for its gale-force winds, rain hammering sideways, waves in thunderous swells. And underneath the water, tons of sand shift and suck, unseen and unpredictable. Nineteenth-century sailing ships sometimes waited offshore three or four weeks before attempting to cross the Columbia River bar. During fierce winter storms, their sailors dared not trust the erratic winds and unfathomable sands. A single gust might pitch a ship into the shallows. A second swell could break a ship in two, leaving captain and crew scrambling for safety.

1841: The *Peacock*, a twenty-two-gun sloop-of-war, tried to cross the Columbia River bar as heavy winds and blinding hail blew fiercely from the north and west. In the pounding surf, the *Peacock* rocked back and forth while her sailors fought unsuccessfully to keep her off the sands. "We have no hope," wrote Midshipman Alonzo Davis in the ship's log, "but of saving the crew."

1846: The *Shark*, a U.S. Naval survey schooner, weighed anchor too hastily and ran aground on the very sands her crew had been charting. Although Captain Schenk jettisoned the ship's twelve cannons and cut down her masts, he couldn't save the *Shark* from extinction. One cannon later resurfaced; hence the name of Oregon's Cannon Beach.

1852: The *General Warren*, a packet steamer loaded with grain, crossed the bar safely but ran into gale-force winds on the open sea. Water deluged the pumps and began filling her holds. Once she ran aground, huge swells battered her sides and leveled her in hours.

1881: The *Lupatia*, a British bark, was lost at the southern end of

OREGON: SAND AND SEA

the Clatsop Spit when her captain and crew were unable to navigate by a starless sky. They sailed directly into the rocky Tillamook Head while astonished onlookers stared at the *Lupatia*'s ghostly silhouette.

With the advent of steam, some of the dangerous uncertainty dissipated, but the actual channel at the mouth of the Columbia remained unpredictable. To funnel the water and sand into consistently navigable routes, the Army Corps of Engineers built the south jetty in the 1890s, extended it in 1914, and finished the north jetty two years later. Even today, dredges must continually deepen the charted channel. Technology has made passage less treacherous, however. Between 1892 and 1979, lightships guarded the mouth of the river, with foghorns and bells and powerful gas and electric beacons as guides. Then radar made the rough channel safer still. Today, shipwrecks are so rare as to be almost unheard of, for electronic buoys oversee the river's mouth and warn the wary away from danger. The ghosts of capsized crafts and drowning sailors, however, patrol the broken Pacific waters beyond the shore.

1899: The *Columbia River Lightship No. 50* slipped her anchor cables. Bow-breaking waves buffeted her toward McKenzie Head. Supposed to guard the bar's entrance and to guide other vessels, *Lightship No. 50* was incapacitated, left high and dry on the sands after the winds and tide receded.

1906: The *Melanope*, her hull listing badly to starboard, floated toward the mouth of the Columbia. Her broken masts, her torn sails, her battered yardarms, and her frayed ropes spoke of a derelict's difficult voyage.

1913: The *Rosecrans*, a tanker carrying twenty thousand barrels of crude oil, ran up and over the south jetty when her captain mistook the North Head for the lightship *Columbia*. "We are rapidly breaking to pieces . . . Good-bye," were the radioman's last words.

1922: The *Iowan*, an American freighter, rammed a British steamer, the *Welsh Prince*. Flames shot through the thick fog. By morning, the *Welsh Prince* and many of her crew lay at the bottom of the channel's entrance.

1951: The *Erria*, a cargo-passenger liner, caught fire while waiting to cross the bar, and smoldered for nearly a week before the steel hulk cooled enough to let Coast Guardsmen aboard. They found eight bodies, dead from smoke inhalation, still sitting in the bar.

1961: The *Mermaid*, a fishing boat, lost her rudder. Battering seas flipped two of the Coast Guard rescue boats, then sank the third, *CG-35454*, alongside the lightship *Columbia*. Five Coast Guardsmen drowned, the worst disaster in the service's Oregon history. Meanwhile, the *Mermaid* and her two-man crew disappeared under the waves.

The Columbia River bar is the third most dangerous bar in the world. A placard inside the entrance to the Columbia River Maritime Museum explains, "The deep river channel, sand spits, rock jetties, changeable weather and coastal surf zones are accompanied by storm waves that can reach a height of 20 feet, and winds often exceeding 50 knots (57 mph)." The entire museum attests to these facts, for its rooms are filled with shipwreck pictures, with skeletal vessels, with artifacts washed ashore. A foghorn sounds over its quiet dioramas, while the red and white flash of a lighthouse beacon colors its walls. Even a Boy Scout troop passes solemnly from one disquieting display to the next.

The retired *Lightship Columbia 604* is docked just outside. Anchored six miles off the Columbia River entrance from 1951 until 1979, she's now a tourist attraction rocking serenely on Astoria's waterfront. Today, a surprisingly bright winter sun makes the *Mermaid* disaster hard to recollect. *CG-35454*, lashed to the side of this very vessel, broke apart in the thrashing winds and seas. Some men clamored up the sides to safety; others were washed away. Handing my ticket to the docent, I cross a deck that barely moves.

Out by the south jetty, tragedy is more palpable. A pair of white crosses mark dunes where men with names no longer readable must lie lost or buried. A railroad trestle, constructed so trains could haul rock while the jetty was being built, has been smashed by an onslaught of waves so powerful that now the jetty itself resembles a grave site. Over and over I listen to the stamp-mill rumble of surf and wonder how I might feel if I were standing spraddle-legged on the deck of a

OREGON: SAND AND SEA

damaged ship. Would I hear a mast crack, see it break into pieces and fall into the sea? Would torn sails shroud my precarious perch? Would my hands, crablike, grip a sea-slick hawser? On a more modern steamer, would the engines go suddenly silent? Would the pumps stop throbbing, too, so that I might hear only the crash of the sea? Or hear a muffled bell, tolling, just before a green wave buries the ship, before a vortex spins the frail vessel and sucks her into a watery grave?

Unwilling to test the force of the waves on the jetty, I backtrack over the dunes and then cross to the seaward side where the soft sandy Clatsop Spit stretches a dozen miles. Yesterday, a scene of unbearable wind and sleet and hail; today, a benign picnic spot; tomorrow, an invisible fogbound trap for the unwary. "On the flood," one old-timer warns, "there is a *dangerous set* toward the Clatsop Spit [italics his]."

1829: The *William and Ann*, a brig owned by the Hudson's Bay Company, lay helpless against a stiffening wind. When the gale hit the breakers outside the Columbia bar, all forty-six crewmen perished. The *William and Ann*'s cargo washed onto the Clatsop Spit, where the Clatsop Indians quickly made away with the goods, and confiscated the empty lifeboat they found overturned on the sand.

1883: The *J. C. Cousins*, a two-masted schooner, tacked offshore, then mysteriously turned toward land. A boat-keeper named Zeiber was blamed for the grounding, and for the probable murder of the four-man crew. No one was aboard ship; no bodies were ever found.

1906: The *Peter Iredale*, 2075 gross tons, 287.5 feet from stem to stern with a beam of 40 feet, became Oregon's most famous shipwreck when she was caught in these breakers. Unlike most vessels pounded between surf and sand, the *Peter Iredale* survived relatively intact, though salvagers never managed to float her carcass free. Until 1951, her bowsprit pointed skyward while her barnacled hull wedged the sand below. Bowsprit fallen now, her skeleton still pickets the beach, like some Modigliani sculpture rusting on the shore.

I draw close to the *Peter Iredale*'s shell. Unlike my nightmarish imaginings, the *Peter Iredale* wrecked herself almost placidly, heaving onto the spit on a sunny afternoon. If her passengers and crew had stayed put until low tide, they could have walked ashore. Some cynics note that, after the advent of steam, a lot of sailing ships suddenly ran aground. The insurance companies, it seems, were very busy at the turn of the century. Still, the *Peter Iredale* is a picturesque reminder of the Pacific Ocean's indifferent nature. Children build sand castles beside the *Peter Iredale*'s romantic hull. Families picnic, and fish, and dig clams, and snap pictures of the Pacific's most photogenic shipwreck.

Offshore, however, unseen sunken ghosts shroud themselves in a curtain of damp sightless fog. I imagine a freighter, lost on a gray horizon indiscernible between waves and sky, her crew listening fearfully to the pitiless echo of a lightship's bell pitched atonally against a deeper, more solemn, hollow horn. My ears strain to hear men's voices. They're hollow, too, otherworldly beyond the fog. "Hard aport!" "Where are we?" "Reverse engines!" Dead ahead, a second steamer cuts across the first one's bow. "Reverse engines!" Steel scrapes steel, as one ship buries herself amidships of the other. More voices cry out, louder, anguished, afraid. Then the foghorn, contrapuntal; a bell, tolling "The Graveyard of the Pacific."

NORTH DAKOTA
TRAIN TIME

During my graduate school years, I often commuted from Seattle to Chicago on the Empire Builder. I especially enjoyed the train in wintertime, when the snow-swept towns of the northern plains hunkered like cattle, their backs to the wind. One year the temperature dropped to fifty below. At 2 A.M. I stepped out on a station platform just long enough to feel the empty chill crackle on my cheeks and echo in my ears. Another year a blizzard stopped the train overnight. As we sat on that North Dakota siding, I stared out the window at impenetrable white swirls and wondered what compelled the occasional automobile to accost the storm. Thirty years later, I'm still imagining the faces of those who live in the towns along the old Great Northern Line. What are their stories? Who were their ghosts?

At Books on Broadway in Williston, North Dakota, proprietors Robin and Chuck Wilder answered in unison: "Talk to Bill Shemorry." A newspaperman for more than fifty years, Bill Shemorry founded the *Williston Plains Reporter*, and served as its publisher from 1953 until 1978. Twenty years later, he still writes a historical feature story every Tuesday for the *Williston Daily Herald*. Since his retirement, Bill has been writing books about Williams County and its county seat, Williston, too. "Talk to Bill Shemorry." Chuck left his bookstore to run some errands. When he returned, he not only brought me some out-of-print books from his personal library but he also brought Bill Shemorry, a man with a passion for people. And so the stories began.

"My dad was a 1905 homesteader. He worked in town for E. C. Carney in the Land Office here in Williston, while my mother, two brothers, and a sister proved up the claim — Truax Township Section 5. The shack was on top of a roll in a rolling land, with a lilac bush alongside. Nothing there now to indicate there was ever a farm. Just a little slope where cattle graze." Bill smiled, remembering the spirit of his Pennsylvania Dutch mother and recollecting homestead days that he himself never knew. Eighty-five now, he was born just a little too late to be a part of the earliest family hardships. He wasn't too late for the depression years, however. "They were tougher than Hell around here," he said.

Bill wasn't born too late to be a part of World War II, either. In March 1944, the army sent Bill to China, Burma, India, and Tibet. His journalism career blossomed when he began writing anecdotes about his wartime adventures for his hometown newspaper. "I always got A's in writing courses," he explained, though "I'd flunk" most of the other ones. "No interest." Bill had a lot of interest in the first-hand stories he was watching unfold, and a growing expertise in photography, too. He became an accomplished aerial photographer for the U.S. Army, a talent that would serve him well throughout his newspaper career. "I have about twenty thousand negatives in the basement," he chuckled. Many of those photos appear in Bill's books. Others accompany the articles he writes for the *Williston Daily Herald*. Some are valuable. "I got a check for a hundred dollars today, from the *Fargo Forum*." His blue eyes twinkled. "They reprinted that oil well picture one more time."

As I listened to him talk, I imagined myself back on that train, looking out the frosty window. I could picture a younger Bill Shemorry out in the storm, a single-minded newspaperman driving through the snow, snapping just the right picture, getting the story straight. I could hear the crossing signal and see its lights reflected as the train plowed through the snow.

NORTH DAKOTA: TRAIN TIME

When the Empire Builder pulled out of the Williston station, heading toward Chicago, it contoured the same land homesteaded by Bill's family and by so many other entrepreneurial settlers. The first tracks were built in 1887 by the St. Paul, Minneapolis and Manitoba Railway—forerunner of the Great Northern. James J. Hill's company laid 698 miles of railroad from Minot to Helena in a record 201 days. Although Williston wasn't officially incorporated until 1894, the coming of the railroad set off a western North Dakota land boom that would continue for a generation. Because steam locomotives needed water every seven miles, new communities were platted every seven miles along the new tracks.

The first stop northeast of Williston was Avoca, where early twentieth-century ranchers shipped cattle, horses, and sheep to market. Like the Shemorry homestead, Avoca is gone. It was gone in the late sixties, too, when I was sitting in the club car that rushed past the fallow fields. Next came Springbrook, just slightly less ephemeral. A vacant store with a faded Budweiser sign now marks the spot, along with another sign pointing the way to a nearby Bible Camp. As I eyed the otherwise empty street, a freight train barreled through, its whistle Dopplering into the distance, mellow and sweet.

Epping sits seven miles east of Springbrook. Closest town to the old Shemorry homestead, Epping once boasted three banks, three hardware stores, two grocery stores, and a host of other small businesses. When train service diminished, and Highway 2 moved four miles to the north, the businesses soon closed. Transportation decisions made elsewhere spelled doom for the economic life of this rural community. People still live in Epping, though. The Lutheran Church fills on Sunday mornings, as does the single local café after services have ended. And residents still care about the past. On the main street, a sign announces the Buffalo Trails Museum Complex: $3 for a tour inside.

Young Lane Thompson is the present curator of and all-around handyman for the Buffalo Trails Museum. Now, I thought, I could counterbalance Bill Shemorry's dulcimer tones with the voice of a man in his thirties. Lane takes visitors on personalized tours of the seven buildings that currently comprise the museum complex. En route, he describes Epping both present and past. "There was a storm last July. Tornado. Hail. Terrible hail. Knocked the windows out of the buildings. Sixty broken windows. I had to replace 'em all."

Lane told me about his predecessor, Elmer Halvorson, who came from Wheelock up the road. The long-time curator must have been a pack rat, an acquisitor who gathered artifacts from every decade of North Dakota life. "Elmer just couldn't say no," Lane said softly, as he led me into the one-time general store. Amid the organized clutter are geology displays, rock collections, a mammoth tusk, arrowheads, an array of beadworked vests, and a stash of old rifles. "Some of the spear points and shell ornaments were found in an old grave on the Thomas farm," Lane explained. "We still have the body. It's maybe two or three thousand years old." He rummaged in a closet and pulled out a large cardboard box. "I found it all unwrapped, so I contacted the Smithsonian. Mice chewed up the notes Elmer made." He handed me a human jawbone, its teeth ground flat. "I'd like to reconstruct it all some day," Lane shrugged, "but there's just too much other work to do." Moving toward more dusty displays, I found myself in front of an Assiniboin village diorama, then a replicated homestead shack interior, then a village store display.

Outside, we walked past huge chunks of petrified wood and a yard full of old machinery to the next building, a log cabin that had been moved from Brooklyn Township. It had belonged to Andrew and Sophie Thorseth. A plaque proclaims: "1908—1928: this was our home." Looking at the table set with Sophie's best dishes, the scrolled oak high chair, the handmade rag rugs, the flowered fly swatter, the washtubs and hand wringer, I pondered the complexities of living in this cabin for twenty years. Raising babies, sweeping aside the prairie dust, heating water, day after day after day. A wall-hanging crocheted in royal purple, HOME SWEET HOME, denied my urban skepticism.

The Machinery and Feed Store is filled with more collections — lamps and lanterns, purple glass, musical instruments, more rocks, hats and hatboxes, army clothes and band clothes, lace and tatting and quilts. A tiny annex holds the trappings of Wheelock Camp #13676 — the Modern Woodmen of America's official stamp, catalogue, robes, cloaks, and secret glasses. To add to the mood, Lane hand-wound a phonograph, sending the sounds of Benny Goodman into the room. I paused for a long time beside a life-size diorama of a doctor pouring a dose of medicine for a bedridden child. "The 1918 flu epidemic," Lane explained. "That's a scene from Elmer's house. He's the little boy with his face turned into his mother's skirt. Elmer made the figures himself. The scene is exactly like he remembered."

In the hardware store across the street, we looked at more fossils, agates, geodes and petrified wood, old license plates, milk bottles, a dozen coffeepots, bicycles and wheelchairs, buggies large and small. "There's almost as much in storage as we've already seen," Lane earnestly reported. Pastor Duane R. Lindberg, who served the local parish from 1961 to 1968, founded the Buffalo Trails Museum. The two Scandinavians, Lindberg and Halvorson, together amassed a collection that would be the envy of any antique dealer. It remains for Lane Thompson and the nonprofit corporation that oversees the property to care for the treasures.

A schoolhouse stands next door to the hardware store. Photos from nearby schools line the walls, along with class pictures and newspaper clippings of baseball and basketball games won and lost. The smallest high school in the state, the Epping Eagles were District 27 Champs in March, 1977. Winner of Region 7, too. I investigated the private library of the Reverend Amund S. Blue (1881–1954), then paused beside a copy of an 1859 Danish Bible and an altar Bible dated 1820. I also looked carefully at another Halvorson-built diorama. This one replicates the schoolroom. "It shows Elmer teaching," Lane clarified the details. "And the faces of the children are those of his favorite kids." By this time I was overwhelmed, not only by the conglomeration of pioneer artifacts but by the very existence of this eclectic museum so far from a major highway. Here was a place that takes its ghosts seriously, and personally.

Before this trip to Williams County, I read some letters, diaries, and memoirs written by women homesteaders in North Dakota. Lucy Goldthorpe, a young single schoolteacher, lived on a claim near Epping. She recalled the winter of 1906–1907, when blizzards came incessantly: "There were many long, cold days and nights in my little homestead shack that winter! The walls were only single board thickness, covered with tar paper on the outside. . . . I covered the interior walls with a blue building paper. Everything was covered, including the ceiling, and the floor. To help seal out the cold I'd added layers of gunny sacks over the paper on the floor and then the homemade wool rugs I'd shipped from home. . . . Regardless of what I did the cold crept in through the thin walls."

Lucy's words foreshadowed Bill's: "One evening while my dad was on his way home, a blinding snowstorm came up. He was far from town and kept going, but when he didn't arrive at the claim or any other place he knew, he realized he was lost. The horse seemed to have ideas on where to go, and somehow Dad had the good sense to drop the reins and let him find his way. They arrived much later than intended, but none the worse for what had happened." Epping's pioneer winters must have been as chilling as I imagined, though the legacy of Elmer Halvorson made the town seem warm to me now.

Elmer was born in Wheelock, the next town to the east, where his father was the blacksmith. Wheelock, or what's left of it, is the highest point on the Great Northern Railway between St. Paul and the Rockies —2387 feet above sea level. Bill says it was named for Ralph Wheelock, a Minneapolis newspaperman. Lane insists it was named for the trains' tendency to "wheel-lock" on the grade. Whichever story is true, the fact remains that today the once-booming Wheelock is almost deserted, though a few of the old residences still seem to be occupied. What once was a central jumping-off spot, "where the land-seekers left the rails and proceeded overland in their search for new homes," now sits idly among fields planted right to the edge of empty foundations.

An abandoned high school, with brick walls and glass block windows, dominates the scene. Leaning downhill from it, empty stores raise hollow false fronts above their facades. Near the railroad crossing, a truncated row of unused storage sheds lines the tracks. Up the hill again, a vacant church neighbors a freshly painted house with a newly mowed lawn. Lane says nine people live in Wheelock now, so the forlorn community can't quite be defined as a ghost town. Nonetheless, its emptiness is evocative of ghosts.

Jerry Engle directs the Williston Council for the Aged. Jerry's grandfather moved from Minnesota to Wheelock, North Dakota, because he hated trees. There he became a banker specializing in cattle loans. Although Jerry grew up in nearby Ray, the next town to the east, he often visited his grandparents in Wheelock. He remembers having to haul water from the community well, and hearing his mother's stories about drunken farmhands breaking horses on the main street of town. He also recalls racing his 1919 Model T with a friend's 1913 version. On the way to Buffalo Trails Day in Epping, they revved their wooden-tire cars up to sixty-five miles per hour on the back roads. Jerry won. The happy-go-lucky man frowns when he thinks of the dilapidated Wheelock high school. "It wasn't vandals," he grimaces. "A windstorm lifted off the roof." Then, good-naturedly, he smiles. "I went to high school in Ray. Wheelock and Epping were our rivals."

After Wheelock, Highway 2 and the railroad tracks run close together again, so present-day Ray is much less deserted. Even though many of its central stores and buildings stand empty, Ray's peripheral streets are lined with prosperous-looking houses and well-kept double wides. Many people, like Jerry Engle, live in Ray and work in Williston, less than thirty-five miles away, an easy commute in decent weather. Ray's grain elevators remain in operation, and the town is the home of the North Dakota Grain Palace, a white boxy building with gingerbread turrets and marmalade facade. The Grain Festival, first held in 1912, is still an annual Ray occurrence.

Ray highlights more than a grain palace, however, for it also is home to an opera house. Built in 1904, the partially refurbished building currently houses the Ray Opera House Museum. When I asked why there were two pioneer museums less than fifteen miles apart, Jerry Engel explained. "Most counties in North Dakota have one museum. Williams has five—one here in Williston, one in Epping, one in Ray, one in Tioga, one in Hanks. I was president of the Williams County Historical Society in the 1980s. There was a shouting match over the funding then." Jerry shook his head. "Williston, the Frontier Museum, they weren't polite at all. The County Commission had the insight to open it up. Now it's routine for every one to get their share."

Walking into the Opera House Museum, I found storied connections. Just inside the front door sits Dr. Walter B. Scott's desk, with an explanation of his importance to the pioneer community. During the 1918 flu epidemic, he treated 876 patients without a death. Looking at his battered desk, I remembered the Halvorson diorama in Epping, where the same Dr. Scott was measuring medicine for Elmer's brother. Past the doctor's desk, I found more familiar memorabilia. A telephone switchboard and a wall-crank phone. A quilt. Altar artifacts from three local churches. A railroad and telegraph display. A kitchen that reminded me of Andrew and Sophie Thorseth's log cabin. A doll house. And, surprisingly, a tiny alcove with uniforms and photos from Desert Storm and Desert Shield, August 1990–March 1991. For the first time I realized that Williams County collecting is an ongoing process.

Another room contains displays from the Roaring '20s, the Dirty '30s, the Wartime '40s, and the Rockin' '50s. I was on my own. No local guide accompanied me through the Ray Opera House, no Lane Thompson interpreted what I was seeing. "Approx 1896–1910," one label partially glossed. "Dress worn by Mrs. Bertha Peterson, grandmother of Phyllis Thoreson. Mrs. Peterson's husband was Frank Peterson, a Methodist Episcopal circuit riding pastor in North Dakota." Looking at the heavy dark material, the high neck, the long sleeves, the long straight skirt, the meager decoration at the throat and wrists, I tried to imagine Mrs. Bertha Peterson in her gown. Proud of her finery, or just uncomfortable?

"Baseball Uniform of Arnold Anderson," read another label. "He played in Tioga 1921, 1922, and 1923." The handwritten card, paper-clipped to the uniform, gave no further information. Was the team a winner, Arnold Anderson the star? I paused before a row of eclectic high school graduation pictures—classes of '32, '38, '39, and '40. Finally, I lingered in front of a heavy brown winter coat. Man-sized, with a fur collar and a wide belt, it was unlabeled. Who wore it, and why was it hanging in this silent room? Breathing deeply, I inhaled the dry antiquated smell of my grandparents' attic. When I was four years old, my cousins and I used to play there, trying on the discarded clothes and pretending to be grownups wearing the dresses and suits with pride. Mentally, I did the same in the Ray Opera House Museum, imagining a story for Mrs. Peterson's gown, or young Anderson's uniform, or the anonymous winter coat, bringing the shadows to life, if I could.

After my train left Ray, it must have passed through Temple, where some of these people might have lived. Now no one lives in Temple, the first real ghost town I encountered on my route east of Williston. Perhaps the weather dictated my reaction, for the morning was overcast with heavy clouds foretelling rain. The road to Temple, already mud-slick, was empty. The endless cultivated landscape felt as deserted as rural Nevada can be. Or was it? As I watched a freight train speed past a crossing devoid of signals or warning lights, a car pulled up on the other side of the tracks. After the train disappeared in the distance, the big American-built car—a Pontiac Brougham—drove on into town, and stopped. "Any problem?" the elderly driver asked. "No," I answered, "I'm looking for stories." The man waved his arm in a broad gesture. "I used to live here." He pointed toward a collapsing building. "We'd have ice cream socials in the basement. And my father knew all about the fire."

Bill Shemorry's book, *More Lost Tales*, tells about the 1916 fire that leveled much of downtown Temple. "It was a blow from which it never recovered," Bill writes. Poor Temple, "it once had all the essentials needed to become a trading center, but somehow it never could keep up with its neighbors." A second vehicle drove into the uninhabited town; the conversational driver rolled down his window, too. "I was raised in that house with the stack and the clothesline pole. My father ran the general store"—Neal Nelson pointed at another building with a sagging roof and weathered siding—"and the post office on the corner." His wife leaned across the car seat. "We lived for a time in that house there. Everywhere we went, we carried hoes and rakes. Not for gardening. To protect our children from rattlesnakes. Snakes lived in all the foundations left from the fire. Seemed like they were everywhere." Her voice drifted off as she smiled at her memories. Neal smiled, too, as he put the car in gear and drove away from his ancestral town.

Not so empty after all, I thought to myself as I walked back past the vacant ruins. Nonetheless, Temple typifies what I might label the "vanishing Mid-West." Where one generation has pioneered the land, struggled to make a living and raise a family, even briefly flourished perhaps, the next generation has moved away. North Dakota's rural population, decade by decade, is shrinking. Those who remain, it seems to me, hold their ghosts dearly, honoring a Sisyphean past that the passage of time obscures.

My next stop was Tioga, perhaps the liveliest community on this nostalgic trek. When passing through on the Empire Builder, I must have been aware of Tioga, must have seen its nightly glow. Since 1951 this town of twelve hundred has been the center of oil exploration and discovery in the Williston Basin. Oil wells dot the flax and wheat fields surrounding Tioga, especially to the south and east, while the nearby Signal Refinery belches fire and smoke into the North Dakota skies. Bill Shemorry took the photo that captures this economic achievement. When the Clarence Iverson well came in, the first productive well in the basin, Bill was there with his camera. "The big Loffland Brothers drilling rig stood before me. Its silver derrick was illuminated by the light of the flare and stood out in stark detail against the black night sky. In the foreground was a big pool of snow runoff water which had gathered in a low place. The night was still. Not a breath of wind. A perfect double image of the derrick and flare was reflected."

Bill quickly "made about a dozen shots, varying the exposures." Then he sped off to Minot where his pictures could be processed, although the highway was dangerously flooded. Back to Williston later that night, he carried the photograph "which has since become the symbol of the discovery of oil in North Dakota," and remains Bill's pride and joy and an ongoing source of income. Oilmen say it is "unique in the annals of the industry."

While Tioga no longer seems the commercial center it became in the 1950s—the oil industry, after all, has a history of ups and downs—it remains a viable place to work and live. Its Main Street buildings boast faded Scandinavian trim, left from the days when Tioga intended to become the "Scandinavian capital of the prairies." Colorful murals front the railroad tracks, one graced with water, trees, ducks and deer, the other picturing a cozy house, its windows warmly lit. Tioga, too, has its own museum.

John Thorburn, once the town's International Harvester dealer and former mayor, now museum president and a member of the county museum board, welcomed me inside the 1926 First Lutheran Church, current home of the Tioga Norseman Museum. He apologized for the mess. "We got a grant for the handicapped access, and to finish the floors," he said. "The younger people are taking over. They're more interested in the building than in the displays," he wryly chuckled. We stepped past the fresh carpentry work into a room so cluttered with stuffed showcases and panel displays and lettered signs and unnamed objects that it was hard to walk between them. "Everything's all pushed together while we're remodeling," John apologized again.

John, like Lane, was a wonderful tour guide. Older, however, nearly eighty-nine, John offered a different perspective. Instead of being somewhat awed by the materials, John embraced many of them as his own. We paused before the World War II uniforms—"this is the one I wore," he announced with pride. At the arrowhead display, he singled out the two he found. Then we skirted the inboard motor taken from his boyhood boat. The retired farm machinery dealer obviously liked motors. Downstairs, he explained the operation of a gargantuan threshing machine. He admired the 1914 Ford in another corner of the big room and commented, "I'll bring my car when this area is finished." Jerry Engel already had told me about John's precious 1908 Cadillac. Pausing alongside the now-defunct *Tioga Gazette*'s linotype machine, John once again detailed the mechanics.

As he spoke, his voice became wistful. "Hard to keep paint on the walls," he sighed. "No heat in the building. Can't afford to heat it." The basement, which smelled damper and mustier than the grandparents'-attic aura of the Ray Opera House, held even more equipment. Harnesses. Neck yokes. A wolf trap. Odd tools. Oil bits of various sizes. When I mentioned the monument commemorating the first Clarence Iverson well, John pulled his blue Kiwanis cap down over his brow. "Bubble, bubble, oil—and trouble?" he quoted a newspaper clipping we had examined upstairs. As Tioga's mayor at the time of the big discovery, John had been in charge of growing a town that had "no drug store, no hospital, no water, no sewer system, no pavement." Another frayed clipping called John the "harried juggler of Tioga's problems." Such responsibility never daunted him. Neither did recent heart surgery nor a bout with cancer. Still going strong, the octogenarian hastily locked the museum when my tour ended. "The Kiwanis lunch starts at noon," he explained. "I don't want to be late."

Were John and his wife, Freada, waiting at the Tioga crossing in their refurbished 1908 Cadillac when my Empire Builder thundered past? Maybe so. I would have been on my way to Stanley, in Montrail County to the east, then on to Minot, Fargo, and St. Paul. At Stanley, however, another railroad option existed between 1911 and 1973. There, the Great Northern opened a branch line almost to the northwestern border of North Dakota. With a "rain follows the plow" kind of logic, James Hill believed that "the wild open plains along his railroad could, and would, grow almost any kind of crop." Through advertising exaggeration and systematic recruiting, Hill drew 64,000 people to North Dakota between 1909 and 1919. The Williams County segment of the Stanley branch line was a key part of his strategy.

Trains today no longer travel the Stanley–Northwest route. When the line originally was extended, though, it brought vitality to what now seems like a sleepy corner of the state. McGregor sits just over the border between Montrail and Williams counties. Because it's at the intersection of two state highways, people still live there. I saw laundry on clotheslines, cars parked in driveways, television antennas, and children playing in yards. A post office operates out of a trailer, though store-front buildings stand empty and a pigeon colony nests on the roof of the abandoned school.

From McGregor, the track aims for Hamlet, which boasts another elegant but idle brick school building. There, the Nelson Grain Company still operates, and the grain elevator remains in use. Most of the other buildings have fallen into weathered disrepair. Bill Shemorry details a different Hamlet. "In 1913, four blocks were platted south on the right-of-way. Paralleling the tracks was Front Street, then First and Second Streets. Main Street bisected the townsite, with 25 foot wide lots facing it and 50 foot lots backing them up and facing First Avenue East and First Avenue West." Today, it's hard to believe that Hamlet once had fifteen business firms and a population of 175.

Wildrose, however, once the western terminus of the now-defunct Stanley–Northwest line, seven miles west of Hamlet and four miles from the nearest main highway, is still thriving. Designed in 1910, Wildrose is squarely plotted, its yards wide and tree-lined, its downtown stores open for twenty-first century business. Flags were flying from a post office, a grocery store, a gas station. Two shiny yellow school buses sat alongside the school.

Between 1911 and 1916, Wildrose was reputed to be "the largest primary grain market in the United States." Bill's *More Lost Tales* cites a contemporary newspaper description of Wildrose's size and importance in those days. Three general stores, with "a first-class stock of goods," crowed the *Williams County Plainsman*. George Cain's hardware business. George Haines's drug store. Dr. Olaf A. Thorvalson. Two banks. Three lumberyards. John Maelstrom, "the sturdy blacksmith." A good restaurant. The Wildrose Meat Market. The Wildrose Tonsorial Parlor. Two billiard and pool halls. Two dance halls. Coal sheds. The Clark Hotel. "Last but not least is the *Plainsman*. Each week's issue will be a spring of newsy news, a bunch of spicy articles and all the current topics of the week. We ask you to subscribe. $1.50 per year. The business men of the city extend to their friends, the farmers, a glad hand and an invitation to trade at the biggest little city in the northwest!"

In 1916, the Great Northern Railway extended its branch farther west from Wildrose. Pre-World War I North Dakota, producing bumper crops, was ripe for further development. Corinth became the next stop, a tiny community that ultimately was home to the second largest grain house in Williams County. "Things went well" until "an early morning fire November 30, 1966 completely destroyed the entire complex. This was the beginning of the end for Corinth." Highway signs brightly point the way toward the erstwhile metropolis, which is just off State Highway 42. Twenty miles directly south, in fact, is Epping. Corinth seems deserted today, but it's not. Two cats peered from a house that had a satellite dish in the front yard. I saw laundry on the line in a second yard, and a yellow Volkswagon bug in a third. Like Wheelock, Corinth looks like a ghost town, but is not quite.

The *Williston Herald* once called the next stop, Alamo, to the west of Cottonwood Lake, "the prettiest place in the country." Larger than twenty-first-century Corinth but less lively than contemporary Wildrose, it's nearer the main highway and has a co-op gas station as well as a post office. I found it interesting for two reasons. Bill narrates the history of Cottonwood Lake's earliest settlers, a Chinese man named Lem Heen and his wife, Nellie. After they proved up their homestead, Lem discovered that the 1882 Congressional Exclusion Act precluded him from owning land. When Nellie married Lem, she lost her citizenship, too. All their hard work might have been for naught, but influential North Dakotans were irate. They circulated petitions attesting to Lem's "honesty of purpose" and describing him "as a man of high moral character," then sent the petitions to Congress. Special legislation was passed by the Senate, the House, and signed by President Theodore Roosevelt. On February 7, 1903, the Secretary of Interior issued a homestead patent to Nellie Etta Heen. When Lem died six years later, the eulogies praised him as "one of the squarest men who ever hit this county" and "the living embodiment of both" the philosophies of Confucius and Christ. Thus did a predominantly Protestant community respect and embrace a hardworking Asian neighbor.

I found Alamo interesting, too, because the Burlington Northern donated the Alamo railway depot to the Williams County Historical Society after the station shut down in 1973. The depot was moved in July that year, and now serves as the Visitor Center for the Williston Frontier Museum. I haven't described the Williston museum grounds because I could never really catch the flavor of the landscape there. The Alamo depot, the Great Northern caboose outside its front door, the Judson School, Snyder's Store, the W. B. Overson House, and the Old Bethany Lutheran Church from Lignite, North Dakota—all were moved to the present site. Each building is freshly painted, each interior cosmetically designed. Their new location—just off a four-lane divided highway with Wal-Mart, K-Mart and Albertson's just down the "parkway"—evokes the smells and sounds of a city, rather than pioneer life. The setting, so very different from the locales of the other four Williams County collections, actually distances visitors, I think.

Back in Appam, the one-time train stop seven miles west of Alamo, I had no such problem. Appam apparently tried to hang onto its ghostly past. Signs naming the original buildings—some still standing, others only a broken foundation or a hollow in the prairie—flank the main street. Sons of Norway Hall—gone. Christopherson's Store and Pool Hall—still there. Cliffords Bar—gone. Oscars Bar—gone. Shilkes Blacksmith shop—gone. Pete Ludwig's Café—gone. Still there—Township Hall, and Herrickson Bros. Hardware and Implement. As I wandered from sign to sign, I perceived no indication of preservation or upkeep. In fact, the signs themselves were faded, many hard to read. Once, someone wanted to celebrate Appam's history, but the ghosts, it seems, got in the way. Although a few people live in Appam today, most of the community has long since moved away. Bill remembers that old-timers thought the Appam café served the best coffee in western North Dakota. In truth, I am certain that Bill's wife, Glo, now deserves that accolade!

Next, WELCOME TO ZAHL—a sign much newer than any of Appam's, and a town apparently more functional. Large trucks were backed alongside the grain elevator, and I could see men moving back and forth between the vehicles and the building. Uptown, a church with fresh white paint suggested an active parish. Although the school was abandoned, several residences were occupied. One place had a boat and trailer, plus two new ORVs, as if Zahl were retaining some of the entrepreneurial spirit exemplified by its founder, Frederick Zahl. "Doc" Zahl, in fact, belongs in GhostWest. Not only was he an accomplished hunter who played a major role in depleting the buffalo herds, but he also was a member of the second Custer burial party at the Little Bighorn.

GhostWest continuities weren't so overt at the next town, but there, in Hanks, the spirits of Williams County coalesced in my mind. More protected from weather and wind than most northern prairie towns, Hanks snugs into a hillside rather like its once-profitable lignite coal mines. The Pioneer Trails Museum, too, shelters into a surrounding eight-foot hedge. A misspelled plaque defines the museum's scope:

> The Praire Was Their Garden
> This memorial is dedicated to the area pioneers, who saw the promise in this land, and had the faith and courage to make it a reality.
> We pray that future generations may have that same courage and spirit of adventure, as did those pioneers. God bless their memory among us.
> Pioneer Trails Historical Society
> 1991

Avis Kohlman went to high school in Alamo. Her husband, Lloyd, grew up in Hanks, where his father, Fred, owned the Hanks Coal Company. For fifty-eight years, Avis and Lloyd have lived in the same house, next door to the old brick high school, next door to what is now the Pioneer Trails Museum. Avis, who was weeding her garden, graciously stopped her chores and took me on another personalized Williams County museum tour. Inside, I found more aging objects of all shapes and sizes and utility. In fact, the Pioneer Trails Museum collection is just as eclectic and just as comprehensive as Epping's Buffalo Trails. The many commemorative plates and carefully lettered labels indicate that families far and near Hanks either loaned or donated their ancestral treasures. I saw the Archie Shaw family heirlooms—bed, stove, coffee grinder, irons, table lantern, organ, marble-topped dresser, and a high chair that makes into a rocker. The wall telephone from the Frank Eberle home. The 1947 uniform of Lt. Col. Carl Thompson, USAF ret. 1984. The safe "from my husband's father's office," stamped Hanks Coal Co.

In what used to be the high school library, the replica of a chapel holds the organ from "the Bethany Church up north," pews from another church beyond Alamo, and censers from Our Lady of God Church of Hanks. I opened drawers of baby clothes and lacework, books of Palmer Method Handwriting instructions. In the hallway, I looked at Grace Maynard's 1929 graduation dress, with peach ruffles and bows. Inside the "newsroom," I strolled past rows of pictures of couples, named but otherwise unidentified. Hyder and Olive Poling. Herman and Marion Rustad. Ivah and Dave Hought. Carl and Mary Sather. Tom and Anna Brisson. Fred and Jennie Kohlman—"my husband's parents." Oscar and Mary Hagge—"my father and mother." Fred and Eva Gotham. Jack and Cecilia Laqua. Duncan and Ida Mclean. Their eyes, forever fixed in time and space, gaze at a present-day audience unaware of their accomplishments. Every couple once lived a precious personal life. Who, in a generation or two, will remember them? I thought about my own grandparents again, their attic emptied long ago, their stories already fading from family memory.

One of the out-of-print books loaned by Chuck Wilder was *Plains Folk: North Dakota's Ethnic History*. In its pages, William C. Sherman analyzes the difficult adjustment to the northern prairie. Life in North Dakota was destined to be forever rural, dominated by small-town and village values. The economics would always be colonial, with crucial decisions made elsewhere. The population would be transitory, an ongoing abandonment of schools, churches, and stores. The landscape itself is one of large dimensions, with neighbors far away and with few visual highlights. "The prairies were too big, too lonely, too cold, too empty. In short, adjustment was too difficult." Many homesteaders left within a generation; others, like the men and women pictured on the walls of the Hanks museum, stayed and flourished. But their individual stories have blurred and been forgotten.

"No one's interested any more," Avis observed in almost the same wistful tone I heard in John Thorburn's voice. "We used to have the Old Pioneer Trail Days, with threshing and food and a program on our makeshift stage. No one comes now. We stopped the Trail Days a few years ago. I don't know if we'll ever have another."

Downstairs, on the gym floor, Avis led me to a real shack—John Dordahl's—moved there from its spot on the prairie. On one side, a coal mine display; on the other, a post office, juxtaposing progress side by side with what must have been incredible isolation. Next, a replica of the General Merchandise store, with commercial scales and shelves of unopened canned goods. I saw sewing machines, wooden wheelchairs, generations of washing machines and wringers, a folding bathtub, and what must have been a dozen cream separators. A huge American flag covers one end of the gym. Avis told me about the day she and a friend hung the flag there. The ladder gave way, her friend fell. "They flew her to Fargo. She lived ten days." Avis's voice was poignant, soft. She must visualize that horrible event every time she enters the old gym. As she spoke, she remembered two other friends who used to help with the museum. "They're both gone," she said.

As in Tioga's Norseman Museum, there was a downstairs to investigate. Old plows and an operative cornhusker machine sit in the high school assembly room. Avis pointed out her grandpa's plowshare sharpener, but was less animated regarding the uses of the other tools. Unlike John Thorburn, she explained nothing about the machinery, preferring to share personal anecdotes instead. Down the hall, we entered The Golden Spigot Saloon—its shelves lined with empty bottles and empty beer cans, its green-felt poker table, its spittoon, its glasses and ashtrays from the travels of H. W. Bublitz, the first Hanks high school teacher in 1933. "He was my teacher," Avis acknowledged. She also apologized for the mustiness of the basement, and thought about turning on a dehumidifier. She didn't. "It's too heavy to empty," she said. "I can't do the work any more."

Outside the old high school are several buildings brought from elsewhere. Bonetraill School No 2. The Hanks Jail, which became the City Hall in a curious reversal of priorities. A Quonset hut that Avis called "the men's space." Again, Avis wasn't much interested in the mechanics of a red ambulance, a fire truck, a mail wagon, a covered wagon, another old threshing machine. Yet she continued talking about the Old Pioneer Trail Days, begun in 1970, when the antique cars and trucks were driven about and people gathered on the lawn to watch.

Apparently the celebration reached its climax each year on the porch of the Zahl railway depot, which has been moved next door to the Quonset hut. Buggies, whips, saddles, harnesses, and church pews fill half of it now, while the other half still resembles the old station office, with leather seats for the travelers and an oil stove for heat. In the depot, too, are stacks of folding chairs, themselves a ghostly reminder of the Old Pioneer Trail Days. "No one comes any more," Avis repeated. "I worry about all the things we have here. Where will they go if no one cares? Who'll take care of the place after I'm gone?"

Midwestern friends tell me that pioneer museums like the five in Williams County dot the prairies. Williams County may be unusual because it has so many (seven, actually, but I omit the fur-trading sites at Fort Buford and Fort Union because they both predate the homesteader influx that followed the coming of the railroads), yet counties all over North and South Dakota, Nebraska and Kansas boast similar collections. Although I didn't say so to Avis, or to John, or even to Lane, I was astonished by the sheer numbers of things. A dozen cream separators. Seven bicycles. Six baby buggies. Eighty-some purple glass bottles. Hundreds of oil bits. Thousands of pictures, many unlabeled. I was surprised, too, by the duplication. Three schoolrooms. Four churches. Five general stores. Avis is right, I thought, to fret about what might happen to the Hanks artifacts. Some, of course, are precious. Others, unfortunately, are commonplace. Still others signify men and women and children long forgotten. Who were these people? I read their names and see their faces, but their individual stories vanish in the ghostly past.

Like Avis in Hanks, John Thorburn frets about the Tioga collection. "The young people, they're more interested in the building," he repeated several times. Even a much younger man, Lane Thompson, worries about Epping. "We lost the gas station last week. It moved to the highway outside of Ray," he said. "Only the café left in town." Jerry Engel collects old cars. Bill Shemorry researches historic events. Bill's wife, Glo, helps old-timers publish their personal stories. Chuck Wilder lives in a house built in 1910; his personal library details the state's history in every aspect. These voices care passionately about the ghosts who came with such optimism to the northern plains, but their children and grandchildren may not be as devoted, and Williston newcomers may actually be indifferent. For those whose families were not personally involved in North Dakota's stories, the "lost tales" remain ephemeral. Titanic events always capture our imaginations, but the "lost tales" of ordinary people evaporate as time passes. Again, I thought of my own relations. My parents named me after my father's sister, who died in the 1918 flu epidemic so personally dramatized in Epping by Elmer Halvorson. After I am gone, who will remember Margaret Ronald?

Grenora—the end of the line. The first work train reached Grenora, a town named for the Great Northern Railway, on October 5, 1916. Land sales, however, took place many months earlier. Bill's *More Lost Tales* reprints one of the original flyers. TOWNSITE SALES, it announces. "Six New Towns Opened in Northern Williams County, North Dakota, Along the New Extension of 'The Great Northern Railway Company' from Wildrose West to Grenora, the Terminus." After listing dates and times for each community's respective land auction, the flyer reminds would-be purchasers: "Splendid openings for all lines of business, in a territory already noted for its productiveness. Each town has an enormous territory, North and South, which means big business and large profits." For further information? "Willard F. Hanks, Sales Agent."

Five years later, the bottom fell out of the market. If times were tough in the 1920s, dry years with plant diseases and insect infestation, the 1930s were disastrous. Dust and the Great Depression brought the farmers to their knees. Half of the North Dakota population ended up on relief. World War II rejuvenated the grain market; oil discovery helped the financial state of the 1950s. Yet real prosperity for everyone

NORTH DAKOTA: TRAIN TIME

never quite materialized. Most of the smaller towns have suffered and shrunk as the young people have moved away, although a few—like Ray and Grenora, for example—tenaciously appear to be holding their own. With the possible exception of Williston, however, none of the communities is thriving in my Sunbelt sense of the word.

The North Dakota landscape paraphrases the economic ups and downs. Stones emerge from the soil with every freeze and thaw. Farmers push them into oval rock piles, then plow the fertile fields on every side. What appeared to be flat countryside from my train window turns out to be undulating, with wind-blown crests and sheltered hollows and grasses of many different heights. Perpendicular roads measure out the acreage; sun shadows, created by clouds, soften the stark colors of wheat and flax and rye. Meanwhile, more ghosts than people are homesteading the snow-shrouded memories of a prairie past.

Bill Shemorry quotes lines from a poem by Hal Boyle. "Memory is the passport / To a land / That never changes.... Where all that did happen, / Is now fixed, and forever changeless." For me, the Frontier Museum, the Buffalo Trails Complex, the Ray Opera House, the Norseman Museum, and the home of the Pioneer Trails are memory passports which take me back to personal moments in North Dakota history. Their stories harmonize in counterpoint to the dynamic Doppler sounds of the train I loved to ride. When I think of my days and nights on the Empire Builder, the changeless music of North Dakota voices resonates in my imagination. But, like the "lost tales" of so many of our everyday ghosts, the harmony finally fades away. Fixed and changeless such individual stories may be, but they live only as long as someone remembers. This is the fear of my friends in North Dakota.

NEVADA
BURIED BONES

Seen from a distance, desert playa resembles endless sheets of parchment paper, ivory pages unfigured by any known language past or present. Closer at hand, the illusion of emptiness doesn't diminish much. A single human being, walking alone on a grainy alkali flat, can circle endlessly under a hot sun. Spiralling away from landmarks, I can lose myself in a mirage of refracted time, lose my connections with earth and space.

Some of my friends like to make desert angels, throwing themselves down on the drifting desert pavement, swinging legs and arms back and forth in corporeal angel designs. Disembodied even as they touch the snowless ground, they enshrine a scattered circle of desert spirits under a sun-white cathedral sky. I used to laugh when we'd play this schoolyard game. I never dreamed that real phantasma might rest just beneath the surface of a Nevada desert floor.

Far from tire tracks and boot prints and even angel wings, a lost tribe lies buried in the alkali cement of time. Long tucked into a womb of blowing sand and dust, a gathering of bodies surfaces slowly from the playa. First the tip of a skull, followed by a jawbone, six teeth, a hip socket, a long thigh bone, slivered fingers, spine chards, radius and broken ulna rubbing side by side. The pace of emergence varies, as does the sequencing of the bones. But emerge they do, these long-lost partial skeletons rising from a long-lost only partially definable past. The unnamed corpses slowly percolate up from where once they were interred. If not rescued by the hands of modern tribal members and trained archaeologists, the bones then disintegrate into fragments and blow away.

Most of the recognizable remains curve into the fetal position. Facing west, knees tucked beneath their chins, their bones are frayed by the wash of wind and dirt. Some of the burial mounds are marked by worked rocks, grinding stones, and dull primitive points. Others are decorated with artificially arranged gastropods, delicate spiral shells that blow away when brushed by my fingers. Still others scarcely seem like burials at all—a bone here, a piece there, a scatter of bones strewn by the wind, ragged edges, long slivers, a fragility of bones.

Three wet years in a row flooded one Great Basin playa with the overflow from a river that normally evaporates as it reaches its sink. When a summer without much precipitation followed the floods and dried out the waters, more than just blowing dust rose from the arid expanse. A 1988 archaeological report reveals that "144 relatively complete skeletons and 272 incomplete skeletons or single bone elements" were found. Nearly a decade later, even more relics have dusted themselves into the parched sunlight.

Dry "osteological analyses" report some interesting facts. More males than females were counted, though archaeologists were unable to determine the sex of many of the burials. The males tended to have large, high cheek bones with prominent nasal bones, large brow ridges and square shaped eye sockets, massive jaws. The smaller females, whose heights ranged from 5'2" to 5'7", tended to have medium high cheek bones, median brow ridges, and medium sized jaws. The pathologies and anomalies suggest there was no marked change of occupants over the course of time—little in-migration, little out. These playa natives generally stayed put.

Most of them suffered from arthritis. Not only do their bones show the normal stresses and strains that would come from gathering food and carrying loads but they also display osteophytic growths on their

NEVADA: BURIED BONES

joints. Although this small skeletal sample may distort the "high eburnation frequencies"—anthropological jargon for the disintegration of cartilage that results in bone-on-bone contact, thus wearing, grooving, and polishing the bones involved—archaeologists generalize that either alkaline water or fungally contaminated food or a combination of the two contributed to the skeletal abnormalities. Or perhaps a lifetime of constant bending and kneeling and scraping and toting exacerbated the skeletal wear and tear. Whatever the causes, and without modern drugstore remedies, the shoulders, elbows, wrists and knees of the older natives must have ached constantly.

I like to think that those bones studied by scientists in the late 1980s rest more easily now. They've been respectfully reburied somewhere, in accordance with modern Paiute tribal wishes. Meanwhile, new skeletal pieces surface each season. The last time I walked through the ancient graveyard, four were visible. One entire skull shadow rested above a folded femur and scapula. Another skull simply sat naked on the playa, unearthed and unprotected. Two other burials were scarcely discernible, one with its eggshell bones already scattered, the other mostly remaining underground.

That particular November day felt properly autumnal. A schizophrenic wind blew cold and warm, while the overhead sky looked washed-out, a flat watery blue. The lowering sun gave my body an elongated unnatural shadow, and my boots crunched a hollow sound on the empty playa. Empty? Not really. Underfoot, a silent cemetery of bones. How many more burials lay below my feet? How many more skeletons could rise from their ghostly graves? While I tiptoed across the uneven contours, I found myself remembering Emily Dickinson's hymnal phrases:

> There's a certain slant of light,
> Winter afternoons, . . .
> When it comes, the landscape listens,
> Shadows hold their breath;
> When it goes, 'tis like the distance
> On the look of death.

Once this playa was alive with people. A group of men, flaking and chipping rocks; others, farther away from the camp, hunting, throwing darts and shooting arrows. Some women sewing skins together, or weaving plant fibers; others, carrying water from a distant marsh, or cooking alongside a smokey fire. If I read the landscape correctly, a spot to my left was the kitchen. Charred bones—the long spiny teeth of a fish jaw, two fragile skeletal wings, a burnt rabbit leg, a half-buried fin, two dozen clam shells, a tiny spine—are strewn across a fifteen-foot radius. The shifting winds, subtle erosion, flood and drought have covered, uncovered, covered, uncovered them countless times. Right now they're half-buried, half-revealed.

So are the mysteries of this isolated Great Basin playa, where so much life—so many years ago—has so quietly departed into a desert slant of light.

CALIFORNIA SAND CASTLES

The Grapevine Canyon road spirals down from Bonnie Clare Flat to Mesquite Springs. Quickly abandoning Nevada for California, it exchanges bitter brush and sagebrush for creosote and mesquite bushes while dropping more than two thousand feet in less than five miles. Most tourists don't approach Death Valley this way. They prefer better-known and more direct routes, highways from Las Vegas to Furnace Creek or from Los Angeles to Stovepipe Wells, not secondary byways such as this one from Goldfield to Ubehebe Crater. So Grapevine Canyon traffic is usually sparse, with more coyotes than cars.

Traffic across Bonnie Clare Flat is sparse, too. Once part of a boom-to-bust mining district, the township of Bonnie Clare began as a tent city in 1906, grew into a railroad hub with a two-story wooden depot, several saloons, and a mercantile company, declined within a year, saw a brief revival in 1913, then faded away after the Bullfrog Goldfield Railroad was abandoned in 1928. The small community originated, in part, because the incorporators of the Bonnie Clare Bullfrog Mining and Milling Company put together a two-million-dollar paper stock venture based on a purported "four million dollars worth of ore . . . ready for immediate conversion into the yellow metal." Brochures, ads, and news stories boasted a hazard-free investment, one safely "underwritten by the forces of nature." For only sixty cents a share, naïve eastern and West Coast investors were told they could earn annual dividends of 60 percent, might see the worth of their stock increase by 400 percent a year. Like many other turn-of-the-century mining flurries, however, this one turned out to be illusory. The Bonnie Clare Company—$43,000 in debt by December of 1907—went into receivership just eighteen months after promoters conceived of it as a "veritable catacomb of wealth."

Some minimalist mining still occurs along the edge of the flat and up toward Gold Mountain to the northwest, but most of Bonnie Clare has reverted to its original spaces and speculations. The old town site is barely discernible. A few miles away, in the middle of this high desert expanse, the foundations of an unnamed building sit alongside a dirt track rarely traveled any more. Across the empty road, an idle windmill spins its bent and broken arms. Far up the valley to the east, a tower marks Rainier Mesa, high point of the Nevada Test Site where scientists regularly detonated nuclear bombs a generation ago. That distant erection of cable and steel—abandoned, bent and broken just like the nearby windmill—marks another outdated burst of the imagination, a Cold War version of space and speculation. I've stood beside that tower, heard its metal pieces groan in the wind, just as I stand near this Bonnie Clare windmill, thinking of promises and profit and illusion and bankruptcy.

At my feet, an intact cement curb curves away from a rectangular foundation. Scoured by desert winds and dust, it looks cleaner than any city street corner I've ever seen. Unlike most urban pavement, however, it goes nowhere. After paralleling the dirt road for a few feet in both directions, it ends abruptly, as if the pourers had reached their sagebrush destination. A broken corral, with relatively new barbed wire attached, extends to the south, but I see no sign of livestock or agriculture, little indication of recent human activity except a battered blue steel water tank with ELV 4300 scrawled on one side, and the windmill, abandoned to the wind that whirrs through its broken spokes. As a jack rabbit pops from behind one sagebrush and springs to the next, I imagine I hear a burro ambling down the dirt road.

CALIFORNIA: SAND CASTLES

That will-o-the-wisp burro runs wild now, along with thousands of others cut loose by early prospectors. Bearded men in overalls led these burros' progenitors while searching for some illusory mother lode. Would-be glory holes, dug mostly at the end of the nineteenth century and the beginning of the twentieth, pock the nearby hills. At the same time but at a greater distance, big-city financiers fancied lucrative and sensational discoveries. Four million dollars worth of ore and 400 percent returns, investors dreamed; empty promises and paper, more likely. For the lucky ones, Tonopah to the north and Rhyolite to the south turned out to be lucrative places to dig, but much of the mining action right here was intangible Wall Street ticker tape, blown by the wind.

Bonnie Clare Flat, in fact, is an illusion of an illusion, a windblown stretch of tumbleweeds and dust devils that, paradoxically, angles toward what I would describe as an illusion of an illusion of an illusion. While Bonnie Clare Flat itself is an emptiness where dreams soon turned to dust, it prefaces a place where dreams transformed dust into a dream fantasy indescribably unique. Not far away, after Highway 72 has left the Bonnie Clare and has corkscrewed down the canyon to the west—elevation dropping, temperature rising, vegetation changing—an odd sign appears. CONGESTION AHEAD. That's where Scotty's Castle stoppers Grapevine Canyon, where sour jug wine turns to Spanish amontillado and California chardonnay.

Although the map prepares a traveler for what lies around the bend, the oasis is startling. Sentinel olive trees, date palms, and imported cholla cactus guard green grass, carefully mowed. Boxy Winnebagos and red sport utility vehicles line up in paved parking lots, side by side with rental Chevrolets. A perimeter fence, forty-five miles in circumference, circles a genuine imitation castle, with red tile roofs, white stucco walls, wrought-iron balconies, three towers, and the stars and stripes flying. From underneath a clock set high on the east wall of the farthest tower, its wrought-iron hands telling accurate time against yellow and blue art-deco tile, a cluster of tourists gawks. Below their feet lies a dirt-filled swimming pool, 270 feet long. Beside them, the words DEATH VALLEY RANCH are chiseled above a massive hand-carved wooden door. Across the courtyard, a 1933 Packard is parked alongside benches waiting for tired grandmothers from Indiana and Illinois. A bell tolls the half hour, calling the next visitors to assemble. As I assemble, I glance beyond the castle, comparing the unvegetated natural browns with this artificial red, white, and green oasis. A slick-covered booklet tells me what to think: "Scotty's Castle, an imposing two-story Spanish villa in Grapevine Canyon near the north end of Death Valley, seems as much in harmony with its locale as are the cottonwood, mesquite, and stunted cactus that dot the wrinkled brown sides of its canyon setting." In harmony with its locale? I think not.

In my opinion, the wrought-iron rails and redwood carvings and the intricate tiled design are out of place in this canyon setting, as dysfunctionally inappropriate as that truncated curbstone now curving through the empty flats of Bonnie Clare. There on the flats, a useless windmill reminded me of the vagaries of the American Dream; here in the canyon, such ostentation visually reinforces the dream's vacuity. Most visitors, I assume, concur with the booklet's generalizations. "One of the best-known and most highly regarded structures in the West," the text begins. "Still another treasure for future generations to enjoy," it concludes. For me, however, Scotty's Castle epitomizes how the American Dream can go astray in California, and how no one seems to notice the irony.

First of all, Scotty's Castle wasn't even Scotty's Castle. Wealthy Chicagoans Albert and Bessie Johnson actually built the edifice as an elegant vacation home in the desert. Scotty himself was an itinerant raconteur and erstwhile prospector named Walter E. Scott who had befriended Albert Johnson in the early years of the twentieth century. After conning Johnson into mysterious mining investments, the Death Valley dreamer then beguiled the midwesterner with fascinating tales and romantic escapades. Since Scotty's flamboyant appeal came more from fiction than fact, sorting the truth of Scotty's adventures was, and is, nearly impossible. But Albert Johnson didn't care. He enjoyed the man's company, and he especially liked the time they spent together in Grapevine Canyon. Scotty lived in a tiny cabin there, where Johnson's wife sometimes visited too. Before long, the Johnsons were buying land in the canyon and deciding to build more spacious accommodations. Modest construction began in 1922, with a two-story stucco house, a workshop and garage. Then the Johnsons imagined a more luxurious retreat. Between 1926 and 1929, what became known as Scotty's Castle evolved—12,000 square feet of Spanish Provincial architecture in the middle of nowhere. Scotty took all the credit. Albert and Bessie Johnson, determined to enjoy their version of the American Dream but content to stay out of the spotlight, remained in the background. Scotty's foregrounding braggadocio amused them.

With the 1929 stock market crash, the Johnsons weren't exactly reduced to poverty but they were unable to continue building their dream house. Construction slowed, then ceased altogether. Thus the empty swimming pool, the vacant rose garden, the random pillars, the unfinished gatehouse, the thousands of unused tiles still stored underneath the castle. When Death Valley National Monument was established in 1933, the dream suffered yet another setback. The Johnsons' multi-million-dollar vacation home stood on government property. Eventually that problem was solved by a congressional bill allowing Johnson to rectify the surveyor's mistake and to purchase the land he thought he already owned, but by then the dream was even more tarnished. The Johnsons came to Death Valley less and less frequently. Finally they turned the castle into a tourist attraction, hiring guides and guards, charging a dollar to those who wished access to the castle's interior.

Scotty remained in residence, however, though even that fact was fiction, too. He actually lived in his cabin down canyon, while paying tourists paraded through what they were told was his room in the castle. There they saw his bed—in which he never slept—with its hand-carved headboard, his autographed pictures of actors and cowboy scenes, his ostensible treasures gathered during half a century of entrepreneurial activities. The bedroom is dark, almost gloomy. In fact, the entire castle is dark, with dark wood, dark leather furniture, and dark lowering paintings on the walls. Opaque windows and heavy leather curtains keep out the desert sun. Today the shades are drawn shut to help preserve the interior furnishings, a park ranger explains, as he hurries his tour group from room to room. Looking toward the massive living-room fireplace, then across to the waterless fountain on the far wall, I think the flowered deco tiles of the Spanish Colonial Revival do little to lighten the interior oppression. American dream or California nightmare? California Gothic, I decide.

Just before Albert Johnson's death in 1948, the financier deeded his Death Valley Ranch to the Gospel Foundation of California. For twenty years the Foundation ran the operation as a guest ranch, finally selling the property to the National Park Service in 1970, which now operates it as a popular Death Valley tourist concession. Our park ranger explains the change in ownership as we move on to the dining room, lined with pottery and heavy glassware, serving no one. Then comes an empty kitchen, rarely used even by the Johnsons because, to keep the castle cool, the cooking was done elsewhere. A 1941 limited-edition publication puts words in the mouths of the early tour guides. "Notice the sink built of imported old Spanish tile," they would recite. "See the quaint figures in the tile—that must be Ferdinand in the center. We have an appropriate pair of fixtures over the sink, a pair of Death Valley rattlesnakes in hand-wrought iron. The bronze doors under the sink show an old prospector with his burro, a pick, a shovel and a 'J' and 'S' stamped out in the door. You will find the 'S' and 'J' everywhere about the Castle, sometimes 'S and J' and sometimes 'J and S'. There is no rivalry between the two men." In 1941 the guides spoke in the present tense. There *is* no rivalry. Just fellowship and flatulence.

As I choose words to describe the pomposity of the two, I wonder about their relationship. I try to picture them sitting together in the darkened living room, perhaps a bottle between them. I try to hear the charisma in Scotty's voice, spinning out another yarn for his listeners. I remember, in fact, my parents telling me they saw Scotty in the early 1950s, when he was an old man. He came upon their tour group, and held them spellbound. The story of a long-lost mine, I think they said, a story spun seductively, an oft-told incantation. Books like Eleanor Jordan Houston's *Death Valley Scotty Told Me* and Hank Johnston's

CALIFORNIA: SAND CASTLES 119

Death Valley Scotty—subtitled *The Fastest Con in the West*—attest to the magic of the old prospector's tales. They say less about Albert Johnson, though his photograph often accompanies Scotty's, and they reveal almost nothing about Johnson's wife, Bessie.

I try to imagine her shadowy presence in a dark castle filled with heavy masculine furniture. Perhaps she sat quietly in a corner of the living room, near the fountain, sipping amontillado, listening to the interplay of rising voices and falling water. I can't see her in the rattlesnake kitchen, for she certainly didn't cook. Perhaps she lounged upstairs in the master suite, where dozens of finely woven Indian baskets line the walls. Someone—maybe Bessie—purchased them from the wives of the Shoshone laborers who toiled to build the castle. The Shoshone lived apart from the other workers, across the canyon in a segregated compound with few amenities. An Indian craftsman earned $2.50 a day; an unskilled Anglo, $5. Baskets necessarily supplemented the Shoshone income.

Modern air conditioners and air humidifiers hum in the background, while Bill Helmer, a 1990s ranger clad in 1930s garb, explains the layout to listeners wearing billed caps and warmup suits. The tour ends in another great hall, as immense as the living room on the other side of the castle and just as dark. "A church-like feeling," our shepherd suggests when he switches on a theater-size electric pipe organ in the darkened sanctuary. Overhead I see more heraldic tiles with painted escutcheons, a deeply carved wooden ceiling, and wrought-iron chandeliers. Did Bessie sit here alone and listen to the 1,121 pipes of the Welte-Mignon organ? Did Albert and Scotty join her? Did she hear more of their dreams? Did she fancy dreams of her own?

Down a steep, narrow circular staircase, we tourists descend from the castle into the hot desert air. With just a few steps, the contrast between the inner sanctum and the outer surroundings is extraordinary. I blink, grope for my sunglasses, and marvel at this cultural anomaly. I don't like it very much. But thousands of tourists come here every month, tens of thousands each year. A sign where I paid my eight-dollar fee says that guided tours leave every twenty minutes but that individuals may have to wait as long as two hours before joining one. I only waited fifteen minutes, but I recall an Easter Sunday ten years ago when I couldn't even find a parking place at Scotty's Castle. Lots of people find their way to this distant desert oasis.

What, I wonder, is the appeal? The ostentation? The obscene display of excess wealth? The fine craftsmanship of the building, the hand-carved ceilings and doors, the handmade furniture, the imported tile? Or is it the oddity of a so-called castle so far from other habitation? The peculiar juxtaposition of heightened Spanish Provincial architecture just an hour's drive from the depths of the lowest geographical location in the country? The American Dream in a valley called Death. Again I think of California Gothic, although this castle seems singularly ghost-less to me. If it's haunted at all, it's haunted by money, by speculation, by Wall Street and glory holes and unfounded claims, by illusory nuggets of silver and gold, not by the Johnsons and their sycophants. To me, Scotty's Castle characterizes itself as a twentieth-century caricature. No more and no less than Bonnie Clare Flat, it's both a promise and an illusion—a pick and a shovel, a glass of chardonnay.

The American Dream in a valley called Death. But just as Scotty's Castle didn't belong to Scotty, so Death Valley isn't really a valley. It's a graben, formed not by the flow of water but by the earth's uplifting. At the opposite end of Death Graben, the same tourists who crowd Scotty's Castle flock to see scenery unengineered by humans. That geologic landscape, however, attracts visitors for similar psychological reasons. It's the lowest, it's the hottest; it's a promise, an illusion. At Badwater, tour buses and motor homes edge the highway, while sightseers trudge across a whitened salt walkway made by their footsteps. Here the elevation is 279.8 feet below sea level. Four miles off the pavement, inaccessible in the July heat, the desert is lower still, minus 282 feet. As I look over the eyebright expanse, I think it makes no difference. Stepping across the salt mosaic toward the low point, I scan the horizon for a tell-tale dip. It's out there, somewhere, but it's too far away, and the temperature is too hot, and I wouldn't see an actual depression in the salty crystals anyway. Like the rest of the tourists I wander back to the parking area without having walked anywhere near four miles across the valley floor. Unlike many of them, however, I'm

CALIFORNIA: SAND CASTLES 121

not distressed by the heat. Two couples argue about the record—134° F, maybe 136°. One woman gestures in disgust. This noontime 107° is too moderate, too ordinary, nothing about which to write home. I turn my ears away from their dispute, and focus my eyes toward the sea-level marker on the hill above me, think briefly about the distance, wipe my forehead, and climb back in my air-conditioned truck.

Backtracking on the pavement and then turning down a well-traveled dirt road, I drive out to the Devils Golf Course. Here, salt and water-bearing gravels are buried more than a thousand feet below the surface. Horizontal forces push columns of salt upwards. Then, a helpful park service sign tells me, the wind and rain carve the "divots" into "fantastic shapes." Mentally chipping a ball from behind one boot-shaped cone and into another, I consider the name of my surroundings—the Devils Golf Course, anthropomorphically inscribed as an incongruous combination of Hades and human design. Then I try out the Devil's neighbors. Badwater. Coffin Canyon. Hells Gate. Furnace Creek. Bitter Spring. Misery Lake. Dry Bone Canyon. Dantes View. Appellations of Satan, these indications of an inhospitable terrain and eternal unrest. The early Anglo pioneers who tried to find short cuts across this valley quickly named its parts. *Agua fria. Jornada del muerto.* Starvation Canyon. The Devils Cornfield. A valley called Death. Supposedly a '49er, after a near-fatal ordeal lasting more than three weeks, turned for one last look and cursed the place the imperiled immigrant wagon train had finally escaped. "Good-bye Death Valley," he—or she, the legend is unclear—shouted.

Native Americans who preceded the pioneers had no such negative descriptors for the land. Instead, the early Shoshone called the valley "tumpisa," which can loosely be translated as red rock, or "tomesha," ground on fire, another historic variant. Today their descendents, the small Timbisha Shoshone tribe, whose name comes from tumpisa or tomesha, still view the valley with affection. I believe they would say, however, that the Euro-Americans have treated them like the devil, or like ghosts.

As soon as President Hoover declared Death Valley a national monument, the Timbisha Shoshone's traditional way of life shuddered shut. Their springs, their hunting grounds, their sacred sites were now off-limits. While they had served as agreeably cheap laborers on such projects as Scotty's Castle and the tourist facilities at Furnace Creek, they no longer were welcome residents in their homelands. In 1936 a small relocation camp was constructed at government expense, but when the tribe—as they had always done in the summer heat—left the valley for higher grounds, the Park Service bulldozed the vacated homes. Of the nine adobe abodes, only four remained. They still adjoin the prefab housing that was added later. Now the Timbisha Shoshone village houses approximately fifty residents. The remaining tribal members—perhaps another two hundred and fifty men, women, and children—must live elsewhere because new housing units aren't allowed in the acreage allotted the community.

Pauline Esteves led the negotiations with the United States government to regain control over at least some of the Timbisha Shoshone homelands. After years of discussion, confrontation and compromise, a "nation-to-nation" agreement has finally been reached, which expands the tribe's Furnace Creek property to 300 acres, adds them to the management team overseeing 300,000 more acres in the national monument, declares them owners of another 7,200 acres outside the boundaries, and grants access to additional lands for mesquite and pine nut harvests. As I write that last sentence, I recognize the verbal incongruity of *expand*, *add*, *declare*, and *grant access* when describing the process of returning what belonged to the tribe for ten thousand years before prospectors, settlers, and tourists suddenly arrived.

Pauline would highlight the irony. Tribal chair for a quarter of a century, she's been described as "hard-bitten" in the newspapers, but I find her just plain determined to reestablish tribal rights and to acknowledge tribal responsibilities. She once left her homeland to attend Stewart Indian School in northern Nevada, then worked in Los Angeles until she discovered she was piecing bombs together for use at the Nevada Test Site. "I didn't like what we were doing to Mother Earth," she told me the first time I met her, "so I quit." A fierce, heavyset, seventy-five-year-old with air-light movements, she flung one arm in disgust. Under a thatched ramada, I joined Pauline and Barbara

CALIFORNIA: SAND CASTLES 123

Durham, tribal administrator, just after they had testified before a congressional committee in Washington, D.C. Tired but exhilarated, the two women circuitously recounted the questions asked and the answers given. "It looks like the negotiations are going to succeed," said Barbara. "About time," Pauline added. Glad to be back home, they both hoped that Death Valley soon would be more like the home of tribal memory. In November 2000, President Clinton did indeed sign their bill into law.

A ferocious spring wind pummels me as I walk the Timbisha village streets. My body leans into the force, then leans away. Like a fighter feinting, jabbing, bobbing and weaving, punching and pulling back, the wind keeps a steady onslaught. Dust particles lend a velvet quality to the landscape, blurring what I see. Modern telephone poles, squaring the village in a rectangular grid, get in the way of my view to the west toward sacred Telescope Peak. As I pace off the grid, I find myself balancing the new and the old, the old and the new. A rusty Ford pickup sits on blocks next to another ancient car with what appears to be its engine sitting on its hood. The car's left front tire is flat. A few houses away, an exquisite red and pink bougainvillea hedges one neighbor from the next. An intricate mesquite fence protects delicate young squash plantings. The playground is floored with dirt and rocks, paved only beneath the basketball hoop. Across the street, a yard has been carefully raked. Two boys toss a ball back and forth, but not in the playground, while a black and white dog dashes between them. Pop bottles and beer can tabs line the ditches. Half a blue Frisbee lays buried alongside a torn brown and yellow shirt.

Bits of sand blow against my skin, that relentless desert prizefighter bruising my body and gritting against my teeth. Through the velvet particles I squint again toward snowy Telescope Peak. From the mountain's summit, the view is equally blurred, smog-shadowed and hazy. Although I stood on top on a relatively clear July day, I couldn't discern any details on the valley floor below, where the sun shimmered obliquely off a salt-flat land. The graben that day resembled a henna-haired hussy, seductively flirtatious, luring prospectors and tourists into her heat. The peak is seductive in a different way—dangerous to climb in winter when an icy cornice knifes the highest ridge, quite accessible in summer when only chukkar and "a garden of bristlecones" guard a trail that contours up and up through thickly flowered meadows. Remembering the breathless beauty of that distant hike, I look around at the low-level housing forced on a tribe that used to spend their hot summers high in the coolness of Wild Rose and Mahogany Flats.

July in the valley is problematic for all but the tribal residents, some Park Service employees, and a handful of foreign tourists. Camping outside in a temperature of 120° F is something to do only once, I believe. Just four other vehicles populated a campground that overflows in springtime. I slept in a wet T-shirt, with another one draped over my head. I drank gallons of water, and wondered how anyone on foot ever managed to carry enough liquid to make the crossing. By morning, the temperature had dropped to 95°. To the Timbisha Shoshone, such palpable discomfort is silly. Pauline and Barbara reacted with indifference to my comments about my overnight experiences. Instead, they wanted to know how the pine nut crop had looked up on the mountain. The fact that I hadn't noticed confirmed their judgment of tourists, I'm afraid.

Now it's spring, and this tourist has returned again to the blustering winds that blow winter desert into summer. Just as Telescope Peak guards the west side of the valley, so the dried Funeral Mountains—another Euro-American designation—line the opposite horizon. What I see isn't Scotty's Castle, which is sixty-some miles to the north, but another mirage of ostentatious wealth and opulence. The Furnace Creek Inn, built in 1927 by the Death Valley Hotel Company (one of their craftsmen was Pauline Esteves's father, a stonemason), nestles greenly against the desiccated landscape. Every time a Timbisha Shoshone glances up, he or she cannot help but see the disingenuous oasis.

From the Inn, though, I wasn't sure I could see the village at all. Non-native tamarisks, planted thickly, block the hotel guests' view in a way that invites them to overlook the village, to lift their eyes instead to the Panamints beyond. Only with effort could I pick out the Timbisha Shoshone dwellings, tiny Monopoly blocks below. Up here, showy petunias, crowded into beds of red, magenta, pink, and white, are de-

CALIFORNIA: SAND CASTLES 125

signed to catch a visitor's eye. While the building's exterior shows its age, with mustard-colored walls and turquoise doors needing paint, the newly remodeled lobby and the grounds are immaculate. I strolled through the horticultural gardens in the early afternoon. When the desert heat reaches its apex, an automatic sprinkler system keeps a manicured lawn green and cool, so moist, in fact, that thick moss grows against the flagstone walkways. Neither moss nor grass grows in the Timbisha Shoshone Village.

That night I camped in a Furnace Creek parking lot euphemistically called the Sunset Campground overflow area. I paid five dollars to stay there. I didn't heat a ten-minute pasta dinner on my one-burner cook stove, however. Instead, I paid considerably more than five dollars and took far longer than ten minutes to dine at the Furnace Creek Inn. A single cocktail cost eight dollars. I grimaced, sipping slowly. When I edged to the dining room entrance, the maitre d' questioned my dress. Black jeans? A fleece vest? Borderline in the no Levis/jackets only dress code, he said, but he ushered me inside anyway. My salmon dinner was slightly overcooked; the table wine pretty good. The dessert tray looked terrific; the view better yet. When I tried to locate the Timbisha Shoshone Village, a sharp orange sunset refracted in my eyes.

Remembering Bessie Johnson, I imagined a cadre of her 1920s society friends sitting at the next table, beside the window, of course. Two women are wearing flapper dresses, one with a string of pearls, both with bobbed hair. One fans herself with her menu as she speaks in a cultured Boston voice. Two men, correctly clad in coats and ties, are sunburned from a day of golf. The one on the left gestures with his cigarette, showing how he holed a putt on the eighteenth green. Four martinis, straight up. The four diners lift their glasses, and toast their desert vacation. Occasionally someone glances across the valley toward the sharp orange sunset glowing behind the golf course, 214 feet below sea level. The dark-haired man signals the waitress for another round.

My imagination veers away. An elderly Timbisha Shoshone woman sits on the front steps of her son's prefab dwelling. Looking across the street, she can see a broken adobe wall, all that's left of the house where her family used to live. Looking across the sand, she can outline the mountains where her family once summered. Dust feints her eyes. Two black hens stalk from right to left, pecking at the dirt. More dust. Wiping her hands on her print dress, she looks at her palms, her fingertips. When she was younger, her arms would ache from cutting mesquite away from the springs, her callused hands painful from the work of splitting, thinning, braiding, and entwining the willow for baskets. She sighs for her memories, long gone, her chin sinking against her chest. Even in the swirling dust of spring, she can picture the Furnace Creek Inn in the distance, with its green lawns, stolid red-tiled buildings, and date palms reaching toward the sky. Every time she looks, this is what she sees.

If she or one of her family members leaves home, he or she immediately encounters the traffic of tourists rushing from one scenic spot to the next. Engines never stopping, the visitors drive down to Badwater, back past Artists Palette, up to Dantes View, down to Mustard Canyon, north to Scotty's Castle, northwest to Stovepipe Wells. Right next door to the Timbisha Shoshone village, the Furnace Creek Ranch sits squarely on the valley floor. Inelegant stepsister to the emerald inn but far fancier than the native village, the ranch appeals mostly to families. I saw children everywhere, especially in the General Store, where T-shirts, cups, mugs, glasses and Indian goods surreptitiously labeled MADE IN PAKISTAN are sold. I thought of borrowing the title of Edward Abbey's 1979 essay, "Death Valley Junk," to characterize the wares. Like the Furnace Creek Inn, the Ranch too was a one-time Harvey's establishment, a resort designed in tandem with the Union Pacific Railroad in a grand plan to open the Southwest to tourism. The plan of course succeeded.

The first Harvey House opened in Topeka, Kansas, in 1876. By 1883, seventeen eating stations had been established. Before the company was sold to Amfac, Inc. in 1968, it had become the sixth largest food retailer in the United States. Many long-time Harvey restaurants, such as the one at Furnace Creek, sit in the midst of national scenic treasures—on the south rim of the Grand Canyon, on the north rim, at the edge of Bryce Canyon. From my childhood I still remember the

CALIFORNIA: SAND CASTLES 127

high beamed ceilings, sophisticated atmosphere, incomparable views, elegant dining. Even in canyon country my parents made me wear a dress. "Where the inhabitants had been used to rooting about in a bean-and-bacon wilderness, Harvey made the Southwest bloom with vintage claret and quail under glass," explains Harvey scholar, Donald Duke. With a motto of "service and quality" for his waitresses, the famous Harvey Girls, Fred Harvey insisted on a "no-coat no-eat requirement" for his customers. Hence the dress code query from the maitre d' the preceding evening; hence my parents' insistence.

Once a vacation to Death Valley was a grand adventure, even a dangerous one. Soaring temperatures, sparse water supplies, and immense distances kept the fearful away. Then Fred Harvey opened the Southwest, "civilized it," in the words of Duke. Now air-conditioning and high-speed roadways invite everyone to play. Driving from parking lot to photo opportunity to signed tourist attraction, it's easy to forget that at first Death Valley spelled disaster for those who tried to cross it. Not for the Timbisha Shoshone, whose ancestors comfortably migrated back and forth with the seasons, but for the pioneers who sought a fast route to California and, later, for the miners who wrested minerals from inhospitable land, this place could be wretched.

One of those marked tourist attractions signals another Death Valley enterprise, the Harmony Borax Works, where Chinese workers labored to scour salt from the playa, shovel it into handcarts, and then wheel it to the steam-powered crusher and massive crystallizing tanks. One source facetiously suggests that "everyone who went there either died within six months or left a broken-down invalid!" An exaggeration, perhaps, but a clear indication of the harsh working conditions nonetheless. Better-known stories are told of the wagons that carried the borax from Death Valley to Mojave. Made famous by the logo TWENTY MULE TEAM BORAX, these immense vehicles weighed over thirty tons when fully loaded. One still stands near the abandoned Borax Works, another in a Furnace Creek display. "The Only Animated Trademark in the World," brags a borax brochure. Radio's old "Death Valley Days" ads said little about the life of a twenty-mule-team skinner, but transporting thirty tons through the Devils Golf Course must have inspired some hellish incantations. "Git hep-th-th-th-th yougithop," followed by language unsuitable for television. I can hear the wagon creaking, mule whip cracking, and the voice of the skinner shouting at the top of his lungs. "Git hep-th-th-th-th yougithop!"

Interestingly enough, in a graben called Death, I can hardly get away from a cast of lively characters. Once, when summer had barely come to Death Valley but the gnats had arrived in full force, I followed most of the two-tracks leading west into the Panamints. Maneuvering the truck as far as its four-wheel drive would take me, I'd then hike the rest of the way. Each road ended at a mine, where someone's dream came true, or didn't. Trail Canyon. Hanaupah Canyon. Johnson Canyon—William, not Albert. Galena Canyon. Warm Spring Canyon. Talc mines. Washouts. Creosote. Juniper. Gully washers. Paintbrush. Gnats. In one century, bearded men in overalls wandered on foot, and pocket hunters led solitary burros under a blistering sun. In the next, more bearded men in overalls eased Model A trucks up grades too steep for the engines. When I compare their existences with Scotty's, I appreciate his self-interested affection for Albert and Bessie. Even Bonnie Clare Flat seems more congenial than the rough isolation of the upthrust Panamint range.

Back in the Funeral Mountains on the other side of the valley, I test some other canyon trails. One is Artists Drive, a one-way road leading through colorful volcanic deposits. The reds, pinks, and yellows come from iron salts; the greens from decomposing mica, the purples from manganese. Together, they make the appropriately named cirque of color, Artists Palette, that I could faintly discern from Telescope's heights. No devil terrain here. A few miles away, I follow another canyon, one without a paved road nearby, and with a more Satanic name. To counteract Desolation's nether image, I recreate it in my own terms. It looks like angel food cake, I decide, angel food cake splashed with crème de menthe, crème de cacao, crème de cassis. An elegant dessert, fit for the Furnace Creek Inn. Farther to the north, in still another canyon with a dismal title, high-walled narrows serpentine back into

CALIFORNIA: SAND CASTLES

the hills. A ranger told me I'd see few flowers this year, but he was wrong. A dozen yards into the canyon, and I was finding prickly petunias with off-white blossoms, yellow daisies, orange mallow, tiny purple composites. I found welcome isolation, too, sharp contrast with the bustle of tourists at Scotty's Castle, Badwater, and Furnace Creek. Elsewhere, I saw the illusions—the costliest castle, the lowest elevation, the hottest temperature, the most elegant dining. Here, a sacred white datura blossoming in the dirt. California grandeur, I decide again, where space and speculation inevitably leads to spectral one-upsmanship.

As I leave the canyon narrows, a hot wind catches my hat brim, strikes a blow to my sunburned face. I walk slowly toward my truck, eyes half-shut against the sifting dust. Back in the direction of Scotty's Castle, though not all the way to its fence line and turrets and chimes, I stop for the night at Mesquite Springs. Somewhere between this campground and the castle, Scotty's rustic cabin sits abandoned. Somewhere between, a now-deserted Shoshone village hides off-limits, too. Unable to find either of them, I wander across the wash and weave my way through mesquite thickets once tended by aboriginal Americans. Under their care, the bushes flourished by design. With Park Service oversight, the mesquite has been left alone to invade the springs and to usurp the precious groundwater. After the new compact is firmly in place, the Timbisha Shoshone once again will tend the native plants in their traditional ways. They hope to model environmental restoration, showing tourists how people can live in graceful harmony with the desert. They plan to sell native artifacts, too, not objects made in Pakistan. As I leave the wash, I turn up a steep volcanic slope, and find spiked barrel cactus, fat from an early spring rain and heavy with orange-red blossoms, clustering down the ridge line. A showy display of life in a valley misnamed Death.

I sketched out this chapter several years ago, when *GhostWest* was just emerging in my imagination and when Pauline Esteves was refusing to give up the tribal vision of a Timbisha Shoshone homeland. At that time, I suppose, those negotiations were as illusory as so many other aspects of Death Valley—the prospects of mineral wealth, Scotty's Castle, the Furnace Creek Inn and the Furnace Creek Ranch, the low point shimmering in the desert heat. Originally, I imagined the tribe as ghostly as Bessie and Albert Johnson or the long-lost Harvey girls. I saw the tiny tribal complex a travesty of what their ancestors once called home. I've changed my mind, however, after talking with Pauline and Barbara so many times. Now I think—I hope—the real ghost is just a haunting memory of the way our government once treated sovereign nations that originally populated our land.

10
ARIZONA
THE OLD PUEBLO

To my right, a car horn blasts exasperation at the slowness of the double-wide left-turn lane. To my left, an orange-vested entrepreneur paces a narrow concrete divider, taps on car windows, hawks newspapers to bored drivers. As he walks, he breathes the fumes from two rows of vehicles waiting for the green arrow light to appear. Anticipating, another horn bleats a higher note. On the far side of the divider, more cars and trucks, bumper to bumper, power into the city while I inch toward the outskirts. Emissions spill into the sky. My windows tightly closed, I twist the air conditioner knob a notch higher, turn up the tape deck volume.

Behind me stretches a six-lane strip mall promenade. Pier 1 Imports, Wal-Mart, Sears, OfficeMax, Blockbuster Video, Bank of America, Carl's Jr., Exxon, Starbucks Coffee. McDonald's, with a red-tiled roof and fake pink adobe walls and accents of turquoise paint. The haute-southwest façade mirrors itself from one block to the next, from shop to shop and from office building to office building, as if the Spanish-American dress of a beautiful flamenco dancer were stitched amateurishly with acrylic thread. In fact, the scalloped blouse and swirling skirt have all but been obliterated by a sanforized patchwork of desert pastels. Now Tucson wears a tattered gown, boasts beads of smog, and dances arhythmically to the clatter of false castanets.

Even so, I've always liked Tucson. Though I've never lived here, I've visited often. For years, I've been searching for the Old Pueblo interred beneath the city, for the real turquoise behind the decorator mauve, for Tucson's ghost dancer twirling in the sun. I know she's there, forlorn and lost on a downtown street once known as Calle de la India Triste. "Street of the Sad Maiden." After the Southern Pacific Railroad arrived in 1880, the Sad Maiden changed her name to Congress Street, and commerce began designing the fabric of the town. Today its central core differs little from the downtowns of dozens of other Sunbelt cities, though the architects pretend. The Norwest tower has aqua glass squares edged bright blue. An older Wells Fargo building bears filigreed wrought-iron trim that matches the turquoise of the neighboring Arizona Bank. But the Tucson Convention Center and the State of Arizona Regional Complex, functional cement structures built where old adobes once edged the unpaved streets, could be almost anywhere.

There are signs of an older Tucson, of course. The Pima County Courthouse, completed in 1929, resembles an elegant little sister, clad in yellow and green and blue tile and looking quite historic. The soot-white San Augustine cathedral is a landmark bridging past and present, palm trees and ocotillos side by side. A block away, a front yard shrine shelters the Virgin Mary behind a thicket of beavertail cactus. Turn the corner, and a brightly painted street-side mural covers an adobe wall. I can even find Tucson's inner self in a row of tiny cribs just three blocks from downtown. But the Old Pueblo is not easily apparent, not when mission-McDonalds line so many car-choked streets and when so many suburban layers disfigure the desert.

Indian Ruins Road pierces one middle-class development, where '50s-style ranch houses sit on forgotten Hohokam mounds. Early homeowners found pottery scraps while excavating their swimming pools and laying down their backyard lawns. Now, less than a mile away, the Medicine Man Gallery prices Maynard Dixon's paintings of old Tucson for $58,000, while the Tucson Country Club augers the lavender ambience of an old duenna. Farther out Tanque Verde Road, with its center divider of posed paloverdes and assorted cactus, the suburbs take on a 1990s guise. A development called Monterey Homes sells waterfront residences fronting carefully excavated cement-lined desert canals. The '49er Country Club comes next; then Bel Air Ranch Estates, where machinery grinds the new ranchettes into proper shapes and sizes. Farther still, after Tanque Verde turns into Reddington Road, lies Camino La Cebadilla, a community of desert estates that appear to be defended by a legion of regimented saguaros. Standing in single file next to green grass and geometric paving tiles, the armed cacti look uncomfortably foolish.

I first set foot on virgin Sonoran desert more than twenty years ago, near the Rincon Mountains not far from present-day Camino La Cebadilla. Familiar with the sparseness of high desert terrain, I could scarcely believe the fecundity of the Sonora. I remember the clutch of cat's claw acacia, and the way the cholla pricked my socks that afternoon. Stepping carefully between thick mesquite and redolent creosote and barrel-chested saguaros, I could hardly walk a straight line. Cactus wrens chittered; banded lizards darted away; a buzzard sailed the thermals overhead. This was a desert filled with life and growth and vitality, hot with the scent of the sun. Just recently I hiked up the ridge that divides popular Sabino Canyon from its neighbor, Bear Canyon. Steep, hot even in December, the route stair-stepped onto a narrow crest with a panoramic view. I could see almost exactly where I'd first touched the Tucson desert. Now, a grid of streets. Houses everywhere. Golf courses. A veiled haze across the valley.

Unless I squinted at the smog-brown horizons, I could see very little undeveloped land. Hiking back down the well-used trail, I thought about a dead saguaro I had seen. Its desiccated ribs, still six feet tall, teepeed together like a shock of tall kindling. More ribs and knots, shattered, lay on the ground. A spin of brown-dry cotton candy was all that remained of the once-pulpy flesh. This particular specimen seemed symptomatic to me, a frail mummy that has breathed her life away.

Like so many modern cities in the West, Tucson exploded after

World War II. In 1998, an average of twelve acres of Sonoran desert were cleared for new homes, offices, and commercial buildings *each day*. More than thirty rezonings, comprising 2600 acres, have been approved in the past decade. Major subdivisions now anchor every corner of the valley. Connecting them is an impossible street system which can't keep pace with a population that has grown from 40,000 to more than 800,000 in less than half a century. Meanwhile, analysts project that the total annual vehicle miles traveled in the Tucson area will grow from two million in 1970 to *twenty-eight million* in 2020. One of the few thoroughfares runs past the Davis-Monthan Air Force Base, where thousands of Second World War planes are cocooned in moth-balls. Planes without tails, fighters without wings, transports without propellers, helicopters without flight—all languish in camouflaged disarray. Their graveyard reminds me of Tucson's pastel-camouflaged past, her exquisite dress moth-balled, her cosmetic embroidery peeling away.

Now, as the twenty-first century begins, the guitars of progress strum faster and faster, crescendoing out of tune. Tucson's once voluptuous figure is giving way to middle-aged fat, her body spreading so egregiously that the desert herself is disappearing. So is the temperate climate and so is the incomparable clean air, two of many reasons why people came and came to Tucson, and stayed and stayed. Of the beautiful maiden who ought to be swaying in soft sunlight, almost nothing remains. I can't see her billowing skirt; I can't hear the rhythm of her steps. I can't even picture her face or imagine her spirit. Overbuilt, overcrowded, and overindulgent, she's danced the night away.

Another horn honks tunelessly behind me. Another vendor raps on my car window. Another red light turns green, amber, back to red. Still caught in traffic, I rewind a Linda Ronstadt tape. Ignoring the incessant sounds of the city, I listen to 'Canciones de mi Padre' play again softly, very softly.

11
NEBRASKA CATHERLAND

Standing in the draft of an autumn afternoon, I was staring down at the Pavelka fruit cave haloed by Willa Cather nearly eighty years before. Reinventing the real Anna Pavelka in my *Ántonia* imagination, I was trying to picture the children—Anna's and, in turn, Ántonia's—"running up the steps together, big and little, tow heads and gold heads and brown, and flashing little naked legs." Daydreaming there at the deserted farmstead, I was envisioning "a veritable explosion of life out of the dark cave into the sunlight." But the present pulled me out of my *Ántonia* reverie. An expensive white car appeared suddenly in the deserted farmyard. A sturdy midwestern family emerged, and marched across the empty grass. They headed straight toward me; I resented the intrusion.

From distant Nevada I had designed a Nebraska essay in my head. Willa Cather's fictions inextricably lace with the real south-central Nebraska countryside. So many of her imagined characters were drawn from life; so much of her imaginative energy still populates the terrain. Trying to understand how an authorial presence so dominates a landscape, I happily was tracing Cather's world from site to site and from page to page. I didn't want garrulous outsiders breaking into my thoughts.

"We're Ántonia's grandchildren," the family spokeswoman loudly announced. Clad in snug Levi's with matching blue oval earrings, high-heeled cowboy boots, wide belt buckled with hearts entwined, she had a voice that boomed in the stillness. My mind repeated the fruit cave "veritable explosion of life" quote, then quickly paged back to another *Ántonia* chapter. Cather in Book II writes of Tony, "Her voice had a peculiarly engaging quality; it was deep, a little husky, and one always heard the breath vibrating behind it. Everything she said seemed to come right out of her heart." Right out of fiction's pages, that same voice echoed again, "We're Ántonia's grandchildren!" And they were. Or at least they were Anna Pavelka's, daughters and son of Lucille, come to the family farmstead during a day-long drive through Cather country, through Pavelka and Sadilek and Shimerda and Cuzak country, through a nostalgic landscape of their grandparents' past made present on this gold September day.

"When we'd visit, we'd play upstairs away from the adults." "We used to sit here and cut paper dolls from catalogues." "Grandma had her washing machine on the porch, in this corner. The porch was open then." "We stayed here after the fire, after our house burned down. I slept upstairs. You did too." "There's where the bee bit me! Remember?" "Sometimes we played in the root cellar. I remember!" Their voices spilled over one another in an explosion of memories that brought Anna Pavelka to a life different from Cather's fiction. For one thing, Wilma and Marcie and George had no recollection of their grandmother as a girl or a wife, only of "grandma" as the family elder, overseeing picnics, working at carefully chosen chores, enjoying her grandchildren at play. For another, their memories themselves were colored by the passage of time, so single episodes like the bee sting loomed large while other more singular events were forgotten. Nearly sixty years had passed since they were children; more than forty since their grandmother had died. Even so, their obvious joy brought the deserted farm to life. I could sense "grandma" on the porch, turning the wringer by hand, could feel her crossing the yard to hang clean sheets in the freshening wind. I could even see Ántonia's ghost in Wilma's eyes, "big and

warm and full of light, like the sun shining on brown pools in the wood." The resemblance made me smile and shiver simultaneously.
I watched and listened some more. Wilma and Marcie and George were remembering Anna Pavelka, not Willa Cather's fictional Ántonia Cuzak, but they announced themselves as "Ántonia's grandchildren." Not Anna's; Ántonia's. So pervasive is Cather's creative presence in Webster County, Nebraska, that even the real-life offspring of her fictional prototypes blur the boundaries between Cather's imagination and their own family histories. With obvious pride, flesh and blood Pavelka scions claim a fictional heritage. One local legend says that Anna's husband, John, once identified himself to a hospital attendant: "I am the husband of My Ántonia!"

Anna and John are buried in the Cloverton Cemetery, just a few miles north of their now-deserted farmhouse. Outside the cemetery gates, a green Willa Cather Pioneer Memorial sign locates the site for tourists. Inside, a sturdy replica of that sign stands next to the Pavelka graves. The replica was set in place by family members. Alongside the familiar plow symbol, the printed words read: "Anna Pavelka Inspiration for *My Ántonia*." Even in death, her literary self defines her, and her family has chosen to honor that definition.

Someone mowed the Cloverton Cemetery recently, though tall prairie grasses still reach around many of the tombstones. Wandering through the grave sites, stepping lightly on a ragged lawn of three- and four-leaf clovers, I discovered that most of the carved marble stones define human lives and deaths in terms of family relationships. Father. Son. Beloved Wife. Lives in connection with others. Anna Pavelka's grave, to the contrary, proclaims her life in connection with a life of the imagination.

So it is with Webster County, a very real landscape characterized as much by a canon of novels and short stories written two generations ago as by a 1990s personality. Even driving there replicates a Willa Cather narrative. From Lincoln south to Beatrice, I then turned west along Highway 136. "On a bright September morning in the year 1899," Miss Knightly did the same. The opening paragraphs of "The

Best Years" describe her buggy ride over "dusty sunflower-bordered roads" that, though paved now and made for high-speed cars and trucks, are still lined in the fall with a blinding crop of yellow-gold. When my eyes weren't fixed on the sunflowers, or the traffic, they looked off toward an unbroken skyline. More used to mountains than prairies, I wondered how far I might drive before the Rockies edged into view. Willa Cather knew the mountains lay far away. "The horizon was like a perfect circle, a great embrace, and within it lay the cornfields, still green, and the yellow wheat stubble, miles and miles of it, and the pasture lands where the white-faced cattle led lives of utter content." Continuing west, I headed into a circle tarnished a bit by the late twentieth century — haze from burning fields hung in the air — but a magic embrace nonetheless. "She seemed," wrote Willa Cather of Miss Knightly, "to be driving through a fineless land." When I reached the Webster County line, a bold gray-green sign told me how "fineless" might be interpreted today. "Webster County Welcomes You to Catherland," it said. A few miles farther, another sign, red this time with another symbolic plow on top, announced "Home of Willa Cather 6 Miles." Red Cloud lay just ahead.

The Cathers came to Red Cloud by train in 1883. Willa was ten years old. After living on a farm sixteen miles northwest of town for nearly a year and a half, her family then moved to 345 Cedar Street, a block from Red Cloud's main thoroughfare. There Willa Cather lived for six years, until she graduated from high school and left to attend the University of Nebraska in Lincoln. Though she continued to visit her parents as long as they were alive, and though she occasionally stayed for a month or two at a time, she never again claimed Red Cloud as her permanent residence. After 1931, she never returned to the landscape made famous by her prose. For only seven years did she actually live in Webster County; only seven, between the ages of ten and seventeen.

In her imagination, however, the small farming community and its surrounding countryside loomed large. This place, as she conceptualized it, developed into different locations in six novels and eight more short stories. The name of the community and its environs changed from book to book: Frankfort, Sweet Water, Hanover, Black Hawk, Haverford, Once Red Cloud, Nebraska, even became Moonstone, Colorado. The terrain changed, too, as Cather fictionally compressed and expanded distances, planted poplars where cottonwoods grew, shifted the bends in a river, added or subtracted a table and chair. Yet the settings retained a Webster County coloration, as if she were painting and repainting a backdrop before which different characters might act.

Many of those characters seemed also to have lived real lives in Webster County. *Willa Cather in Person* notes the author's insistence that her fictional men and women were "all composites of three or four persons" she had known, but in truth, some of her best-known portrayals were drawn very closely from the personalities of her Red Cloud neighbors. Anna Sadilek Pavelka, for example, grew into Ántonia Shimerda Cuzak; John Pavelka into Ánton Cuzak and then into "Neighbor Rosicky"; Cather's own Grandmother Boak into "Old Mrs. Harris." A complete list would cover this page and more. So it is little wonder that the Red Cloud community became fascinated by seeing itself in print. Not everyone liked the results, of course, but in a small midwestern town—population about 6000 when Willa lived there, population about 1200 today—the printed word became food for thought, gossip, bemusement, even resentment, and finally—as years passed and a generation died—acceptance.

Into that small-town milieu stepped Mildred Bennett. Daughter of strict Seventh Day Adventist parents, Mildred Rhoads left home and moved to south central Nebraska in the early 1930s. Her first teaching position took her to Inavale, a tiny farming community just seven miles west of Red Cloud. When she told her American literature teacher that she had signed an Inavale contract, the teacher replied, "Oh, that's Cather country." Mildred "didn't know what she was talking about." She soon read her first Cather novel, however, *Shadows on the Rock*, and soon met Wilbur Bennett, the man she would marry. The couple settled in Red Cloud after he completed his medical degree.

While raising her children in this small rural Nebraska community, Mildred was looking for ways to keep her mind occupied. Though she no longer accepted the church teachings of her youth, she still sought something in which to believe. During a 1989 television interview, she explains that she found her meaning in Willa Cather's fiction. Although Mildred never met Cather, she knew the men and women of Red Cloud, and she knew their parents' stories. Mildred talked with her neighbors, listened, gathered tidbits of local color, then quickly expanded her horizons. She read and reread Cather's prose, then traveled more widely and asked more questions. The result was Mildred Bennett's 1951 publication of *The World of Willa Cather* with its details of the people and places and local lore that shaped the novelist's childhood and, later, her Nebraska fiction.

Willa Cather's death in 1947 and the appearance of *The World of Willa Cather* four years later generated more interest in Red Cloud. Visitors planned side-trips there, walking the uneven sidewalks, looking for the sites and sounds of Cather's world. Soon Mildred and her friends decided they needed to do something to preserve the most special places. Eight of them met in March of 1955 to discuss possible projects. Contributing twenty dollars apiece, they incorporated the Willa Cather Pioneer Memorial and Educational Foundation (WCPM). The first acquisition was the City Hall—previously the bank building—which Mildred and another housewife bought with "our husbands' money" for a thousand dollars.

As Mildred's enthusiasm spread, the fledgling WCPM successfully sought other acquisitions of literary significance. Today Red Cloud visitors can enjoy the former Farmers' and Merchants' Bank building, which is administered as a branch museum by the Nebraska Historical Society, the old Catholic Church, the railroad depot, the Cather childhood home, the Episcopal Church. Outside of town, they can stroll the contours of a 610-acre tract of virgin mixed-grass prairie managed by The Nature Conservancy. Or they can follow a well-signed driving tour which meanders north past the location of Charles Cather's first farm, past the site of the infamous suicide grave which figures in *My Ántonia*, to other lonesome Midwest cemeteries, to abandoned churches and vacant schoolhouses, and of course to the Pavelka place. A convenient brochure points the way, complete with timely quotations to remind tourists of Cather's descriptions.

Red Cloud's residents seem to know the tour spots and the quotations by heart. Or at least those intimately involved in the WCPM have memorized the stories told by Mildred Bennett in *The World of Willa Cather* and have adopted the scenes of Cather's childhood as something special. I first saw Red Cloud in the company of two busloads of English professors. Mildred designed our tour, greeting us with a homemade buffet in the now-vacant Lion's Club building and then sending us out to see the important places. Between stops I, like so many before me, walked the distinctive red brick streets and thought about the personalities of this tiny rural community. Alongside two out of every three houses, a large red N flew near the front door; sounds of Nebraska football — the Cornhuskers were playing Oklahoma — filled the air. Then, in a disjuncture of time and space, my colleagues and I would step from the bright sunlight of the present into the dim shadows of a building preserved from the past.

Best-known is Willa Cather's childhood home. Now a registered historic landmark, it was built in 1879 and housed the Cather family for twenty years. Willa lived there between 1884 and 1890, spent vacations with her parents there, and lovingly described its rooms in "The Best Years" and "Old Mrs. Harris" and *The Song of the Lark*. Responsible for the home's purchase and its basic restoration, an outdoor plaque explains, was W. K. Bennett, MD. No mention is made of Mildred, but I felt her presence there as powerfully as I felt Willa Cather's.

Mildred admired *The Song of the Lark* heroine, Thea Kronborg, perhaps more than any other Cather protagonist. She felt a spiritual connection with Thea's fictional struggles to break loose from her parents' religious domination while not breaking away from their love. Working to restore Cather's childhood home was for Mildred a way of touching Thea Kronborg's life, especially in the darkly quiet upstairs room, where Thea found refuge and "thought things out more clearly." No one actually lived in the Cedar Street attic after the Cathers left, so total restoration was not an insurmountable task. Once the Bennetts' generosity enabled the WCPM to purchase the house, Mildred proceeded to recreate the upstairs room exactly as dictated by *The Song of the Lark*. Today's visitors hear a mellow taped voice reading:

> It was the end room of the wing, and was not plastered, but was snugly lined with soft pine. The ceiling was so low that a grown person could reach it with the palm of the hand, and it sloped down on either side. There was only one window, but it was a double one and went to the floor. In October, while the days were still warm, Thea and Tillie papered the room, walls and ceiling in the same paper, small red and brown roses on a yellowish ground. Thea bought a brown cotton carpet, and her big brother, Gus, put it down for her one Sunday. She made white cheesecloth curtains and hung them on a tape. Her mother gave her an old walnut dresser with a broken mirror, and she had her own dumpy walnut single bed, and a blue washbowl and pitcher which she had drawn at a church-fair lottery. At the head of her bed she had a tall round wooden hat-crate, from the clothing store. This, standing on end and draped with cretonne, made a fairly steady table for her lantern.

Like Thea Kronborg, Willa Cather papered her Cedar Street room with "small red and brown roses on a yellowish background," hung her own white cheesecloth curtains, and kept a wooden hat-crate beside the head of her bed. Mildred Bennett scraped layers of wallpaper to reveal those roses, scrubbed the pine board floor, found replicas of missing items and put everything in place just as if Willa had stepped away overnight, just as if Thea had stepped from the pages of her novel. Hovering both inside and outside the tiny room in the darkened attic are the ghosts of all three women—the fictional heroine, her creator, and the re-creator of their space. Others, feeling the ghostly affinity too, unfortunately acted out some urge to touch the past. Now a glass barrier prevents visitors from entering the room. Because too many souvenir hunters found scraps of wallpaper irresistible, the WCPM had to take measures to keep tourists at bay. No one is allowed to cross the threshold of the tiny sanctuary; no one can even go inside the house without a WCPM guide.

Born and raised nearby, recruited and trained by Mildred Bennett, these guides repeat the stories of Willa Cather's world. In fact, they tell no other stories, though given their Red Cloud connections they well might share some other memories or facts. They have been well-taught, however, to recount those anecdotes that are the substance of *The World of Willa Cather*, doing so with a decided twist. The guides' gentle voices speak of the fictional characters as if they were real-life denizens of the local community and, as often, describe real people as if they were products of Cather's imagination. "That's the Rosen house in 'Old Mrs. Harris,'" not Mr. and Mrs. Weiner's in Red Cloud. Here's the St. Juliana Falconieri Catholic Church, "where My Ántonia was married and where her first child was baptized." "Remember Wick Cutter? I'll show you his house."

Before long, I heard myself making the same mistakes. It's all too easy to blur the distinctions in a community that defines itself by the presence of a writer's imagination. The wall of the local laundromat, for example, displays a poster of Jessica Lange starring in a 1992 Hallmark Hall of Fame presentation of *O Pioneers!* Next to the poster, an entire wall is painted with a map of Red Cloud territory. Important Cather sites are labeled—sometimes with real names (Pavelka Farmstead in *My Ántonia*); sometimes with fiction (Wheeler House in *One of Ours*). Across the street, in the Red Cloud Café, a tattered 1913 map of Webster County hangs on the wall. Prominent are Cather names in Catherton Precinct; the family owned a lot of property. The Red Cloud Cemetery holds Cathers, too. In another demonstration of the importance of familial connections, bulky marble tombstones mark the graves of Willa's parents and her Grandmother Boak while smaller ones signify the resting places of the next generation. Not far away, a tall marker shows where the body of Francis Sadilek was finally interred, and where his wife, Anna, and their son, Ánton, are also buried. Anna Pavelka's parents and brother—or are they somehow Ántonia's?—rest in peace.

Throughout Red Cloud the presentation is low-key but omnipresent. None of my visits has been orchestrated, exactly, but I've never quite escaped the Willa Cather-ness of the place. Signs keep reminding me of significant locations, and sometimes of less important sites. The church "where Ántonia was married," for example, is not directly mentioned in the novel. Actually, it's the church where Anna Sadilek married John Cuzak—a nearby WCPM sign confirms the fact—but the lore long since has superseded the actual event. Uptown, there's an Episcopal Church that was built after Willa Cather left Nebraska. Though her parents later worshipped there, and the Cather children donated stained-glass windows in their parents' memories, and Willa herself became a member in 1922, the church per se had no impact on the youthful novelist-to-be's spiritual development. Nonetheless, because it was meaningful to the Cather family, it's a key stop on any Catherland tour. The guides, in particular, generate a fondness for its beauty, and I know many Cather scholars find solace there.

So Mildred Bennett succeeded beyond her wildest expectations. As time passed, and as her children grew to adulthood, she devoted all her energies to the preservation of Willa Cather's Webster County world. The churches, the railroad depot, the Pavelka farmstead—Mildred was responsible for starting every negotiation, for facilitating every acquisition. She was passionate about her life's work.

A dozen years ago, in Fort Worth, Texas, I returned to my hotel room just before midnight. Expecting my conference roommate to be fast asleep, I tiptoed into the room as quietly as I could. No one noticed my entrance. The room was filled with people, maybe twenty of them, and they were mesmerized. Sitting on a hard-backed chair, Mildred Bennett was telling stories. She was recounting interviews with Cather's friends, conversations with her fictional prototypes, encounters both planned and accidental that became the vignettes underlying *The World of Willa Cather*. Occasionally someone would ask a question, and a new set of anecdotes would follow.

We—I say "we" because I soon was as fascinated as they—hardly breathed, while Mildred's soft voice held us captive. Her firm mouth bespoke her resolve and her steadfastness of purpose. Searching her memory for fresh details, she would frown for a moment. Then a quick deep smile would light her face with the enthusiasm that had always

NEBRASKA: CATHERLAND

propelled her on her Cather quest. She must have talked for at least two more hours, there in that harshly lit, sterile Texas hotel room in the middle of the night. To describe the scene as "worshipping at the shrine" would be unfair, but the whole ambience was characterized by reverence and respect. I've never seen anything quite like the adoration on the listeners' faces and their rapt attention to a storyteller in her seventies speaking softly of another woman's world.

The last time I visited Nebraska, I ventured on another pilgrimage. John C. Neihardt, Nebraska's poet laureate, lived for many years in Bancroft, a small farming community eighty-five miles north of Lincoln. Now Bancroft is the home of the Neihardt Foundation, and boasts a Center operated by the Nebraska State Historical Society. I decided to see how a tour there might compare with one to Catherland. The differences were extraordinary. At the Neihardt Center, the director told us what we were to see and what we were to think while we were seeing it. His preacher-voice rhetoric told us of Neihardt's profundity and greatness as a philosopher. His gestures showed us how to proceed through the sacred hoop garden, how to "go clockwise in the circular exhibit room." When Neihardt's daughter read selected passages aloud, the director explicated the poems precisely as he wanted us to understand them. With such controls in place, I never felt a Neihardt spirit, never connected with either his writing or his landscape, never was imaginatively touched by the Neihardt stories.

Less heavy-handedly but just as insistently, Red Cloud irresistibly invites a close Cather connection. Even for the uninitiated who know little of Cather's stories, real spirits walk the Red Cloud streets and byways. Willa Cather's; Mildred Bennett's; the Cather family's; spirits of the men and women who shaped Cather's imagination and who appeared in some guise in her fiction; spirits of those who came later, and have joined the ongoing preservation efforts of the WCPM. And those efforts continue. The WCPM recently acquired the Opera House, where Willa Cather's high school graduation was held and where Willa proudly gave the graduation speech. Inside, it looks little changed —plank floors, a bare plank stage, a chandelier, old scenery leaning against itself. One dark dusty wall bares part of a Cather signature.

Douglass's? Roscoe's? Willa's? I can't be sure. Pat Phillips, long-time director of the WCPM, said the now-empty Opera House was the place "where the world came to her," but didn't elaborate.

When I last toured Catherland, Pat kindly accompanied me. We started at the old stockade site, where Silas Garber later built his mansion and where Cather adopted the setting for *A Lost Lady*. The house that "stood close into a fine cottonwood grove that threw sheltering arms to left and right and grew all down the hillside behind it" isn't there any more (I wrote, falling into the Red Cloud rhetorical trap). What I saw instead were four large bulls munching grass while warily watching us walk in their pasture, two concrete blocks that must have been part of the house's foundation, a rusted '49 Ford chassis, purple poppy mallow instead of the lilacs described by Cather, and an impressive accidental crop of low-grade marijuana plants.

I wanted to talk about the landscape, to learn the difference between a catalpa and a mulberry tree, to smell Nebraska farm country as Cather must have smelled it. Pat and Alberta, my other guide there, chose to define the space by what man had built. The broken foundations; a dugout site; a sunken lane overgrown with grass. "Where the boy broke his arm," said Alberta. "In *A Lost Lady*," Pat added. While I remember the scene from the novel, I more clearly picture the replica of the scene in the Bank Building museum. Upstairs is a gloomy red wallpapered room, where a blue-gowned department-store model woman gazes down in perpetuity at the figure of an overalled boy stretched on a brocade bedspread, his arm bent at an awkward angle. I meant to think about "snow-on-the-mountain, globed with dew," and "swamp milk-weed spread[ing] its flat, raspberry-coloured clusters." Instead, my guides took me back to the stories, away from the soil beneath our feet.

Readers acknowledge the strength of Cather's landscape portrayals. *O Pioneers!*, a testimony to the Nebraska prairie, is the story of "few scenes more gratifying than a spring plowing in that country, where the furrows of a single field often lie a mile in length, and the brown earth, with such a strong, clean smell, and such a power of growth and fertility in it, yields itself eagerly to the plow." In fact, when Pat and I ap-

NEBRASKA: CATHERLAND

proached the Divide in northwest Webster County, a watershed where the earth flattens and long cultivated swells carry the eye far away, she paused while I walked to the edge of a field and touched its naked furrows, "the material out of which countries are made." Largely unfamiliar with such calibrated midwestern contours, I nonetheless felt its naked geography and for a moment sensed how a settler must have imagined turning the soil into the present scene. My perception of the landscape was helped, I must admit, by Willa Cather's descriptive phrases.

Mildred Bennett said, "The thing about Cather that really struck me was how well she put this country into words. More than the plot or the story or anything else was the description of the countryside, and you wouldn't see the beauty of it until Cather showed it to you." I agree. One *Ántonia* paragraph gives a snapshot of the photo opportunity I saw when we paused alongside the Cathers' first Nebraska home. While the farmhouse has long since vanished, the vista remains. "All those fall afternoons were the same," Jim Burden observes,

> but I never got used to them. As far as we could see, the miles of copper-red grass were drenched in sunlight that was stronger and fiercer than at any other time of the day. The blond cornfields were red gold, the haystacks turned rosy and threw long shadows. The whole prairie was like the bush that burned with fire and was not consumed. That hour always had the exultation of victory, . . . It was a sudden transfiguration, a lifting-up of day.

If I were to describe the same view, I would do so without an emotional connection, in words inadvertently passionless and distant. In contrast, Cather's heartfelt diction brings the reader close to the soil. Even when her recollections—or her characters'—are less romantic, the intensity remains. Music at "A Wagner Matinee," for example, evokes for the narrator a less idyllic but nonetheless powerful portrait of the past.

> I saw again the tall, naked pond where I had learned to swim, its margin pitted with sun-dried cattle tracks; the rain gullied clay banks about the naked house, the four dwarf ash seedlings where the dish-cloths were always hung to dry before the kitchen door.

> The world there was the flat world of the ancients: to the east, a
> cornfield that stretched to daybreak; to the west, a corral that
> reached to sunset; between the conquests of peace, dearer-bought
> than those of war.

Given the way Cather regularly offers "a sudden transfiguration" of the visual imagination, especially in wide-angle scenes like the preceding two, I can't help wondering why Cather pilgrims spend more time in buildings than in deserted pastures.

The WCPM, its mission committed to fictional historicity, skews visitor responses. Their tour signs lead to what is tangible, to cemeteries, to houses and deserted churches, to scenes but not to scenery. Their sense of place stops at the bottom of the printed page. Where the Republican River country edges up to the Divide lies the fertile *O Pioneers!* landscape where the real G. P. Cathers and the fictional Alexandra Bergson made their homes. The *fictional* Alexandra Bergson! Alexandra's character grew wholly from Cather's imagination, so there is no specific farm site to visit, no *Pioneer* personalities to trace, no map from the past to overlay on the present. While the rich distances of the Divide are part of Catherland in general, nothing there can be traced to the 1913 novel. The lack of a precise location has deterred the WCPM from investing in the landscape. Another deterrent, of course, is a simple economic one. Such prime farmland would be far too costly to purchase. But it seems to me that the WCPM has made more effort to capture interiors than exteriors, to direct visitors to scenes instead of scenery, to focus—as does the Little Bighorn monument—on the people and the stories.

I especially thought about this duality near the Republican River, where Willa and her childhood friends played and picnicked, where "The Enchanted Bluff" and "The Treasure of Far Island" are set, and where the sun sinks behind the plow in a powerful *Ántonia* paragraph. I knew I wouldn't find the inspiration for the WCPM tour signs, the plow "heroic in size, a picture writing on the sun," but I thought I might be able to find the same view. Up a dirt road scarred by water run-off and debris, I drove onto the bluff and got out of my rental car. I looked down on the river. "Out in the stream the sandbars glittered like glass, and the light trembled in the willow thickets as if little flames were leaping among them. The breeze sank to stillness. In the ravine a ringdove mourned plaintively, and somewhere off in the bushes an owl hooted."

Not any longer. I trudged to the river's edge through gray mud, carefully avoiding a torn mattress, rusted bedsprings, empty plastic oil containers and a tin can dump. Someone recently had built a campfire, of city-bought charcoal. Cather's "enchanted island" disintegrated with the big 1935 flood, but smaller sandbars still surface above the mud-brown flow. Because the Republican is a managed river these days, the water was flood-high, and I didn't dare test its limits. So I stayed onshore, listening to cicadas sing out of tune with the fast-moving current, watching a buzzard swing overhead across the sky. Invisible bugs crawled in my ears and behind my glasses. Before long, the itching vanquished all romantic notions of a plow at sunset.

When I asked Pat if I could at least see the site of Cather's magic sandbar, she explained that the road had washed out. There was no way to get there. She took me as close as she could, to the Murphy grave, where the prototype of *Ántonia*'s Larry Donovan lies buried in a small plot of Catholic ground. The white picket fence badly needs paint; the WCPM tour marker is, in Pat's words, "shot all to hell." The marble tombstone reads: James William Murphy "Gone but not forgotten." Like the treasured island, I thought ironically, "dazzling white, ripple marked, and full of possibilities for the imagination." A river and an island gone but not forgotten by Cather's readers, yet ignored by the WCPM. Here, at a long-abandoned cemetery, a human-battered sign once again directed me toward the land in human terms. Mildred and her followers marked places defined by human or fictional activity; I, a westerner who relishes untouched open spaces, just wanted more landscape.

As I stood by James Murphy's bedraggled gravesite, I didn't know I would meet *his* grandchildren at the Pavelka farmstead just a few hours later. I didn't know how proudly they would claim Lucille as their mother, *Ántonia* as *her* mother, and the Cather heritage as their own. People and places and memories and fiction intersect everywhere in Catherland. People and places intersect throughout the Midwest, in fact, where the landscape has been hand-hewn and plowed by people and where the view is always circumscribed by human success or failure. In the intermountain West, I can gaze at snow-lined ridges or red-walled canyons where human intervention would be foolish. In Nebraska, where human activity is everywhere, I have to accept a different definition of place. Necessarily, then, the Catherland distinctions between scene and scenery—"the conquests of peace"—replicate the prairie pioneering point of view.

Later that day, watching Wilma and Marcie and George cross the Pavelka yard, I actually was thinking of the first time I saw the empty house. I remember Mildred Bennett climbing up from the fruit cellar and posing for my camera, just so, "a veritable explosion of life." I joked with her, then more seriously looked around a place no longer resembling the house buried in hollyhocks that Cather described. "At some distance behind the house," she wrote, "were an ash grove and two orchards: a cherry orchard, with gooseberry and currant bushes between the rows, and an apple orchard, sheltered by a high hedge from the hot winds." The fruit trees were winter-killed years ago, and more wretched marijuana weeds fill the distance between the house, a broken pump, and two tin barns.

I went back to the farmstead alone, without my copy of *My Ántonia*, without her grandchildren, without Mildred, without Pat, without (I hoped) an impossibly naïve Nevada conception of how I should define a Nebraska landscape delimited by human beings. Prowling around the house, I contemplated a healthy crop of milo to the east, then looked south through dead sunflower stalks at the "sleeping fields" described with affection in "Neighbor Rosicky." A barbed wire fence kept a patch of bluestem out of the farmyard, but other grasses grew randomly over the fruit cellar mound. So did a desolate crop of mushrooms. The farmhouse, like Murphy's picket fence, needs a coat of fresh white paint. The broken cement porch needs fixing, too, and the outbuildings are beginning to fall in upon themselves.

NEBRASKA: CATHERLAND 151

Xylophone grasshopper sounds, twilight sounds, met gusts of wind that blew hotly up from the south. Frigid from the north in the winter, these breezes of autumn brought only the sadness of season's end. Ántonia, the woman who "had not lost the fire of life." Mildred, who understood the sacrality of this place, who never lost the fire of her quest. Willa Cather, a figure defined in our literary imaginations and now, for me, by my recent Red Cloud experiences.

Were they really absent from this checkered Nebraska land? Or were they alongside the stubbled cornfields, the dying goldenrod, the bluestem, the humming cicadas? At the isolated Catherton Cemetery, where ladybugs clustered thickly on the tombstones and the G. P. Cather family lies buried beneath grasses growing six feet high? At the Cloverton Cemetery, too, amid the Pavelka graves with the poignant sign and its proud *Ántonia* connection? There, Neighbor Rosicky thought to himself, "a man could lie down in the long grass and see the complete arch of the sky over him." There, at the Cloverton Cemetery, stretched the arching spaces Cather never forgot.

Willa Cather first characterized this country as a place where "the air and the earth are curiously mated and intermingled, as if the one were the breath of the other. You feel in the atmosphere the same tonic, puissant quality that is in the tilth," she pronounced, "the same strength and resoluteness." Mildred Bennett gathered strength and resoluteness not only from that terrain, but from Willa Cather's words. Almost single-handedly, she forged a real landscape with a literary one, turning scenery into scenes so effectively that those scenes now define Catherland for the tourists who visit there. Now Mildred's ghost joins with her favorite author's and with a host of Cather characters. Intimately connected forever, they together haunt the streets of Red Cloud, the empty buildings, the fertile Nebraska fields outside of town, and every visitor's imagination. "We're Ántonia's grandchildren!" the ghosts proclaim proudly. And they are.

12
NEW MEXICO
LAND OF ENCHANTMENT

I see a steeply eroded cliff, seared with rubble and scarred by avalanches red and yellow. Georgia O'Keeffe saw apricot swirls and trails of jade pleating into shamrock that might be cottonwoods, or might not. I see a geological amphitheater cradling a Ghost Ranch scene of adobe buildings, a parking area, two horses and half a dozen sheep grazing. Georgia O'Keeffe saw, without narrative, an ashen-layered cliff dusted with turquoise. I see chimney shapes I want to name—a yellow sea horse, a dragon spine, lumped towers of red. Georgia O'Keeffe saw the endless sky, yellow washing into blue, blue edging darker, midnight edging darker still.

An artist's vocabulary differs from a writer's. O'Keeffe patently preferred the former and scorned the latter. "The meaning of a word—to me—," she wrote in 1976, "is not as exact as the meaning of a color. Colors and shapes make a more definite statement than words." For O'Keeffe, a canvas was more provocative than a piece of paper, a brush stroke more profound than an adverb. Visually, not verbally, she spoke with pictorial energy and precision and passion.

I see a tiny flower on the desert floor, dwarfed by nearby cholla, Indian rice grass, and sage. Georgia O'Keeffe saw a curl of petal so large that it filled her perspective and extended beyond. I see a hint of color, off-white. Georgia O'Keeffe saw creams touched by subtle greens and blues, with electric stamen twining toward the sky. I see a nearby wash, damp from yesterday's rain. Georgia O'Keeffe saw aquamarine whorling between maroons and reds that reach, but do not touch. I see the S-shaped stream. Georgia O'Keeffe saw a rainbow on its side.

The long-awaited Georgia O'Keeffe Museum opened in Santa Fe in July, 1997. A line of eager viewers snakes back and forth in front of the adobe building, waiting until the exhibit partially empties and the next group is admitted. Children shuffle on the sidewalk, while adults crush single file along a street where buildings block the desert view. Another line forms inside where I wait to buy my ticket; still another, where postcards and picture books can be purchased. Just past the entrance to the first gallery, I must choose. "Black Cross With Red Sky, 1929" to my immediate left; "Jimson Weed, 1932" on the long wall; "Black Place III, 1944" on the half-wall ahead. I stand alone in front of the bleakly textured cross, trying to find words to describe the blue-black mountains behind the penitente shape, the hellish red glow. Others turn to the right instead, where a ten-minute film will define the spectrum of their visit.

I can hear the narrator's words, can occasionally hear O'Keeffe's voice, too. "My mind creates shapes," she says, as I move slowly through the gallery. Ahead, black and grey and white thunder splits the canvas, a pile driver from the sky, while pale magenta—called Mars violet by O'Keeffe and other painters—tints the foreground with a contrast some might call surreal. I see an arid landscape billowed with sleet and rain. Georgia O'Keeffe saw a horizon bisected into sheets of hueless color, angular and sharp. I see a lowering thunderous sky. Georgia O'Keeffe saw sensuous banks of clouds, repeating the tyranny of the terrain. I see a desolate horizon, more dismal than disturbing. Georgia O'Keeffe saw an ominous chasm of lightning burn incandescent through earth and charcoal.

Yesterday I hiked to Kitchen Mesa, that long vibrant cliff southeast of Ghost Ranch where O'Keeffe spent so many happy hours. A single startled doe, three Gila woodpeckers contesting snag space, two hyperactive lizards, and a butterfly were there before me, but no people walked the trail. I followed a wash at first, then stepped heavily over the cascade of jumbled rocks that leads up a sandstone ledge. Green-painted coffee cans mark the route where O'Keeffe often found her way alone. I climbed warily, my eyes seeking the dry waterfall she sketched and painted so many times, my feet purchasing balance on the uneven terrain.

Two rifts in the sheer wall—either one might be the place. I see a coiled juniper on the skyline above a streak of desert varnish. Georgia O'Keeffe saw sandstone skyscrapers shaping themselves flat against the cliff. I see a glow of sun reflected by the canyon. Georgia O'Keeffe saw rectangles, squares, and triangles ruled by pen and charcoal. I see the scenery as if doubled in my vision for, as I gaze at this red rock country perimetered by my words, I simultaneously picture the folded landscape of Georgia O'Keeffe's art.

Can anyone now look at the northern New Mexico distances without overlaying O'Keeffe's special artistry on the scenery? Is it possible to hike the Chimney Trail at Ghost Ranch, or to meander toward Box Canyon, or to climb up Kitchen Mesa, without following in O'Keeffe's visual footsteps? Where I perceive rocks and angles, and imagine the geology, Georgia O'Keeffe looked inside that landscape and measured the scope of the earth. She had what might be called a magnetic resonance imaging of the land. Or, if not MRI vision precisely, at least a resonance of magic when she sought mystic shapes and forms that nominally escape my eye. Where I see panorama, O'Keeffe saw intersecting lines and repetitions of curves. Where I see buttes and boulders, O'Keeffe saw beneath the skin of the earth, disinterred the skeleton below.

Bones were her trademark, of course, but I'm thinking of something more epochal than a pair of antlers or a single horse's skull. She turned the earth inside out, interiorized the exterior, somehow saw behind the strata. She focused, not on details but on the primordial shapes and colors that lie beneath the foreground of our visual awareness. She taught us, I believe, to interpret the high New Mexico desert landscape more evocatively than before. I, for one, cannot hike a Ghost Ranch trail without constantly re-envisioning my surroundings on O'Keeffe canvases. As I walk, I find I'm aware of the crumbling earth beneath my boots and then the view, the cliffs and colors, the escarpment swelling north and west, nothing in between. O'Keeffe knew that "spatial ambiguity," too. Like any hiker, she ignored the middle distance and understood intuitively the layering of foreground against background.

Climbing up toward Chimney Rock, I muse about the ways she laid the scenery bare, the bare bones of her imagination. I see the badlands below the cut of the trail, their shadowed hulks in a colorful land. Georgia O'Keeffe saw folded breasts of magenta, pink, and mauve. I see shaped and shapeless mounds oxidized by desert air. Georgia O'Keeffe saw the earth's axis, spinning in slow motion. I see the obvious. Georgia O'Keeffe saw the land's sinews and muscles exposed. A crow flies past. I see a flat black flap of wing. Georgia O'Keeffe saw an angled silhouette that, with just a brush stroke or two, could repeat the horizon line as well. I see what I can touch. Georgia O'Keeffe saw inside the imagination.

On this warm October day, I sit atop a lonesome Ghost Ranch butte and smell the scents of fall, the juniper, the lemon grass, the dried sage. A freshening wind ruffles my hair, while the hot sun counterpoints the cool texture of my rock. I take off my fleece vest, and sit on it. For lunch, chamayo chili, cheese, and an apple—a fiery taste, a crunch, more fire, water, then more cheese. Another crow joins the first one. Cawing loudly, the two catch a downdraft and disappear below the cliff line. Their crow voices continue their crow conversation, a loud drum-roll over the fluted sounds of traffic on the busy Abiquiu highway. I can see the cars and campers if I lean out over the rocky defile, but I ignore the sounds of commerce. Like the painter, I try to focus on the rocks.

But a writer uses all the senses—the cacophony of crows and highway sounds, the rumpling wind, the tang of chili and crisp apple, the hint of sagebrush pollen, the cold rocky ledge measured against

NEW MEXICO: LAND OF ENCHANTMENT 157

the still hot sun. Georgia O'Keeffe drew all this in brush strokes, reduced the senses to a single line. I see escarpments side by side, red pushing up to blue. Georgia O'Keeffe saw two hills conjoined in an embrace more metaphysical than measured. Those special hills, she said, "so beautifully soft, so difficult." I see a sweep of sky above the sandstone, clouds forming overhead, a canyon wren flitting east. Georgia O'Keeffe saw time stand still in colored cups of wrinkled burgundy. My scenery moves, it tells a story; hers, in equipoise, balances the eternal.

From almost anywhere on any Ghost Ranch trail, the Cerro Pedernal is visible on the southwest skyline. A massive humpbacked mountain fringed with juniper and mottled with piñon pine, the Pedernal is impossible to ignore. It dominates the horizon, just as its silhouette ruled the artist's eye. Changing Woman, Spider Woman—the stories abound. "It's my private mountain," O'Keeffe announced in pithy phrases now quoted widely. "It belongs to me. God told me if I painted it enough, I could have it." Back in the new Santa Fe museum, I find her words come true, for the Pedernal lines one canvas after another. Sometimes blue, sometimes green, sometimes orchid or deep purple, sometimes a pale hue or color for which I cannot find the words, the mountain recurs more often in her scenery than any other landform.

My favorite example, I think, is "Ladder to the Moon, 1958." There, the moon, the mountain, and an earthtone ladder pause in eternal suspension, conjoining what cannot be connected. While the three images never touch physically, they come together intellectually. Transfixing the Pedernal in textured turquoise, O'Keeffe then ranged it below the ladder in the sky so that the two forms would be forever reaching and yearning, forever consummating themselves visually and spiritually, if not physically.

Suddenly uncomfortable with language and its achromatic inadequacies, I bring myself back to my Ghost Ranch lookout rock. Again, I let my eyes drift three hundred and sixty degrees. I see shadowed cliffs pulsing in an autumnal reflection of sunlight. Georgia O'Keeffe saw beneath their chalky outline, a horizontal sweep of orange melon and yellow citrus and sweet lime. I see, and hear, a rock tumble down the hillside. Georgia O'Keeffe saw, and knew, where it came to rest. Across the shining valley, the Piedra Lumbre as it's called, an afternoon haze blurs the sky. I see a trickster mountain discolored by the smog. Georgia O'Keeffe saw a sacred place, its outline crisp and clear, its silhouette a solemn source of energy and myth. I see the Pedernal, still in the distance, and know it can't be mine. Georgia O'Keeffe saw its inner spirit, its resonance, its enchantment, and knew the opposite.

13
SOUTH DAKOTA
SCULPTURED STONE

Somewhere behind the presidential faces of George Washington, Thomas Jefferson, Theodore Roosevelt and Abraham Lincoln, a fractured mountain called Rushmore still rises in spectral silence. Visitors to the monument barely notice, for their eyes are drawn solely to the sculptures. Most people ignore the scattered rubble that attests to the power of explosives but reveals nothing of the mountain's original profile. Their visit instead is shaped by the vision of the Ozymandian designer of the behemoth heads. Gutzon Borglum's stenciled words stamp their experience. "Mount Rushmore is eternal. It will stand until the end of time. Ten thousand years from now our civilization will have passed without leaving a trace. A new race of people will inhabit the earth. They will come to Mount Rushmore and read the record we have made." I read that record somewhat differently. For me, Mount Rushmore is yet another western ghost, another mother lode mined by proponents of anthropocentric progress.

Doane Robinson, a regional historian and a South Dakota booster, initially proposed some sort of massive carving as a tourist attraction—a western hero, perhaps Kit Carson or John Colter or Jim Bridger, memorialized on a granite spire. He invited the well-known sculptor, Gutzon Borglum, to come to the Black Hills, to look at some of the oldest rock in North America, to project what would become "a work of art for the ages." Borglum agreed, though he imagined a sculpture with more national than regional import. In 1925, after a lengthy horseback tour of the terrain, Borglum spotted the peak that would inspire him. "There it is!" he announced to his companions. "American history shall march along that skyline."

From the outset, Borglum's conception was larger than life—heads sixty feet tall, eyes eleven feet deep, mouths eighteen feet wide. He sought to commemorate men of major importance in the carving of America itself, and he intended to do so in dimensions larger than the Great Sphinx of Egypt. A combination of imagination and energy made the enterprise possible. After President Calvin Coolidge dedicated the cornerstone on August 10, 1927, the work began. Borglum built studio models to scale, then guided workmen to replicate his artistry on the cliffs of Mount Rushmore's sunlit southeast face. Drillers and powdermen soon mastered the art of implanting charges large and small to sheer off honeycombed slabs of rock. Once a presidential profile was rough-hewn, stonecutters using chisels and pneumatic hammers completed the remaining work. Progress was sporadic, one face at a time. Money, during the Great Depression, was difficult to raise; skilled men, hard to find; the South Dakota weather, hazardous and unpredictable.

Borglum persevered, however, and his monument to democracy slowly took shape. First George Washington, then Thomas Jefferson on his right. When the Jefferson design proved unworkable, Borglum blasted his face away and repositioned him to Washington's left instead. After that, Abraham Lincoln's head, dedicated in 1937; Theodore Roosevelt's, in 1939. Work continued for two more years—Borglum wanted each figure finished to the waist, a grand staircase and a Hall of Records constructed, the unsightly rubble removed. Then the sculptor died unexpectedly. Although his son, Lincoln, took over his supervisory role, construction flagged and finally halted on October 31, 1941. With impending crises overseas, government funds would no longer be available. The project was finished, at a total cost of $989,992.32.

Rex Alan Smith, in *The Carving of Mount Rushmore*, calculates the achievement, "carved upon a cliff that has changed but little since mankind first appeared on earth. The faces will still be there," he asserts, "looking much as they do now, long after man has gone. All things considered, Mount Rushmore National Memorial is not only America's greatest and most enduring monument, it is all of mankind's as well." Scholars like Albert Boime disagree. In a chapter titled "Patriarchy Fixed in Stone," Boime concurs that "Mount Rushmore allegorizes the idea of Manifest Destiny." However, he concludes, "In trying to subjugate the earth as the old pioneers had tamed the frontier, Borglum carved deeply into the Native Americans' holy mountain an eternally tangible yet spiritually shallow magisterial gaze." Gazing at the row of wrinkled lips and sneers of cold command, I compare these two diverse opinions, and wonder if I'm seeing a sacred shrine, or a sacrilege, or some ironic postmodern combination of both.

To decide for myself, I first had to negotiate a multilevel parking garage. Although admission to the monument is free, an enterprising business concession gleans eight dollars for every vehicle parked anywhere near it. Beyond the parking labyrinth, I strolled along a concrete Avenue of Flags—one banner waving for each state and territory. There, I could purchase a tour guide for a dollar, if I wanted one. Following the promenade, I came to Grandview Terrace, which is actually the roof of the Visitor Center. An impressive straight-ahead scope of the four enormous faces looms ahead. I first approached this monument more than thirty-five years ago, when a two-lane country road curled up to the base of the sculptures, when the "welcome" center was so nondescript that I can't remember it. That day I stood alone in the rain while water cascaded like tears from the presidential eyes. But solitude on Grandview Terrace today is no longer an option, so I elbowed my way along the newly ramped Presidential Trail, where there were as many ice cream cones and VCRs as there were people. At the far end of the "trail," a staired section leads down to the sculptor's studio, with models of Borglum's original conception, including the cravats and collars, and a gypsum Lincoln fully formed. After that, Borglum's terrace, with another view.

No Rushmore visit is complete without attending the evening ceremonial performance. To the accompaniment of martial music by John Philip Sousa and George M. Cohan, that ceremony unfolds as a patriotic pageant. One night I watched the sun shadowing gold to the left of the mountain, heard the murmur of families quietly conversing, listened to a uniformed ranger ask the audience to recite the final lines of the Gettysburg address. Golden granite darkened to magenta, deepened to black. Another night a royal purple cloud-bank bulged above the carved faces while lightning zigzagged from left to right and rumbles of thunder punctuated the ranger's storm-shortened spiel. Both times, spotlights brightened a row of waving flags but simultaneously deflected the angles of the faces and flattened their dimensions. Even when the spotlights lifted onto the sculptures, the effect was pallid and lifeless. Meanwhile, it was impossible to see Mount Rushmore behind Borglum's artistic achievement, for the mountain itself remained wholly in the dark.

Remembering Robinson's and Borglum's search for the perfect granite location, I decided to follow their tour. In the 1920s, few roads penetrated the Black Hills. When the actual site was chosen, in fact, Rushmore could only be reached on foot or by horseback. Today modern highways grid this popular vacation destination, although some old narrow curlicues still exist. Driving through a formation called the Needles, for example, I barely kept the truck mirrors intact. I was on my way to Harney Peak, 7242 feet above sea level, the highest point between the Rockies and the Pyrenees. As such, it provides a popular hiking destination, attracting hundreds of walkers each summer day. The Black Hills themselves still resemble vertebrae, rockribbing the darker evergreen trees. I could imagine them as natural sculptures, in fact—a buffalo, a mountain goat like the one I had seen grazing near the Needles, a porcine mushroom, a scarecrow. But the surroundings have changed since the 1920s. Unlike Robinson and Borglum, today's sightseer cannot stand on the top of Harney Peak and look at a landscape relatively untouched by human intervention.

Helicopter flights, at regular intervals, punctuate the distant sky. I could see them circling what must be Mount Rushmore, though the faces themselves tip the other way. Below the unseen sculptures, an immense white and tan clearcut slashes the flank of the mountain. The monument's parking complex, I realized, is the dominant human feature of the landscape. Lesser clearcuts from logging are visible on the ridge lines, too, but their colors blend in with the characteristically dark hues of the Black Hills. An abandoned fire lookout tower, built by the Civilian Conservation Corps in 1939, silently guards Harney Peak's summit. While its intricate rock work is of course a human construct, it somehow fits visually into the terrain. Where the summit ends and where a manmade cistern begins, for example, is hard to discern.

I sat alongside one of the tower walls, my feet on Harney Peak, my eyes on the granite, the quartz insets, the feldspar, the chalcedony. I touched the irregularities and imagined blasted faces instead. Two middle-aged hikers paused to chat. "My mother and my aunt climbed these mountains for years," one woman said. "They even walked around on Lincoln's nose. But they liked Harney Peak better. That's why my cousin and I came up here today, in their memory." Dozens of other hikers scrambled up and down the tower's circular stairs, jumped from rock to rock below, and exclaimed about the scenery. I ran my hand across a patch of stubbled lichen bleached into shades of lemon and lime. We could touch this mountain. No more than a stroll for a hiker used to higher places, its summit seemed almost neighborly. I felt more intimately connected with the Black Hills here, more than just a spectator. Even through my boots I could detect the softness of the trail contrasting with a solidity of granite.

Hiking back down the mountainside, I took a circuitous route, wandering past the spires that Robinson first imagined might be carved. After close inspection, Borglum found them too fractured, "full of rock rot," with major faults. I suspect they lacked the required grandiosity, too, but I personally liked walking there, where the serrated ramparts of Cathedral Spires picket the sky. I scrambled into a circle of ten-story boulders. What if they all had been carved? A ring of rock art, a group sculpture of sorts? A mountain man? A granite rendezvous? Climbing alongside an anvil of stone, I wondered if it could be improved. Right now it resembles something Thor, the blacksmith, might have used. Might humans hammer it more artistically? As I edged up the shoulder of a spire, I let my own anthropocentric imagination run wild. The spires themselves? Elongated shafts of playdough puttied side by side. The reticulated rock? Bits of chocolate stuck in a birthday cake of stone. Back at Sylvan Lake—I later learned it was manmade—I leaned against my truck and counted picnickers. Six or seven dozen, several hundred or more played along the shoreline and lounged in the shade. Some swam, some drank beer, some even closed their eyes. "Hey, we made it!" shouted a group of hikers returned from Harney Peak. Here was a sort of possession, too. Just as I had fingered the lichen-stained granite on the summit, so these scattered groups of summer visitors were touching the sandy beaches and tree-lined trails. I thought I breathed clearer air than at Grandview Terrace, though, and heard more laughter than along the Presidential Trail; I knew I judged less harshly than amidst the Avenue of Flags. I didn't miss the theme park at all. In the center of this quasi-wilderness, however, a queue of cars waited for my parking space.

In truth, lines of cars clot Black Hills parking lots and highways alike. Summer camping spots are almost impossible to find; isolated trails are nonexistent; even the animals seem tame and well-adjusted to tourists. Custer State Park draws a remarkable number of hikers and campers, while Mount Rushmore attracts even more. Nearly three million people gaze upon those immense stone sculptures every year. So Doane Robinson wasn't wrong when he prophesied the appeal of a massive carving, and Gutzon Borglum wasn't wrong when he foresaw a patriotic shrine. "My plan is to make Rushmore a center in the heart of America so attractive, so comprehending, that the inevitable visiting world will assemble there with something more than curiosity, and go away with something more than wonder," the sculptor proclaimed. Millions of Americans have since agreed.

Behind the façade, however, that mountain called Rushmore partially remains. Invisible from the parking lot or from the terraces, part of Rushmore still can be seen from across the valley—a humped ridgeline of fractured granite. Or from Highway 244, where the blasted side to Washington's right now accidentally resembles a gnarled old man of the mountain. I couldn't get any closer to the once-real Rushmore, though. Out of bounds to hikers, off limits to climbers, irrelevant to tourists who focus on Borglum's creation, the mountain itself has gotten lost behind the synthetic shrine. "The buffalo, the hills and the rock have all given way," writes Tom Charging Eagle. "Sacred places have become state and national parks, places of tourism and curiosity." Borglum invokes curiosity as a prelude to wonder, but Tom Charging Eagle uses the term pejoratively, and reminds us that the United States government once promised the Black Hills to the Sioux.

The Fort Laramie Treaty, signed on April 29, 1868, established a reservation in very explicit terms. "The United States hereby agrees and stipulates that the country north of the North Platte River and east of the summits of the Big Horn Mountains shall be held and considered to be unceded Indian territory, and also stipulates and agrees that no white person or persons shall be permitted to settle upon or occupy any portion of the same; or without the consent of the Indians first had and obtained, to pass through the same." When gold was discovered less than a decade later, however, the 1868 treaty was broken immediately. Forever turned out to be finite. What had been guaranteed in perpetuity to the now-displaced Indians was rapidly overrun by white miners and settlers. George Armstrong Custer's Seventh Cavalry smoothed the way.

Between Spearfish and Rapid City, one place still retains a measure of its sacred heritage. Bear Butte, or Mato Paha, rises from the plains of South Dakota just out of reach of the Black Hills. Here, many tribes believe, the creator communicates with the Indians through visions and prayer. People like me are allowed to climb to the summit, but only if we stay on the trail and only if we respect the ceremonial nature of the place. On a day of heavy clouds and dripping rain, I made my way to the top. I passed prayer cloths tied to the bushes and trees, rainbow colors of bright pink, red, blue, green and turquoise. I passed tobacco ties draped like rosaries. I passed almost no people, though their remembrances lined the way. I hiked in silence.

Near the crest, wooden platforms keep non-Indians off the roof of the mountain. I could peer at the clouded view, but I couldn't step onto the earth, couldn't physically touch the land. Even so, I felt connected in a spiritual way, felt the intensity as I stood above a ritual hourglass of shale, felt the wind vibrate the air. In contrast to Rushmore's rectangular revision of a mountain, Bear Butte's natural shape is circular. The trail spirals to the summit, and circles back down. The view extends outward, in all four directions. In fact, the A-frame visitor center opens east, west, north, south, too. Off to one side, a circle of tents dotted a grassy meadow and a circle of Indians pressed tightly together. On the trail, a pencil-thin snake had coiled away from my boot. While I stood on top of the highest platform, the morning sun broke through mounds of cumulus clouds.

The moment lacked eco-perfection, however. In 1996, one man's ceremonial fire got away. On a day of hot dry winds, the flames spread quickly. Before the fire could be extinguished, it had burned nearly 90 percent of Bear Butte's trees. So my hike to the summit and back was slightly surrealistic, with the prayer cloths and tobacco ties actually hanging from charred skeletons no longer evergreen but starkly blackish brown. While the grasses had turned green with the coming of spring, the trees had not yet re-seeded themselves. Again anthropocentricity had changed the character of the place, inadvertently had made Bear Butte into a ghost of itself. Not like Mount Rushmore, but still altered somehow.

Thinking about ghosts and *GhostWest*, I wondered if my chapters were becoming repetitious both in my imagination and on the printed page. First the pioneers, the miners, the ranchers, the settlers, had usurped the Indians' lands. Then they made 'improvements.' Now, as I try to see the original outlines of the landscape, the hand of anthropocentrism keeps getting in the way. There on Bear Butte I had a sense of an ancestral bonding with the land, but I knew that I myself was an interloper, that others had been there before me and that I didn't quite

SOUTH DAKOTA: SCULPTURED STONE 167

belong. Was I in fact perceiving the real mountain, or was it as hidden from my view as Mount Rushmore? The dichotomy came together for me at the Crazy Horse Memorial, located on the western side of the Black Hills, closer to the presidential sculptures than to the sacred Mato Paha. In 1939 a sculptor named Korczak Ziolkowski received a letter from Henry Standing Bear, a Sioux chief. "My fellow Chiefs and I would like the White Man to know the Red Man had great heroes, too." He asked if Korczak, who had briefly been on the Borglum team, would be interested in carving an Indian memorial in stone. World War II intervened before any commitment could be made, but throughout the war years the sculptor kept picturing a Crazy Horse design.

In 1947, he finally had time to do the work and so the project began. The two visionaries, Korczak and Chief Standing Bear, secured the necessary land for the sculpture by filing a mining claim on the mountain. A year later, on June 3, 1948, the Crazy Horse Memorial was dedicated and the first blast detonated. Unlike Mount Rushmore, Thunderhead Mountain was to be sculpted in the round—a circular figure of gigantic dimensions. All four presidential heads would fit inside Crazy Horse's. His outstretched arm would be 263 feet long and 42 feet wide; his hand, 33 feet thick. He would ride a steed whose head would be 22 stories high. His shape would be fluid, emerging from the rock rather than carved onto the stone, dynamic rather than static. From the outset, Korczak considered himself a storyteller. He called Crazy Horse his "granite epic," and said "I write in stone." He imagined the Indian leader "with his left hand thrown out in answer to the derisive question asked by a white man, 'Where are your lands now?'" Korczak wanted to narrate Crazy Horse's answer—"My lands are where my dead lie buried"—a response ironically antithetical to Mount Rushmore's democratic theme.

By the time Korczak died in 1982, almost seven and a half million tons of rock had been removed from Thunderhead Mountain. Under the supervision of his widow, Ruth, his ten children have advanced the project. June 3, 1998, marked the fiftieth anniversary of the dedication with a large blast to initiate a second half-century of progress. Today, the work continues. The face, the headdress streaming behind, the arm extended are all clearly articulated in stone. The shape of the steed is painted on the mountainside, so visitors can picture the fully finished sculpture. Unlike Mount Rushmore, the Crazy Horse is being carved without benefit of federal dollars. Signs everywhere proudly proclaim: "No State or Federal Funds have ever been used."

This memorial differs from Rushmore in more than monetary ways, however. The visitor center is constructed of native materials, rather than marbled concrete. The closest view isn't from a Presidential Trail, but from a dilapidated school bus that takes tourists nearer to the base of the sculpture. The ride is a dusty one and, because of the hues of pegmatite granite, the dust is blood red instead of governmental gray. One weekend a year, on the anniversary of the dedication, an annual Volksmarch actually encourages visitors to touch the mountain. Rather than look at the sculpture from a distance, thousands of hikers contour from the base, through the trees, and up the switchbacks to stand on the arm of Crazy Horse.

The event is what I would call "a happening," with more emphasis on congenial conversation than on conquering a mountain. I started my hike as soon as the trail opened at eight in the morning, stopped often along the way, and reached the arm less than two hours later. Blue sky and sunshine brightened that fifteenth annual Volksmarch, so most people—men, women, and children of all ages—strolled at a leisurely pace. Before long, hikers serpentined along the entire route. Couples walked hand-in-hand; one family of twenty wore matching T-shirts; three teen-aged boys brushed past a balding man with a red daypack; an elderly woman paused after every four or five steps; yellow-shirted officials tallied the visitors; Cub Scouts hawked apples and Kool-Aid; bare-legged girls handed out tiny cups of water. By the time I neared our goal, hundreds of hikers already gazed down from Crazy Horse's sculpted arm.

In fact, the arm was almost overcrowded with people posing for pictures and vying for viewpoints along the fenced edges. It seemed more like a football field than an objet d'art. Near the flat fist, I joined other onlookers to take in the panorama across the valley, to watch the many hikers still slogging up the rutted route, to peer over the sharp edge of the dynamited rock. At the opposite end of the arm, the view inspired wonder in a much different way. Standing close to the face, I looked up at the nostrils—thirty-five feet in diameter and fifty feet deep, I later learned. Here "the wrinkled lip and sneer of cold command" that I had sensed at Mt. Rushmore felt even more eminent. This sculpture's lip actually does curl, the nostrils flare, and the arrogance is palpable. The face is pegmatite pinkish, almost mauve in places, and fool's gold flecks the jaw. Black and gray fault lines faintly stitch the features together with seams that line the fractured face.

I found myself walking back and forth between the visage and the back of its head, where the unblasted part of the mountain is covered with mining camp detritus, with sagging sheds, rusted equipment, and junk heaps of iron and wire. Despite this unsightly clutter, the rock there looks more like Harney's summit. It's grayer, darker rather than flesh-pink, with pale green lichen clinging to the cliffs. The irregularities are rougher, more natural, without honeycombed blasting marks etching the rocks. Although I tried to imagine a fully sloped Thunderhead Mountain prior to that first 1948 explosion, I, like all the other Volksmarchers, found it hard to focus on anything but the compelling immensity of the sculpture. I kept returning to the face, tipping my head to measure visually its extraordinary physical dimensions. I kept thinking, too, that I actually was standing where the rest of the mountain used to be. In truth, I hadn't climbed a real mountain at all—just an ingenious concept artificially engineered.

Hiking back down the road, I rehearsed the apparent differences between Crazy Horse and Mount Rushmore—Korczak Ziolkowski's wider vision, the privatization of the project, the importance of narrating an Indian point of view. But I could not reconcile the obvious similarities—the artistic arrogance, the dissolution of stone, the absolute conviction that a mountain carved is more meaningful than a mountain untouched by human hands. I think that poet Peter Blue Cloud would fundamentally agree. Taking a point of view quite counter to Chief Standing Bear's, he sardonically suggests a Crazy Horse response to the monument created in his name:

> And what would he think of the cold steel chisel,
> and of dynamite blasting a mountain's face,
> what value the crumbled glories of Greece and Rome,
> to a people made cold and hungry?

I found myself wondering the same thing. Philosophically, as well as physically, this particular memorial sculpture can be faulted, too; like Rushmore, a complicated conjuncture of sacrilege and shrine.

For me, however, it's the physical ghost of a displaced mountain that's at the heart of my story here. Sculpture relies on absences as well as presences, on space as well as structure, drawing the eye to what is not there as well as to what is tangibly visible. At these enormous human constructs, my eye always was drawn to what was missing—the mountains themselves. From my point of view, then, Thunderhead Mountain is no less a ghost than Mount Rushmore, its original size and shape now a costly pile of rubble. That the Crazy Horse Memorial, for many people, makes a strong Native American statement is important, of course, but it does so at the expense of the very land it holds dear.

On a wall of the Crazy Horse visitor center, next to a window facing the gigantic half-wrought sculpture, next to a spate of statistics comparing this achievement with Mount Rushmore, the Washington Monument, the Great Sphinx, and Egypt's largest pyramid, the Ziolkowskis have put the words of White Antelope, a Cheyenne brave, in a place of prominence. "Nothing lives long," he apparently said in 1864, "Only the Earth and the Mountains." Nothing could be further from the truth in South Dakota.

14
OKLAHOMA
SHADES OF THE PAST

In my imagination, four columns of winter-clad cavalrymen emerge from the fog that shrouds a valley in western Oklahoma, angle toward a Cheyenne encampment alongside the Washita River, and charge. George Armstrong Custer, characteristically impetuous, leads the way, riding over bleeding bodies as they fall. His Seventh Cavalry exterminates the village even more quickly than the soldiers themselves will be destroyed at the Battle of the Little Bighorn, seven and a half years later. Custer and his men kill 103 Indians, capture 53 more. Of the total, eleven Cheyenne were warriors; the rest, women and children. "The only good Indians I ever saw were dead," remarked General Sheridan, who ordered the engagement. The Washita River incident in 1868 followed the Bear River encounter, where 90 women and children were killed, and the Sand Creek massacre, where 200 Cheyenne men, women, and children died. It preceded the Marias River debacle, where 173 Blackfeet deaths included mostly women and children, and the better-known Battle of Wounded Knee, where more than a 150 Sioux were slain. Reporters characterized each bloody confrontation as a necessary step to civilize the American West.

In my imagination, a posse of men on horseback clusters in a Texas gully choked with mesquite and chaparral. Before them flows the Clear Fork of the Brazos. Two men hang from the lower limb of a pecan tree, their bodies swinging in the hot afternoon sun, their necks stretched by the ropes knotted across their throats. A single horseman rides forward, and pins a note on one of the bodies—"anyone moving these men will fill their places." The riders admire their handiwork, then canter back into the picturesque hills, and disperse. "The best way to end stock thefts," announced John Larn, the sheriff of Shackelford County, "was to end the thieves when caught." Brother-in-law of Sallie Reynolds Matthews, Larn and his deputies were responsible for at least sixteen vigilante forays that ended in multiple "eliminations" of cattle rustlers and horse thieves. Then the Albany, Texas, citizens discovered that Larn was only eliminating the competition, while he personally directed a highly lucrative rustling operation of his own. Forcing him to resign as sheriff, they put him in chains and locked him up. That night, a dozen men wearing bandanas delivered their own brand of vigilante justice, shooting Larn to death while he sat helplessly shackled in the Albany jail. No one ever learned the identity of any of the twelve regulators. No one ever tried.

In my imagination, two gunfighters face each other at noon on the main street of a vacant western town. Their lips curl in contemptuous bravado. A camera zeros in on their holsters; their trigger fingers are poised. The close-up fades to a panoramic emptiness, then focuses back on the sheriff and the outlaw, alienated together from a society content to let them savagely fight alone. The men draw their six-shooters. They fire simultaneously. That old-fashioned shoot-out, so glamorized by Hollywood in the 1950s, fast-forwards to 1968's *The Wild Bunch*, which opens with a horrific massacre. The gun-slinging bunch and a well-armed posse blaze away at each other, across and through the bodies of innocent citizens, every shot traced explicitly in an almost pornographic amount of bloodshed and brutality. No one is innocent; everyone is guilty; heroes are monsters, and vice versa. Such silver screen depictions, I'm afraid, reinforce a narrow view of western settlement and voice tacit approval of violent recourse.

The West, of course, was won in part by real violence—violence to the native peoples, violence to the powerless, violence to the law, violence to the land itself. Looking back at the centuries that precede our own, I would like to ignore that heritage, and to assume such extremes of brutality and force have been left in the past, that violence is but a ghost, a shadow we no longer engage. The bombing of the Alfred P. Murrah Federal Building, however, can be interpreted as an illogical extension of nineteenth-century violence and vigilantism. The perpetrators were carrying out a sinister act of vengeance, synedochically destroying a symbolic agent of oppression while in truth administering grievous destruction, lashing out at the government by murdering a host of unwitting victims. This maniacal mission, randomly monstrous in its execution, was a deadly exorcism indeed. Now Oklahoma City is home to a specter that haunts us.

One hundred and sixty-nine human beings, along with their families, their friends, and an entire nation of people who watched from afar, were victimized. When the Federal Building collapsed in on itself at 9:02 A.M., its nine stories disintegrated in a hideous extrapolation of vigilante violence. To read about the subsequent minutes, hours, and eternities that followed the explosion, is to confront one unconscionable way in which the past has terribly informed the present.

"You could smell the bomb," said one eyewitness. "You could smell the death." One of the walking wounded cried out for someone to go to the day care center on the second floor. There was no second floor, however, only a huge crater in the floor. First-hand accounts by the survivors of the blast are excruciating. "I remember a brilliant flash of light and the sensation of an invisible force pressing me out of my chair and to my knees before everything turned pitch black," one man sighed. "An incredible force pushed me forward and all I could see were white flashing sparkles," recalled a woman who worked on the fifth floor and suddenly found herself below the second. "I was on my stomach, with my face twisted to the right. My head was wedged tight and I had no luck moving my legs or my right arm." In truth, the actual intimacies of violence, transcribed by eyewitnesses in a collection entitled *We Will Never Forget*, are more intense than any film could capture, more graphic than modern cinematographers might imagine, more immediate than recounted episodes from the past.

Where the Murrah Federal Building once stood, the Oklahoma City National Memorial now covers 3.3 acres. Empty chairs line a grassy slope. Each individual bronze and stone chair—150 full-sized, 19 small—bears the name of a victim etched on its glass base. Monumental gates flank either side of the memorial, the one to the east with its clock fixed at 9:01 A.M., the one to the west with its clock fixed at 9:03 A.M., the minute before and the minute just after the moment of the explosion. Between the gates, a reflecting pool has replaced Fifth Street. One "Survivor Tree," the elm that miraculously endured the holocaust, still stands, surrounded and protected by a newly planted grove called "The Rescuer's Orchard." A children's area, made of hand-painted tiles, offers a place for youngsters to chalk their feelings when they visit the memorial. A fence along Harvey Avenue displays personal remembrances left continuously by thousands of visitors; thousands more tokens of grief have been archived. The half-destroyed *Journal Record* building, reconstructed, is a Memorial Center to display those precious objects and to house an Institute for the Prevention of Terrorism.

Pacing, I am visually bombarded by the host of symbols, each with its distinctive memory, each with its particular meaning. The mission statement of the memorial explicitly defines my field of vision.

We come here to remember those who were killed,
those who survived and those changed forever.
May all who leave here know the impact of violence.
May this memorial offer comfort, strength, peace, hope and serenity.

An accompanying brochure interprets the stations of the site, but I prefer to conjure up my own connections. Pausing by the reflection pond, dramatically orange-red from sunset's glow, I watch crowds of visitors move from one side to another, their voices hushed in the evening air. I listen to their questions, their thirst for narrative, their hunger for stories both painful and heroic, and the pond blurs with multiple reflections. Along a chain link fence, "the fence where we hang our hearts," I look at T-shirts and ball caps, flowered wreaths and banners, trinkets and flowers left in sadness and in memory. The atten-

OKLAHOMA: SHADES OF THE PAST 175

dant phrases, some anonymous and some very personal, are terribly poignant.

Restless, I climb a short flight of stairs and cross another cement walkway where I can stroll behind the empty chairs. Above, in the harsh twilight, I discover a square of grass where the day-care children often played. I find that this spot touches me more deeply than the official memorial construct. Here, alone, I personally feel the force of the innocence so emphatically extinguished.

Standing quietly, I consider the implications of a monument to violence. "May all who leave here know the impact of violence," exhorts the memorial's mission statement. I wonder—could the men and women who settled the West ever have conceived of the legacy they left behind? As the evening darkens around me, a rumble of thunder gathers itself more forcefully. In a few hours, I'll return to the memorial to watch zigzags of lightning in the sky, to see harsh rain reflected in the pool, to reflect again on the Washita and Wounded Knee in a very real West, on sheriffs and shoot-outs in a West that we imagine. Here in Oklahoma City, in a solemn hour before dawn, I will muse— how did violence and vigilantism ever lead us from six-guns to sacrilege?

15
UTAH
GLEN CANYON RESERVOIR

Lake Powell, "The Jewel of the Colorado." Glen Canyon, "The Place No One Knew." The lake, an emblem of the entrepreneurial ingenuity and anthropocentric energy that sought to tame the landscapes of the American West. The canyon, a powerful symbol of the environmental movement's failure to articulate a timely plan for preservation. The lake, a thriving economic enterprise. The canyon, now a ghost. Together, one visible before me and the other accessible only via old photographs and other writers' words, Lake Powell and Glen Canyon mirror the antithetical ways we treat and talk about and use and remember the land.

Today, as I sit on red rock and stare at an immensity of blue, I recall that Wallace Stegner imagined the half-filled lake looked rather like a picture of Miss America with her legs cut off. Now only part of her head shows above the water. Across the way, two alcoves arch like eyebrows, while her forehead runs with the mascara of desert varnish. Tamarisk, dyed pink with a greenish tinge, must be her hair. The Waterpocket Fold, her boxy hat, perhaps. Despite her make-up, she's still a good-looking gal, though a little artificial. Underneath, however, where I can't see below the water, her once striking figure may be crumbling, her waistline sagging, her legs less shapely than before.

White lines must girdle her body, squeezing her comely flesh. Though her bones are still good, she's lost her muscle tone. Some will say it doesn't matter—she's wearing such a lovely aqua dress.

Metaphoric exaggeration is outrageous, of course, but the aging beauty queen highlights the central problem of the following pages. What rhetorical choices do people make when they write about a politically sensitive place that has disappeared? What do they happily remember? What do they conveniently forget? What kind of diction do they use? And, most important, how are they skewing their own memories and thus our subsequent interpretations? How do *their* words define *our* ghosts?

I never saw Glen Canyon. I visited Lake Powell in the mid-1960s, long before it pooled to its present high-water mark, but I never saw the canyon in its pristine pre-dam state. I've seen scores of faded slides taken by a colleague who, as a young grad student, worked on-site with archaeologist J. D. Jennings. I've seen videos made from 1950s and '60s home movies. I've seen Eliot Porter's glowing photography. I've read more words than I can count—the recollections, the comparisons, the contrasts, the scientific reports, the congressional hearings, the editorials, the press releases, the impassioned enthusiasm for the lake, the elegiac regret for the glens, the objective analyses, the prejudicial propaganda. Out of this eroding sandstone emerges a landscape gone but not forgotten, a rhetorical specter and spectrum.

The outline of the canyon's ghost story is probably familiar—the 1922 Colorado River Compact to allocate water to both the upper and lower basins, the federally funded Colorado River Storage Project and the Bureau of Reclamation's commitment to building dams, the environmentalist passion to prevent encroachment within national parks and monuments, the inevitable compromise. Specifically, in saving Dinosaur National Monument, the settlement doomed Glen Canyon farther down the river. Construction of the Glen Canyon Dam started on October 1, 1956, with a ceremonial 'first blast' two weeks later. Despite ensuing political machinations, work continued almost nonstop. On January 21, 1963, workers closed the west diversion tunnel and Lake Powell began to shape itself. On June 22, 1980, the lake first filled to its capacity—1960 miles of shoreline, 252 square miles, 27 million acre-feet of water. While its level fluctuates from year to year, the legal accords and a thriving recreation industry dictate that the Bureau of Reclamation keep Lake Powell as full as possible. By 1998 the area was attracting three million visitors each year, producing more than $400 million in revenues. Meanwhile, the dam annually was generating between 500 and 800 megawatts of electricity. Economically speaking, Lake Powell is a success.

Some would call it a failure, however. Even as the dam was being built, wilderness supporters were discovering the special nature of the canyon that would soon be submerged and were regretting the devil's bargain they had struck. When last-minute efforts to prevent the lake from filling to capacity were foiled, preservationists vowed to negate the Bureau of Reclamation's achievement. Critical environmental support has grown with each decade of the dam's existence. Arguing from both scientific and aesthetic points of view, founders of the Glen Canyon Institute now advocate draining the lake. Lake Powell, filling with sediment, eventually will be nonfunctional; the reservoir wastes nearly one million acre-feet of water each year through evaporation and bank seepage; downstream environmental damage is "harrowing." In 1996, the Sierra Club's board of directors voted unanimously to endorse the Institute's position. Newspaper headlines, and congressional hearings, soon followed. After more than forty years, the dam controversy is still very much alive.

To counter the 'drain the lake' movement, a new coalition recently was incorporated. The Friends of Lake Powell's mission statement voices a strong commitment both to the beauty *and* to the economic aspects of the lake, the dam, and the surrounding Glen Canyon National Recreation Area. "People who have visited Lake Powell know it is one of the most stunningly beautiful places in the world," the Friends' first newsletter explains. "Converting it to a 200 mile long mud bog framed by a gigantic white bathtub ring on the formerly beautiful red sandstone cliffs could only be contemplated by someone who has never visited the Lake." Julia Betz, director of the John Wesley Powell Museum in Page, seconds the Friends' evaluation. "I know what's under water because I dive," she reports. "The muck on the rocks, once dried out, would blow debris and dust everywhere!" Friends of Lake Powell unanimously agree that a lake drained would be unimaginably ugly. Opponents retort that a free-flowing Colorado River would soon replenish the landscape.

I read the newsletter's pronouncement while sitting where I could see sun glinting off sparkling water, could hear a constant drumroll of inboard and outboard motors, could watch red rock cliffs reflect themselves in turquoise water. That evening, the moon rose in a shimmer of currents; the next day, the sun did the same. Too many boats and campers for my taste, but everyone there had sufficient sandstone space with direct access to the sloping shoreline. The place, alive with happy voices, was the kind of cove imagined by entrepreneurs a generation earlier. Looking at the scene and the scenery, it was easy to forget the ghostly silence, the muck beneath the waves, and the violence to the land that caused this place to be haunted.

Instead, I focused on the newsletter's words, for they inadvertently articulate what puzzles me most about Lake Powell rhetoric. They admit that the dam must have created "a 200 mile long mud bog," and they acknowledge "formerly beautiful" red sandstone cliffs. At the same time, they praise the lake as "one of the most stunningly beautiful places in the world." How can a single locale simultaneously be both "stunningly beautiful" and "formerly beautiful"? Wallace Stegner gave a reasonable answer. "In gaining the lovely and the usable," he wrote, "we have given up the incomparable." In building the beautiful, we necessarily destroyed the beautiful. In arrogantly managing the landscape for ourselves, we necessarily transformed it from one kind of aesthetic entity to another. Friends of Lake Powell prefer one vision; canyon purists, another.

Purists would deny the present panorama, preferring to picture Glen Canyon a hundred years ago—"a curious ensemble of wonderful features—carved walls, royal arches, glens, alcove gulches, mounds, and monuments." John Wesley Powell, leader of the first Euro-American expedition to boat this Colorado River canyon, poetically described what he saw. "Past these towering monuments, past these mounded

UTAH: GLEN CANYON RESERVOIR

billows of orange sandstone, past these oak-set glens, past these fern-decked alcoves, past these mural curves, we glide hour after hour, stopping now and then, as our attention is arrested by some new wonder." Edward Abbey's glen imagery—perhaps my favorite of all canyon passages—is no less striking. "Down the river we drift in a kind of waking dream, gliding beneath the great curving cliffs with their tapestries of water stains, the golden alcoves, the hanging gardens, the seeps, the springs where no man will ever drink, the royal arches in high relief and the amphitheatres shaped like seashells. A sculptured landscape mostly bare of vegetation—earth in the nude." For me, these two idealistic quotations help shape the ghostly garb of the late Glen Canyon.

Many more nonpareil descriptions can be found alongside Eliot Porter's photographs in *The Place No One Knew*. Published by the Sierra Club in 1963, this coffee table collection commemorates the canyon in both pictures and words. David Brower's foreword sets its elegiac tone: "The closing of Glen Canyon dam in our time was a major mistake to learn from, and our purpose here is to help the world remember these things lost." Porter briefly describes the canyon as he experienced its simultaneous grandeur and intimacy, as he watched how its "opaque river converts light reflected from rocks and trees and sky into a moire of interlacing lines and coils of color," then lets his photographs speak for him. Accompanying his pictures are the words of other writers. Although not necessarily referring directly to the canyon, each quotation suggests a relevant artistic analogy. For example, Clarence E. Dutton observes:

> Very wonderful at times is the sculpture of these majestic walls. There is an architectural style about it which must be seen to be appreciated. The resemblances to architecture are not fanciful or metaphorical, but are real and vivid; so much so that the unaccustomed tourist often feels a vague skepticism whether these are truly the works of the blind forces of nature or of some intelligence akin to the human but far mightier; and even the experienced explorer is sometimes brought to a sudden halt and filled with amazement by the apparition of forms as definite and eloquent as those of art.

On the page opposite Dutton's paragraph, Porter pictures the now submerged Dungeon Canyon, here a waist-wide slot between walls stained charcoal brown and burnt umber. So narrowly is this side canyon defined, so steep its walls, that no sky appears above. Subterranean specters surely must haunt this sculptured crypt.

In 1995 Eleanor Inskip published *The Colorado River through Glen Canyon before Lake Powell*, subtitled *Historic Photo Journal 1872 to 1964*. Inskip, too, was looking for ghosts. Like *The Place No One Knew*, Inskip's book matches words with photos, but here the photos were taken by a number of different people and the accompanying paragraphs always relate directly to the places pictured. In addition, each page adds the appropriate Lake Powell buoy number. If I were so inclined, Inskip tells me, I could anchor directly over Buoy #38, peer down on invisible Dungeon Canyon, examine Sarah Moench's photograph, read an excerpt from Bruce Berger's *There Was a River*, then imagine what no longer can be seen.

Moench shows a couple strolling hand-in-hand away from the camera. Light filters from above. Like Porter's version of Dungeon, no sky is visible, although sunlight does reflect off the canyon floor. Unlike Porter, Moench emphasizes cavern walls that arch, so the effect appears more medieval to me. Berger's description extends that feeling. "The vaulting walls closed in, squeezing ever closer, letting only the faintest trickle of light ooze from the far sky while we filed through as phantoms. Ever twisting and convoluted, the passage lengthened to a long nave of staggered piers in the style of late English gothic. There was no sound but the thread of our voices, our feet disturbing the pebbled floor, and the silence of eras gripped in stone."

Katie Lee, one of the best-known river-runners and Glen aficionados, describes Dungeon even more graphically. "The few places where a tiny slice of sunlight struck the fluting or the floor, I fancied some poor soul shackled to the wall and almost heard the clank of chains as he moved to gaze up at the only source of shredded light. Ritual bled from the walls. In that sepulcher, color spoke—blue, blood red, aubergine, violet, gold, rusty orange—all were deeply bruised." I examine Lee's words, compare them with Berger's, read them again.

The clank of chains, the style of late English gothic, the walls deeply bruised, the silence of eras gripped in stone. I look at Porter's photograph once more, then Moench's, then Porter's. Where I could walk Harriet Fish Backus's Tomboy hillside or follow her through Leadville streets, where I could enter a darkened castle great hall and envision Death Valley Scotty there beside me, I cannot ever set foot in Dungeon Canyon's tomb. Berger rightly points out that, "in another generation or two, no one alive will have a personal memory of Glen Canyon." My own generation could have seen the canyon; most of us did not. So my canyon ghosts must take shape from other writers' words, and old photographs discoloring with age. My father bought *The Place No One Knew* when it was first published in paperback. That dog-eared copy, now more than thirty years old, has lost its vibrancy—its reds and greens faded, its pages yellowed. Like the canyon I'll never see.

To counter the somber message of *The Place No One Knew*, to highlight Lake Powell's euphoric beauty and recreation potential, the Department of the Interior and the Bureau of Reclamation cooperated to publish their own propaganda. *Lake Powell: Jewel of the Colorado* appeared in 1965 and sold for seventy-five cents. Orchestrated by Floyd Dominy, then commissioner of the Bureau of Reclamation, *Jewel* is active rather than passive, inclusive rather than exclusive, more like an *Arizona Highways* magazine than a coffee table centerpiece. It's accessible. Holding *Lake Powell: Jewel of the Colorado* in one hand and *The Place No One Knew* in the other, I'm reminded of another book, *Encounters with the Archdruid*, where John McPhee invites Dominy and Brower to visit Lake Powell and the Grand Canyon together. In McPhee's pages, Dominy accuses Brower of elitism while Brower accuses Dominy of arrogance, characteristics apparent in their two Glen Canyon publications.

David Brower's funereal foreword to *The Place No One Knew* begins, "Glen Canyon died in 1963 and I was partly responsible for its needless death. So were you." Interior Secretary Stewart Udall opens *Jewel of the Colorado* with a much livelier tone. "Once in a blue moon we come upon almost unbelievable beauty. Such was my reaction at my first sight of Lake Powell and its setting of incomparable grandeur. Lake Powell holds working water, but it also is a new and major national recreation area. The blue waters and the sculptured shore hold something for all—the fun and excitement of fishing, boating, and water sports, or healing solitude in the midst of natural beauty." The ensuing pictures have an anthropocentric focus—the dam itself, speedboats on the lake, water skiers, scuba divers, fishermen, campers grilling dinner on an open fire, children laughing. High red canyon walls sheering into clear blue water provide the background for every photograph, but the emphasis is on people at play. Such colorful spreads are anachronistic, however, because at full pool Lake Powell now overtops many of the formations shown in *Jewel of the Colorado*.

Floyd Dominy's effusions, if not anachronistic, are at least ironic:

> How can I describe the sculpture and colors along Lake Powell's shores? Every time I go back, I search again for a new set of words. And they always seem inadequate.
>
> Over eons of time, wind and rain have carved the sandstone into shapes to please ten thousand eyes. The graceful, the dramatic, the grand, the fantastic. Evolution into convolution and involution. Sharp edges, round edges, blunt edges, soaring edges. Spires, cliffs, and castles in the sky.
>
> Colors like a symphony of Nature's music. Bright orange, brick red, ocher, pink, deep brown, vivid purple, granite black, mustard yellow—and a soft, pale green so delicate no artist could ever capture it with paint.

In truth, Floyd Dominy isn't describing Lake Powell at all. Sculpture and colors? Spires, cliffs, and castles in the sky? Bright orange, brick red, ocher, pink, deep brown, vivid purple, granite black, mustard yellow? He's describing Glen Canyon over eons of time, before the water's inundation. Intending to praise his human construct, Lake Powell, he instead chooses words that describe the vanishing canyon. Today's publicity materials perpetuate the same mythology. *Lake Powell Magazine*, for example, contains pages of photographs with red sandstone rising behind expensive boats. A close examination reveals that if there's a cliff, there's also a white bathtub ring circling its girth. With water at

UTAH: GLEN CANYON RESERVOIR

full pool, the ring vanishes. But so do the cliffs. A double entendre of sorts, when Mrs. America's clothes must artfully disguise a body no longer buxom.

My 1998 visit to the lake coincided with a water level less than seven feet below the maximum 3700 feet. Standing on the bridge beside the dam, I scanned a shoreline with no real cliffs, just creamy sandstone rounded above the water line. The sweeping view only vaguely resembled the *Jewel* pictures. When I stood here in 1966, the lake was two hundred feet lower and the cliffs, although they didn't exactly tower any more, still reached high above the rising water. Now, with the cliffs diminished, it seems as if the major Lake Powell attraction is solely the water—the houseboats, the swimming, the fishing, the jet skis. Wahweap, at least, has become a destination resort for humans in relation to machines rather than for humans in relation to the environment. Walking back and forth above the dam confirmed my reasoning. Of the thirty or forty other sightseers also on the bridge, no one walked on the downstream side, no one stopped to gaze at the steep sculpted canyon walls below the dam, no one even took a picture in that direction. Instead, they turned their eyes and their cameras on the dam itself, and on the lake tucked into the soft orange hills. I'm told that the downstream side of the dam reflects the way the entire canyon used to be. No one noticed.

The next day, I hiked a lonesome Utah canyon that twists down to the lake through chiseled sandstone and crumbling boxcar blocks, past a natural bridge and a few white flowers past their prime. Although hot and dry in June, the canyon must occasionally course with flooding run-off. The sparse vegetation all leaned downhill. I guess I expected to come to a beach where I could cool my feet in gently lapping lake water. And my first glimpse of Lake Powell held such promise. To my right, beyond a low narrow arch, an unreachable jade green pool tucked into the sandstone. Jewel of the Colorado, I thought to myself. The canyon hung left, however, so I followed its curve. Underfoot, caked dirt. Then mud. Then silted lake, with tamarisks hip-high in the water and splashing spawning carp.

The canyon never opened into the lake. Instead, the lake encroached into the canyon, and died. No shoreline, no swimming hole, no sandy beach. I climbed cliffside, scrambling up a yellowing track of broken rubble. From the top, I could see the pieces of the puzzle. Corpselike tamarisks wallowed in mud. Brown water finally gave way to artificial jade, with a dark swirl of dirt blotting the transition. Not a real jewel after all, but a gem as synthetic as a lab-grown Chatham emerald. "Where's the lake?" A melodic Parisian voice broke my concentration. I shrugged. From the visitor center, the shoreline looks sharply etched against the rock. From a hiker's perspective, the fine etching blurs and fades. Where's the lake? I tried another canyon, only to find more clotted mud and more invasive tamarisks, with just a hint of Lake Powell and no panoramic view.

Back in the visitor center, insulated from ghosts, I examined the National Recreation Area's indoor focal point, with its wall-size pictures of spires and alcoves and buttes. Keynoting this photographic display is a quotation from August Frugé. "When your spirit cries for peace, come to a world of canyons deep in an old land, feel the exultation of high plateaus, the strength of moving waters, the simplicity of sand and grass, the silence of growth." Of the millions of tourists who come to the dam-site, few realize that these very words grace the page opposite Eliot Porter's first photograph in *The Place No One Knew*, that the Park Service covertly has borrowed the opening chord of Glen Canyon's requiem. I suspect few stop to think of the overt implications, either. No longer a world of canyons deep in an old land, Lake Powell laps at plateaus that don't stand as high any more. Neither moving waters nor sand nor grass can be seen. And engines drown the silence.

Stan Jones, affectionately called "Mister Lake Powell," would contradict my analysis. At the 1997 hearings in Washington, D.C., his statement was read into the Congressional Record. "I submit to you, the Glen Canyon area and its 100 or more side canyons do not need to be restored, why, because they were never lost or destroyed by the waters of Lake Powell. Every canyon is still there and in its full splendor. Yes, there may be 100 or even 200 feet of water on their floors, but when the walls go up, sometimes straight up over a 1000 feet, it actually enhances them. Rather than think of it as spoiling them, think of them as having a reflective base that appears to double their height." Jones's well-known book of essays, *Stan Jones' Ramblings by Boat and Boot in Lake Powell Country*, affirms his perspective. "What is past is past. It cannot be redeemed." When a favorite arch submerges, for example, he sheds a metaphorical tear and remembers it fondly, but immediately boats on to a new attraction in the next canyon. Clearly he loves the changing Lake Powell terrain as much, if not more, than he liked Glen Canyon. Ghosts do not trouble Stan Jones.

Nor do they haunt any of the writers who enthusiastically embrace the lake's beauty. In still another collection of pictures and words, this time by a single individual, Colin Warren writes: "The Colorado River once raged through mountain wilderness, its turbulence so intense that the land was transformed into a melange of mesas, buttes, arches, coves, and cliffs. Then, with the construction of the dam, the ravaging onslaught of water was transformed into the gently flowing Lake Powell, a deep, blue mirror, its tranquil surface reflecting the constantly changing panorama of clouds, sky, sun, and moon." His words sound fairly typical to me. Like Floyd Dominy's, they casually characterize the ways time and the river shaped this canyon country, then move serenely to the tranquillity of the lake itself. Without regret for the loss of the natural landscape below, they take pleasure in a lovely utilitarian creation.

If lake enthusiasts think about ghosts at all, they generally recall the human ghosts who preceded them. Larry L. Meyer, in a 1987 *Arizona Highways* article, voices a genuine interest in Glen Canyon history. He describes as "houseboat reading" both the *Dominguez-Escalante Journal* and Powell's *Canyons of the Colorado*. He likes the old Anasazi ruins, and is saddened that the old trees are "inundated out of sight." Such specific ghostly relics don't daunt him, however, because he just appreciates their company. "I knew I belonged there with the haunts. I was home."

Meyer expressed his interest in the historic past just a year after C. Gregory Crampton published a whole book on the subject, *Ghosts of Glen Canyon*, which traces the human history submerged beneath the lake. Crampton details events and personalities, keying his stories to old black-and-white pictures and to numbered locations on a map of Lake Powell. He tells of the Indians who abandoned their lofty dwellings, the missionaries who traveled hastily through, the early explorers like John Wesley Powell, the Mormon settlers who wrestled with the inhospitable rocks, the surveyors, the gold-seekers, the first river-runners, anyone who left a mark in one part of Glen Canyon or another. Will Rusho's introduction to the revised 1994 edition of *Ghosts of Glen Canyon* calls Crampton's work "an impressive panoply of other ghosts and illustrations from the past."

To write of human ghosts would be to retrace what Crampton has already done effectively, to write a different *GhostWest* chapter. Although the human ghosts of Glen Canyon are compelling and charismatic, I personally am more intrigued by the unnatural "river" ghost that humans violently created. The phantoms of Dungeon Canyon, for example. Or the ghost of Music Temple, Number 21 in Crampton's catalogue. *Ghosts of Glen Canyon* pictures four names carved there in sandstone—C. Powell, J. K. Hillers, F. S. Dellenbaugh, and F. M. Bishop—stressing, once more, the human presence. I prefer to think of the words that actually named the place, a "hollow in the rock filled with sweet sounds. It was doubtless made for an academy of music by its storm-born architect; so we name it Music Temple."

Katie Lee describes it twice. In 1954, "A song can be heard from beneath that dome to the river, nearly half a mile away. A nostalgic spot, so full of whispers of the past, so lovely—the pool, the stone estrade, the bank of ferns and columbine backing the pool, hanging baskets of them overhead clinging to a seep, and the sandstone spire twisting mysteriously out of sight way above, from where pours a crystal ribbon of water that drops musical notes into the pool." In 1967, "Half the dome, and most of the spiral that had fed the pool, was under water. . . . I was able to climb the remaining narrows to open canyon. There'd been another drawdown, and for several hundred feet all was scaly, dead, ugly—blurring my vision for the hundredth time." Reading her descriptions, I finger Eliot Porter's photographs of this spot so varnish-stained it looks like a Jackson Pollack painting, an amber stream rusting the caustic sand, another wall seeping tears of black. Now it's scaly, dead, ugly. If I have tears for a place I never knew, I shed them at Buoy #55.

Katie Lee says that she sang in Music Temple every year for ten years. In all that time, she never heard anyone shout. I appreciate the reverence she expresses, the understanding and acceptance of a small human presence in a canyon larger than life. Some might say that the act of naming is an act of possessing, that I'm idealizing Powell's exploratory voyages and ignoring the economic reasons propelling them down the river, but ghosts *are* nonpareil, aren't they? Isn't *GhostWest*, after all, an act of rainbows? An alive red-running river, when the reality is a dead reservoir of blue?

"Man has flung down a giant barrier directly in the path of the turbulent Colorado. . . . It has tamed the wild river—made it a servant to man's will." So says the Bureau of Reclamation. Some authors, unlike Katie Lee, are boastfully anthropocentric. Some, like Bob Hirsch, aren't even subtle. "I owned the lake and all the soaring cliffs and purple buttes around it. It was mine and each of my canyons was more intriguing than the last. I shut off the engine back in one of those glorious wrinkles in the ancient earth and I breathed the golden air and thrilled to the scream of a bald eagle that soared across the face of a buff cliff." Just as government engineers turned the turbulent Colorado into an obedient servant, so Hirsch masters the lake and calls the canyons his own. Such self-aggrandizing rhetoric isn't surprising. Lake Powell's very inception invited man-centeredness, first by diverting the Colorado's force and then by making its "seeps where no man will ever drink" more accessible, its high-walled side canyons more down-to-earth.

Not every lover of the lake writes so egotistically, of course. Larry L. Meyer is much less high-handed when he defines man's position in relation to the scenery. "Azure sky and red cliff and blue water can change with sudden swiftness through the intervention of a cloud. Sky turns a nacreous gray; the scarp dull to a pale pink; the water stirs into alternate patches of pale green and purple sapphire. Let the sky suddenly thicken with the scud of an approaching storm and the cliffside dulls to brick red; the water churns with a chocolate chop, and the passing underside of the rushing nimbus picks up the rust tint of earthly sandstone." Welcoming the surges of nature, Meyer appreciates its challenges, too. For him, Lake Powell is a natural wilderness extension.

Many writers ostensibly agree, but their rhetoric says otherwise. In poetry, as well as prose, they measure the old river and the new lake by a different yardstick.

> I was brick-red, mud-laden:
> Big Red, the River Colorado;
> Trickle or flood at Nature's whim
> Since time began.
>
> To the sea my waters are wasted
> While the lands cried out for moisture.
> Now man controls me
> Stores me, regulates my flow.
>
> The wild red outlaw river
> Tamed.
> Now flowing clean and blue
> Unmaimed.

Nature's whim, a wild outlaw; unregulated water flow, a waste; usufructuary control, a territorial imperative; the ghost of Big Red, pinned to a drafting table. In *Jewel of the Colorado*, the poetic syntax and diction is essentially martial, with strong feet, accented syllables, and an occasional internal rhyme. When the verses soften, I read the lines ironically, although I don't believe the author—quite possibly Floyd Doming himself—meant to be ironic at all.

> Sculptured beauty
> Shaped by nature.
> To her
> A million years
> But the flick of a page
> In the endless book of time.

Since it took only six and a half years for the Bureau of Reclamation to close off the canyon, to flick to the back of the book, this paean is oddly phrased. Endless, either literally or metaphorically, only until the engineers arrived.

More intentionally ironic and double-edged by design are the rollicking campfire ballads of Vaughn Short, who blends personal observation with good humor and rhythmic refrain. Here is an excerpt from a much longer narrative song about the ghosts of the glen.

> So give three cheers for the Bureau boys
> And a special rah for Floyd.
> He buried them all deep under his lake
> But he did it for the people's sake
> He did
> He did it for the people's sake.

Katie Lee consciously makes fun of the Bureau of Reclamation, too.

> Three jeers for the Wreck-the-Nation Bureau
> Freeloads with souls so pure-o
> Wiped out the good Lord's work in six short years.
> They never saw the old Glen Canyon
> Just dammed it up while they were standin'
> At their drawing boards with cotton in their ears.

Many of Lee's songs are much more serious, however. One woeful lament ends with an italicized refrain to let the river run undammed— *Set him free . . . ! Set him free . . . ! Set him free . . . !* And so ends her book, *All My Rivers Are Gone*.

Tess Gallagher penned a different kind of poetic "Farewell to the Canyon," one which addresses the canyon directly and begs for elegaic guidance.

> Do you want me to mourn?
> do you want me to wear black?
>
> Or like the moonlight on whitest sand
> to use your dark, to gleam, to glimmer?
>
> I gleam.
>
> I mourn.

Gallagher's poem, found in the Museum of Northern Arizona's *Plateau* series, concludes a prose farewell that exhorts, "Let us keep this remembered place alive in legend. Let us make the story of Glen Canyon a myth, or a parable, for the twenty first century." Two fiction writers, whose characters cloak themselves in disguises of humor and high tech machinery, have tried to do just that.

The Monkey Wrench Gang first popularized notions of the dam's vulnerability. Although the monkey wrenching quartet never directly sabotages Lake Powell's plug, the four schemers talk about the possibility. While they wreak havoc on every slickrock construction project they can find, they never stop dreaming of the dam's demise. Edward Abbey published *The Monkey Wrench Gang* in 1974, nine years before Glen Canyon dam almost failed on its own, so he couldn't foresee how novelist Steven Hannon might blend that real-life possibility with imaginative techno-eco-terror.

Because the Colorado River Storage Compact prizes water storage over flood control, and because Lake Powell marinas and vacationers prefer high water to low, the lake of the last two decades has been a full one. In 1983, warm spring snowmelt combined with unseasonable rains to produce enough run-off to endanger the Bureau of Reclamation's premier accomplishment. While water threatened to flow over the flashboards atop the dam, cavitation threatened the integrity of the tunnel spillways. Engineers calculated a delicate balance between the two outlets until the rains finally stopped and the emergency ended. Unclassified technical reports suggest that the problem, then solved, will not recur, but the novel *Glen Canyon* assumes otherwise. At the same time some of Hannon's characters struggle with the weather and structural design, others busy themselves with bomb-making and infrastructural terrorism. I won't give away the ending, but the plot is highly imaginative, the scientific details plausibly inventive. The on-site physical descriptions mirror the reality of what I know exists. "You ought'a see all those little side canyons up on the reservoir. At the upper ends of nearly all of them, there's just a mass of scum and driftwood and shit floatin' around. They look like cesspools. You sure don't see pictures of that in the promotion brochures for the *Jewel of the Colorado*." The

Friends of Lake Powell newsletter labels *Glen Canyon* "a book of disgust" that should not be purchased.

So far the Friends have not reviewed Colin Fletcher's newest nonfiction book, *River: One Man's Journey down the Colorado, Source to Sea*, but I don't think they would applaud it either. Although *River* contains none of the physical violence found in *Glen Canyon*, Fletcher's descriptions of Lake Powell's bathtub ring reiterate Hannon's images of scenic violation. What may be unobtrusive from a distance becomes a stigma: "a thick white scabrous crust that coats the cliff's skin like desiccated fungus. The rock is sick. It has leprosy. And in this zone of sickness nothing lives. Or almost nothing. If you look long enough you may detect an occasional insect and even one or two small lizards that no doubt subsist on the insects. But otherwise you have moved into a Death Zone." Thus Fletcher characterizes another kind of ghost, this red rock band faded to bloodless scabrous white.

Many writers, sympathetic to the Glen Canyon of the past, have launched themselves on the Lake Powell of the present. Fletcher, for example, floats the lake's length as part of the journey that traces the entire course of the Colorado. Edward Abbey's, Wallace Stegner's, and Bruce Berger's essays are all well known, describing raft trips down the un-dammed canyon, retracing their routes on the waterways above. Comparing and contrasting their memories and their misgivings, each denigrates the most obvious blemish on the old queen's complexion. "Lake Powell by Houseboat," printed in Abbey's last collection of essays, might be called his sequel to "Down the River," in *Desert Solitaire*. In contrast with the idyllic canyon landscape, the Dead Zone is horrible to Abbey: "an extensive area of drying mud and mud-covered trees and shrubbery—all dead." He adds, "A ten-foot vertical drawdown, for example, can expose a hundred square miles of barren waste where nothing survives but tamarisk and tumbleweed. And flies. And maggots."

When Stegner was writing his descriptions, the lake had filled only to 210 feet below full pool level. He predicted the water would never reach much higher. Cliffs still rose above Stegner's Park Service patrol boat, and no bathtub ring yet encircled the canyon walls. So he found Powell considerably less Zola-esque than Fletcher or Abbey, beautiful even, in a sad sort of way. "The contact of deep blue water and uncompromising stone is bizarre and somehow exciting. Enough of the canyon feeling is left so that traveling up-lake one watches with a sense of discovery as every bend rotates into view new colors, new forms, new vistas." When Stegner projected his thoughts into the future, should the lake continue to rise and fall, his imagination darkened. "Then indeed the lake would be a vertical-walled fjord widening in places to a vertical-walled lake, neither as beautiful nor as usable as it still is. And the moment there is even twenty or thirty feet of drawdown, every side canyon is a slimy stinking mudflat and every cliff is defaced at the foot by a band of mud and minerals." He unhappily anticipated what turns out to be true.

Bruce Berger, traversing the lake on a tour boat, makes fun of a guide who actually calls the blood line to the customer's attention. "Think of Lake Powell as a giant holding tank. Today the bathtub ring is 78 feet high," the Wahweap employee blithely patters. Berger eyeballs the shoreline, and isn't impressed. "The complex textures, gradations, and stains were sheered at the high-water mark, beneath which all was unvarying whitewash. The Jewel of the Colorado, as the Bureau of Reclamation called the lake in its brochures, may have been star sapphire in the middle, but at the edge it was decidedly paste." Once again, it seems to me, Katie Lee has the last word. "Cesspowell, the Stool of the Colorado." In *All My Rivers Are Gone*, she annotates her own journals and provides a multi-layered, multi-decade view of a ghostly terrain that comes to life with her words, and then slowly dies.

Given so many descriptions of Glen Canyon and Lake Powell, a certain repetitive incantation recurs. Jewel of the Colorado. The Place No One Knew. Big Red. The Dead Zone. One conclusion is clear. Everyone reveres this special landscape. For every author who eulogizes the submerged canyons, another praises the glories of the lake. That their encomiums are accompanied by a reverence for canyon walls now damaged and diminished is an irony escaping most of the Lake Powell acolytes. That draining the reservoir will not, in their lifetimes, result in a Glen Canyon restored is an irony escaping most of

UTAH: GLEN CANYON RESERVOIR

the cult of the wild. To fairly evaluate both sides of the rhetorical war is to say that histrionics almost always accompany partisan interpretation. To dismiss the passions, however, is to do a disservice to the Floyd Dominys and David Browers alike. On the other hand, to pretend that Glen Canyon's ghost no longer haunts the waters of Lake Powell is to be very narrowly focused. The Glen's sculptured walls, vaulted alcoves, and keystone arches will shadow the anthropocentric dreams of developers and most certainly will plague the destiny of future water projects in the West. I hope.

Somewhere in Escalante country, a box canyon folds into a picturesque river that eventually runs into Lake Powell. Well above the high pool mark, this particular canyon is in no danger of inundation. It looks like a hundred other slickrock destinations, with vibrant Navajo sandstone cliffs, creamy beehives, a miniature arch, and more than one granary tucked vertically where horizontal red gives way to white. At my feet, June flowers cluster everywhere. Bright orange globe mallow, pale desert primrose, vibrant shooting stars, dry prickly pear and leafing thistles. Walking softly, I alarm only a single deer.

Where the canyon boxes itself in, a slim hundred-foot waterfall glissades down a mossy notch. On either side, tiny columbine blossoms cling to pale green seeps. Below, a ruffled pool reflects lacy water and crocheted sand. From different points of view, the windblown waterfall elongates, broadens, flattens, curtains the ocher wall, rainbows its surroundings. Its jasmine sounds never crescendo, never miss a beat. I sit alone, half-mesmerized. Can I imagine darkness? Thick drifts of silt? Skeletal tree branches draped in muck? Granaries crumbling and pictographs bleaching. A soup ring of white? My box canyon, another uneven spot on the reservoir floor? My waterfall, consumed?

Haunted by ghosts I never knew, I'm also haunted by the rhetoric that shadows and highlights them. Dungeon Canyon. Music Temple. Grotto Canyon. Hidden Passage. Forgotten Canyon. Basket Maker Cave. Balanced Rock Canyon. Gregory Natural Bridge. Moqui Canyon. Cathedral in the Desert. So many places I can read about but can never see. The real Jewel of the Colorado—the late Glen Canyon.

16
IDAHO LAVA LAND

A volcanic rift, dormant for centuries, belies violent beginnings. In the morning light, in ghostly remission, there is nothing infernal about this place. Under my boots, the cinder-path trail crunches like chocolate Rice Krispies; overhead, two nighthawks whiffle chevron wings across a sun-blue sky. Otherwise, Craters of the Moon is as silent as its crescent namesake. Because hundreds of hoof-prints pepper the ground, a herd of deer must have preceded me today. Now I can see nothing but hard-edged lava, crumpled cinders, and an occasional star-flower burst of yellow.

As I walk, I hum a refrain from Alan Hovhaness's Mount St. Helens symphony. Composed in 1983, the three movements musically replicate the only volcanic eruption I've ever personally experienced. And I didn't actually witness that explosion. I saw only a fine green filter of volcanic dust mysteriously layering the air, covering the northern Cascades trail where I was hiking and where a single deer had left Vulcan hoofprints before me. Here, in Idaho's Craters of the Moon, I remember that Washington trip, and that haze of ashes, and the immense quiet of that distant morning. In my head, I hear Hovhaness's gentle Spirit Lake violins.

To my left stretches a cinder-field punctuated with more blazing stars, bright yellows dotting mauve-gray. Fifteen thousand years ago, a grove of trees grew on this barren slope. One cataclysmic day chunks of lava enswirled their trunks, captured them where they stood and turned them into charcoal. Like plaster of Paris, the molten rock spattered the trees and steamed them alive. Centuries later the trees have disappeared but their empty molds remain, edged with bark-scaled scallops. Nothing else breaks the monotony of that cindered slope, though a pica shrills a hillside alarm across the tree-ghost emptiness.

The adagio-allegro movement, which follows the Spirit Lake movement of Hovhaness's symphony, begins quietly, too, with a trill of flutes and a pica piccolo. Then, as must have happened here in this silent grove, a timpanic burst deafens the air. A sliding brass crescendo interrupts. Like drowning trees, the French horns moan a landscape dirge. More timpani. Throated cymbals. Trombones. Drums, and more drums. Rhythms irregular, rhythms staccato, rhythms insistent, the timpani explode with atomic force, then subside slowly, regularly, as if the lava were hardening on the earth's surface. Finally, soft violins silence Mount St. Helens.

Alongside the empty tree molds, I rehearse the volcanic sequence in my memory. Percussion and brass explosions; echoes of woodwinds and strings. Drums, trumpets; oboes, cellos. Where I hear a symphony, however, my Craters of the Moon predecessors imagined a more martial tune. The absent grove of lava trees stands on Trench Mortar Flat, named for spiral openings that twist like riflings in a gun barrel. So-called cinder bombs once littered this place with fiery lava. When a piece of molten basalt tumbles and spins, it solidifies into a teardrop shape called a pear bomb or a spindle bomb. When clotted lava pulls apart in the air, a ribbon bomb results. When the molten exterior cools before the hot interior finishes expanding, the surface fractures like a loaf of fresh sourdough. A breadcrust bomb, it's called. Today's peaceful expanse, empty of bombs because early twentieth-century collectors picked it clean, hardly resembles a Trench Mortar munitions dump at all. Instead, it's a war-zone cemetery, centuries after battle.

Other visitors have also been struck by the silence here. R. W. Limbert, writing in *National Geographic Magazine* in 1924, first invokes the military and then acknowledges his own inarticulate response. "The

IDAHO: LAVA LAND

ascent to this point, known as Big Cinder Butte, was through a conglomerate of lava bombs and pancakes, where still plastic lava had fallen and flattened out," he wrote. But at the top of the cone, he was speechless. "We yielded to the influence of silence." Limbert, a Boise taxidermist, returned again and again to Craters of the Moon. His articles and his unabashed boosterism were at least partially responsible for the preservation of this lava landscape as a national monument.

Like Death Valley, Craters of the Moon inspired hellish appellations. Devils Orchard and Infernal Cone, for example. Mr. Dante's country, said Ernest Hemingway, who lived in nearby Ketchum. Limbert avoided such demonic descriptions, however, choosing words more picturesque than satanic.

> Were I gifted with the art of word painting, I might in some small way suggest the wonderful coloring of these craters. Picture yourself standing in some vast amphitheater whose towering walls are a riot of yellow, green, orange, brown, and black, with brick red and vermilion predominating. Imagine, too, an awesome, enveloping silence. I had noticed that at places like these we had almost nothing to say.

Even when he descended into some of the countless caves that tunnel through and beneath the lava flows, Limbert's language was more uplifting than dark. He admired the stalactite and stalagmite formations shaping the ceilings and floors of the frozen lava tubes, and he enjoyed crawling across icy floors to peer through cracks and into crevices. I, on the other hand, felt claustrophobic underneath the lava. Not even rose-colored names like Beauty Cave or Boy Scout Cave compelled me to investigate more than a hundred yards in the dark.

The vented cinder cones, however, and the neighboring lava flows, were marvelously enticing. Climbing alongside North Crater cone, I found limber pine tentacled to the slope, miniature arches of blackened rock, red cinders underfoot, tiny drifts of desert parsley. Below me, hardened lava had pooled into *pahoehoe*, which braids out into the valley. *Pahoehoe* means 'ropy coils' in Hawaiian, and features such quixotic characteristics as toes and pressure ridges and squeeze-outs and collapses. Crocheted and knit together, the tubular rock gives off a blue-black sheen. It froze, I believe, at 2000 degrees Fahrenheit. Balancing my way across the threads like an uneasy tightrope walker, I imagined Limbert and his friend Cole inching their volcanic miles across "strange shapes and twists, as if a rapid in a mountain stream had suddenly congealed."

The *aa*—another graphic Hawaiian word meaning "hard on the feet"—must have been excruciating. As the *pahoehoe* cooled, it fragmented into shin-sharp surfaces, boulder-sized pincushions of rock needles and rubble. Some *aa* is huge, such as the Chinese temple goddesses sculpted nearby; more often, it's only knee- or chin-high. A master potter, perhaps, threw his wet clay to the ground, where it stuck in blistered blackened clumps and scythes. I can't fathom crossing *aa* on foot, with its "bubbles, rolls, folds, and twists, as if a giant's frying pan of thick gravy furiously boiling had been frozen instantaneously." Cole's tendons hurt so badly that, finally, he couldn't walk. Limbert says he almost wept as he watched their Airedale try to negotiate the route.

Shuffling across a lava flow or peering into an ice-filled spatter cone—called sputter by Limbert—I thought about the two explorers and their dog. Scaling a hollow red-black crater, especially one with its side blown out, or looking across unbroken miles of black and brown plateaued lava, I soon forgot their ghosts. Craters of the Moon excludes an earthly presence. Indians generally avoided the place, though they traversed its northern edge now and then. White settlers found it useless. Humans and human ghosts are irrelevant here. The real specter is the cataclysmic force so powerful that it shook the land irrevocably and reshaped the landscape forever, an unimaginable cacophony of timpani and cymbals and brass.

I watch clouds build in the sky. Cream-colored cumulous with ominous accents billow against the blue, while black anvils gather and tower behind them. In the center of the earth, magma must fold and unfold in much the same way. White-hot, red rainbows of orange, the molten interior must shape and reshape itself. Later today the sky will erupt in a thunderstorm of gigantic proportions. Blowing off energy, cracks of lightning will illuminate Inferno Cone so that it seems unat-

IDAHO: LAVA LAND

tached from the earth, in motion with the dust streaming from its nether side. Figuratively, the sky and the land will explode. Cinder dust will obliterate my view, then rain, surging sideways, whipped by the wind.

Underground, where magma boils like molten clouds, the earth eventually will explode, too. Spatially less forgiving, however, the earth's eruption will be literal, not figurative. Fourteen million years ago, volcanic activity on the Snake River Plain first occurred. Between two thousand and fifteen thousand years ago, Craters of the Moon specifically was formed. When the Great Rift, a volcanic crack nearly sixty miles long, pulled apart, a curtain of gases, magma, fluid lava, and seething froth detonated and sprayed. Once the expansion of the gases decreased, the flow sputtered to a halt, but not before the *pahoehoe* and the *aa* had buried everything in their paths. At some point in the next millennium, the process will recur, today's strings giving way to tomorrow's percussions.

Meanwhile, silence. After the gargantuan thunderstorm blew through my campsite, the sky began clearing. By midnight, a lunar landscape had emerged. Black lava reflects no light, but I could see jagged moon monsters hiding in intricate shadows. I walked among them, picking my way between dark and dangerous knobs and knolls. Volcano dust was still settling in the air, so the volcanic formations seemed unattached, ghostly and phantasmal. I tiptoed. Nothing moved.

Beneath the surface of the rock-hard lava, however, deep in the earth, the magma must be blistering, bubbling, coiling and curling. Somewhere below, at this very moment, the molten liquid is writhing into life. Some day the Great Rift will erupt violently again, spurting liquid geysers of hot cinders and ash, smothering southeast Idaho and Craters of the Moon in more *pahoehoe* and *aa*. Some day percussion and brass will bury the blazing stars, the hoof-prints, and the limber pine. Some day this quiescent volcanic plain will explode back to life. Of all the *GhostWest* specters, in fact, Vulcan is the only one assured a future as well as a past.

17
WASHINGTON ANCIENT FORESTS

A trail of ghosts shadows each one of us, and haunts with personal particularity. Family photo albums remind me of my own wraithlike self. A round-cheeked three-year-old on her brand new skis clutches oversize ski poles to keep from falling over. A skinnier nine-year-old staggers under a Trapper Nelson strapped to her back, the wood-frame pack stuffed with a misshapen World War II surplus sleeping bag. Four years older, sailor hat cocked over one eye, a young teenager steps into a green canvas canoe. She waves her paddle defiantly. Older still, a fluffy-haired sorority pledge looks uncomfortable in blue cocktail dress, white gloves, and heels. A page later, another snapshot shows a slouched twenty-year-old in cut-off blue jeans and dirty scuffed tennis shoes. She is staring dreamily at a snowy peak reflected by a tiny lake, and she looks happier than the accessorized college freshman.

My favorite young ghosts are conjured from the camp I attended for almost a dozen summers. Stretched along Washington state's Hood Canal, we had salt water in front of us and the Olympic Mountains behind. We picked oysters off the beach and ate them raw. We backpacked up the Dosewallips River and slept under the stars in a place called Enchanted Valley. We washed down buckets of huckleberries with water dipped straight from the streams. We regularly encountered elk and bear. Once I saw a cougar pad fifteen feet away, and once I imagined I heard a wolf howl far in the distance, and then a second wolf.

At first the camp had little electricity or hot water. I remember a violent storm when the dock broke loose and began floating away. The nine-year-olds got to stay up late that night, standing side by side along the beach, shining flashlights on the counselors who were trying to haul the boom logs on shore. We only took showers once a week, heating water by firing up a boiler with wood we cut ourselves. I had pigtails, which I never ever unbraided. Mostly we just stayed dirty, in a muddy Pacific Northwest sort of way. Primitive? Yes. But that never seemed to bother anyone.

When I was ten, we hid a whole unit of little girls—twenty-four of us—behind a single Douglas fir. Someone snapped a picture, I recall. Though I never saw a copy of it, I know we wanted to show that no one was visible behind the massive trunk. Years later, I was a counselor in the same unit. The huge tree was gone by then, turned into firewood I'm afraid, but another stump, almost as large, jutted out from the bluff above the water. I sat on that stump nearly every night, my feet propped against its gnarled roots, my back resting comfortably along the twisted wood. From my perch, I might see the moon rise, or watch scattered lights twinkle across the water, or smell the salt breeze and listen to it whiffle the summer air. I learned to love poetry, there on that stump, and I learned to love the tired feeling that comes after a long day of hiking.

I loved backpacking most of all, though our gear was heavy and the powdered dinners dreadful. Aluminum frames were still in the future; freeze-dried food too expensive for the camp's budget. I didn't even have a pair of hiking boots—just worn-down tennis shoes, and blisters. Along the Dosewallips, up the Duckabush to O'Neil Pass, bushwhacking past the Hamma Hamma toward the Brothers, from Lake Cushman to the Flapjacks to Mount Gladys and beyond. I followed the same trails so many times I thought that, if I were dropped almost anywhere on the Olympics' eastern slopes, I would know immediately where I was.

WASHINGTON: ANCIENT FORESTS

During college, when the Girl Scouts actually paid me to go to camp, we even hiked on our days off. I climbed Mt. Constance, did the Bogachiel, and dreamed of scaling Mt. Olympus some day. Once I watched a forest fire crest over the next ridge, with flames popping and embers flying in the wind. Sometimes, especially during fire season, we stayed closer to the salt water, stuffing ourselves with cracked crab and garlic bread, or dancing with the loggers in Hoodsport on Saturday night. When we curved around the peninsula to the ocean, we encountered little traffic and could toss down our sleeping bags almost anywhere. On the Makah Indian Reservation, a favorite spot on Washington's northwest tip, we might walk the beach for hours and never see another person.

Aldo Leopold wrote that one should never revisit a wilderness: "the more golden the lily, the more certain someone has gilded it. To return not only spoils the trip, but tarnishes a memory. It is only in the mind that the shining adventure remains forever bright." Fearing the truth of his words, I avoided the Olympic Peninsula for thirty years. To find my own ghosts, however, and the ghosts of the giant trees, I needed to return to Camp Robbinswold and to the valleys and mountains that sweep up from Hood Canal. I needed to look for the cedars and hemlock and the huckleberries and that squat little bush whose green leaves I liked to chew. To understand *GhostWest* past and present, I needed to walk the same trails once again; I needed to see another cougar, and hear another wolf.

Different writers describe the Olympic Peninsula as an island, an island of rivers, a series of concentric islands, a series of circles, a doughnut, a castle inside a moat. In keeping with my Girl Scout indoctrination, I might call it a nest of pots in a camp cookware set, the smaller pans fitting inside the larger kettles. The perimeter is water—the Pacific Ocean to the west, the Strait of Juan de Fuca to the north, Puget Sound to the east, a salt-water finger called Hood Canal fishhooking between Puget Sound and the mountains. Next comes an interior patchwork of public and private lands that includes Indian reservations and pieces of a national park but is mostly owned privately or by the state of Washington. Within that ring sits the Olympic National Forest, multiple-use public land which contains stands of timber that may or may not be logged out, occasional preserves of designated wilderness, and the variety of natural resources crucial to a healthy Pacific Northwest ecosystem.

What William Dietrich calls the castle inside the moat is the London Tower of the peninsula, the crown jewel. The Olympic National Park fills the heart of Washington's northwest corner. In 1909 President Theodore Roosevelt set aside an Olympic National Monument of 620,000 acres, holdings nearly halved when World War I triggered a market for additional natural resources. Then President Franklin Delano Roosevelt visited the area in 1937, just before World War II would have propitiated incentives for additional timber production. FDR was so impressed that he lobbied Congress to set aside the region forever. On June 29, 1938, the Olympic National Park was created—648,000 acres, slightly larger than the original monument, a preserve encircled by land designated and appropriated for other purposes. Because the ostensible intent was to save sufficient terrain for the Roosevelt elk and because no one had yet conceptualized ecosystem well-being, much of the park lies in the high country—the peaks and glaciers, the subalpine lakes and unforested meadows. Trees in the surrounding rings of the Olympic National Forest and the state and private lands have always been available for commercial timber harvest.

The history of the Olympic Peninsula is interesting because of its contradictions. One of the last parts of the contiguous United States to be explored, it quickly became an attractive vacation destination—at once remote and accessible, primitive and popular, wild yet surprisingly well developed. Until the late nineteenth century, it drew few visitors. Even the American Indians, for the most part, avoided the interior. In the 1880s, however, several expeditions set out to explore the unknown territory. A report by Joseph P. O'Neil, who headed an 1884 foray south from Port Townsend, details the inherent complications of cross-country travel in the overgrown mountains of western Washington. "The dense forests and denser undergrowth around the base of these mountains extending about twenty miles back from the water render all attempts to enter, but the most systematic trail cutting, abortive. The rivers can not be ascended to the interior of the mountains on account of the swiftness of the current and the numerous impassable falls, and it is [owing] to this that some portions of these mountains are alive with game having no fear of man." At the lower elevations, as I well recall, shin-tangle absolutely stymies cross-country hikes.

O'Neil's second exploration in 1890 turned out to be as problematic as the first. Along the North Fork of the Skokomish River, his men had to hack a stair-step trail out of solid rock to accommodate their mules. As they did so, they made travel easier for a second party that headed into the same territory that summer. James Wickersham, a Tacoma probate judge, had ventured up the North Fork the preceding year, but turned back when his food supply ran low. Learning about the O'Neil expedition, he was determined to see the high country first. So he and his wife, along with two other couples, utilized O'Neil's man-made trail through the densest parts of the forest, then foraged on ahead across the scenic—and more open—mountainous terrain. "Everywhere lie snowbanks, glaciers, flowery meadows, lakes, and groves," Wickersham wrote. "Magnificent waterfalls roar and splash down the mountain buttresses, reaching the canyon bottom in fine spray, and with the action of the winds, make music on nature's own aeolian harps. Here, music, flowers, birds, sunshine, and spring; there, fogs, ice, rocks, and drear winter—every variety of scenery and climate in a few minutes from our high porch." The six young adventurers slid perilously across dangerous snowfields, ascended numerous peaks in the high country, then waded raging streams and slogged through muddy bogs to descend the unmapped Dosewallips River.

I like to think about the undaunted spirits of the three women in particular, clad "in soft felt hats, blue ducking short skirts, blue ducking overalls, drawn tight around the ankle, and heavy leather shoes, with soles filled with hobnails." For three weeks, the three couples tested their abilities to their limits. The first tourists to overlook the headwaters of the North Fork of the Skokomish, the Hamma Hamma, the Dosewallips, and the Duckabush, they pioneered the very rivers that Robbinswold campers know the best. Their trip also signals how the park developed so incongruously. By 1900, little more than a decade after the initial incursions, vacationing outsiders were coming to the Olympics with increasing regularity. Fancy hotels at Lake Cushman and Lake Crescent made roughing it quite easy. Alpine clubs like the Seattle Mountaineers made summer outings irresistible. Because of the difficulties of cross-country travel, established trails quickly became the norm. What was impassable soon became almost easy to hike. Government employees erected wooden bridges across the unfordable rivers and streams, built log cabin lean-tos to shelter hikers from inclement weather, and kept the trails relatively free of fallen trees.

(Just recently, the National Park Service replaced some of the old wooden bridges. Two years later, the new metal bridges buckled under the weight of heavy snow. Since an impoverished Park Service can't afford to replace the bridges soon, some of the high country is as inaccessible today as a hundred years ago. I'm told that the route through Enchanted Valley is blocked by so many trees that it's impassable, too. This year, at least, the high country must be nearly as isolated as the Wickershams and their friends found it, every waterfall and peak and meadow "one continuous surprise.")

At the same time the government was making the monument and then the park more user-friendly for hikers and horses, its policies blocked excessive highway construction. To this day, only the Hurricane Ridge Road pierces the high country of the Olympic National Park. In the southeast corner, which is closest to Camp Robbinswold, a few roads wander up some of the wider drainages but, inside the park itself, all visitors must walk. From the outset, the monument and now the park always attracted vacationers who "took only pictures and left only footprints." It's no wonder the Girl Scouts took advantage of the opportunities there.

Outside the park, however, the utilization story is quite different. William Dietrich's book, *The Final Forest*, gives an outstanding overview of forestry practices on the Olympic Peninsula. In its pages, Dietrich considers a critical conundrum. Known best for its ancient trees, many parts of the Olympic Peninsula have been logged so thoroughly that its old-growth has nearly disappeared. What once might have merited our veneration has, in large part, vanished. Dietrich's fair-minded discussion centers on the community of Forks, the northwestern quadrant of the peninsula, and the rain forests of the Pacific slope, so his stories do not exactly parallel those of Hood Canal settlement and the concurrent commercial logging there. He does, however, explain the complications caused by excessive clearcutting, by political machinations, by economic imperatives, by the Endangered Species Act, and by subsequent court decisions. An emerging public enthusiasm for preservation now confounds a hundred years of environmental exploitation, leaving the residents of Forks in an emotional and economic limbo that would have been inconceivable a generation ago. To a lesser degree, that anthropocentric roller coaster is true of Hood Canal, too.

For the twenty years or so when I thought the Olympic Peninsula was mine, logging seemed an integral part of the place, as natural as the trees themselves. Because the forests seemed inexhaustible, no one questioned the way foresters conducted their business. During the 1980s, however, operations changed. Fear of environmental regulation led to wholesale opportunism, as timber companies rushed to get out the cut before new governmental regulations shut them down. In 1987, for example, "a record 5.6 billion board feet were cut on national forests" in Washington and Oregon. Environmentalists, incensed by damage they thought irrevocable, invoked the Endangered Species Act. In May 1991, U.S. District Judge William Dwyer of Seattle ruled that the operative federal agencies "had committed 'a remarkable series of violations of the environmental laws' by treating the forests as timber reserves rather than ecosystems." After his landmark decision, the federal cut dropped 87 percent.

A death knell, silvaculture businesses insist, but Dwyer's ruling has not been single-handedly responsible for the recent vicissitudes of Pacific Northwest logging. Increased mechanization has reduced the overall number of timber workers necessary. Corporate takeovers have restructured the parameters of the cut, imposing new imperatives to show immediate profit and showing little concern for the long-term health of the land. Science, too, has had an important impact on forestry practices, teaching us to think of ecosystems as coherent wholes. Forests are more than just trees, we now understand more fully. Forest health means a sustainable habitat for the four-legged residents, for the birds, the understory plants, the ferns and the berries, even the fungus and moss. All these forest constituents somehow interact. If one piece of the puzzle is missing, the picture is incomplete.

For example, the last confirmed sighting of wolves on the Olympic Peninsula occurred in 1924. What I heard at Marmot Pass in 1959 must have been coyotes. In ways I surely didn't understand at the time, the ecological puzzle picture was damaged long before I started going to camp. Even then, ghosts from the past were haunting the land, were howling in the imagination. And now I am a ghost of sorts, too, as distanced from my Girl Scout days as that youngster was from the flesh-and-blood wolves, from the ancient forests that once grew to the edge of Hood Canal, and from the intrepid Deborah Susan Bell Wickersham with her husband and their friends. I've often wondered what the ghosts of history would think if they could see the present-day West. Surprised or uneasy? Delighted or horrified? Proud or contemptuous? Amused or simply intrigued? Now I can test my own premises, on the shores of Hood Canal.

Just as prop planes have given way to jet liners, and locking hubs to automatic all-wheel drive, so the dilapidated Kingston ferry has turned into a gas-guzzling SUV of a boat. Agile attendants, their arms rapidly pointing right, then left, wedge cars and vans and eighteen-wheelers bumper to bumper, row after row, so close together I can hardly open the door of my truck. This behemoth must transport two or three times as many vehicles as fit on one ferry in the past, I decide, as I pry myself out and climb to an upper deck. Upstairs, outside, I can smell salt spray instead of diesel emissions, can hear the distinctive keening of quarrelsome gulls, but I can't see five feet in front of me. Thick summer-white

WASHINGTON: ANCIENT FORESTS

Puget Sound fog curtains the water. While I sense blue sky overhead, even sunshine, the ferry itself slides along through damp invisibility. Thirty fogbound minutes later, a clouded shoreline emerges. I've crossed over to the Olympic Peninsula, but I haven't seen a thing, except for the glimmer of an arched rainbow oddly hued white, black, and gray, the erstwhile Pacific Northwest sun already playing tricks on my imagination.

Between the landing at Kingston and the Hood Canal floating bridge, more rays break through the mists. In just a few miles, the visibility clears enough for me to begin comparing my memories with what I can actually see along the highway. More cars and trucks, of course, and a straighter road than I remember. And clearcuts, some an ugly brown, others fuzzed with the light green of new-growth Douglas fir. And taller trees, though not as many as I think there ought to be. After the turn-off to Quilcene, the highway narrows and the traffic thins appreciably. In fact, I'm surprised at the empty stretches. Even driving on south from Quilcene, where I expected a clog of recreational vehicles seeking the water, I find old Highway 101 relatively uncrowded. Most visitors to Hood Canal seem to cluster at the ends easily accessible from Seattle—Belfair outside of Bremerton, the roads to Port Townsend and Port Angeles to the north. So the miles in the middle, although more heavily traveled than thirty years ago, are much like I remember.

There's a new bridge across the Dosewallips, convenience stores at Brinnon and Lilliwaup, a bigger resort at Pleasant Harbor, and clusters of vacation homes in places called Seamount Estates or Olympic Canal Tracts, but the meandering twists and curves are just the same. I used to play a game on Highway 101—all the way to Robbinswold without dropping below 50 or touching my brakes. I'd win, more often than not. This morning I played by the rules for almost ten miles, then slowed behind a pair of Wisconsin motor homes. Daydreaming, I wonder if I've missed the turn-off. Then, miraculously, the set of the highway looks familiar. An unbanked curve; a short straightaway; a pedestrian crossing in the midst of forest. Even though thick trees block my view of the water and heavy branches overhang a sign that spells

CAMP ROBBINSWOLD, I know exactly where I am. When I turn down the driveway, I feel as if I've stepped back half a century.

From the porch of the lodge, a bell signals time for the hoppers to set the tables for lunch. A group of ten-year-olds, collapsing with giggles, skips along to noontime duties. Two older girls, clad in baggy pants and oversized sweatshirts, their heads tipped together in serious conversation, dawdle behind. Beyond the girls I see the beach, the salt water, and a pair of canoes cutting through the waves. Closer, a wooden bridge still crosses the stream that has cascaded through camp for generations. The bell rings again. I smile at a menu of tomato soup, toasted cheese sandwiches, carrot and celery sticks, and chocolate brownies. The girls, talking nonstop, tell me about their morning. Crafts, canoeing, passing their tippee-tests, rehearsing for a play. When I ask where they're staying this week, they name units forever unchanged. Timber Trails. Cedar Ledge. Little Creek. Enchanted Forest. My own special favorite—Barnacle Bay. Magical places, every one. I am haunted by the happiness here.

Camp Robbinswold lines Hood Canal for a mile and a half. Originally a part of an 1890s logging operation that cut those trees accessible from the water, and a later 1920s operation that in effect stripped the rest of the marketable timber, the property wasn't worth much during the Depression. The Robbins family, who owned the Hama Hama Logging Company and who were having trouble paying the taxes on their tree-less and thus unproductive land, sold 360 acres to the Girl Scouts in 1936. The Girl Scouts paid $5000. As the years passed, more acreage was added, bringing the dimensions up to the current 430 acres. Camp life has always centered on the strip of land between highway and salt water, where the units spread like outstretched arms from the more permanent buildings in the center. In 1939, for $7700, the main lodge was built from materials barged in from Seattle. Other core buildings—the rotunda, a staff house, a nurse's facility, a caretaker's house, another caretaker's house when a falling tree smashed the first one, and a boathouse—were added gradually. Despite the changes, however, the ambience remains the same.

Jim Messmer, camp properties manager, explains his philosophy. "Keep it like it was, but with modernization." When the lodge needed remodeling, for example, Jim argued successfully for retaining the original façade. The part that faces the water, with its encircling porch and its all-encompassing windows, looks just as it did sixty years ago. Even the scrolled woodwork trim is the original or, in a few places, an exact replication of the original. Inside the dining room, the same tables and benches scrape the same old-growth fir floor, although an all-new kitchen with up-to-date appliances extends off the back side of the lodge. The girls no longer wash dishes out back, as I did when I was little, scrubbing pots and pans in the rain.

Actually, the girls don't have to do much of anything in the rain any more. Now Camp Robbinswold functions as a year-round facility, used as much by troops in the spring and fall as by the campers of summer. So several weatherproof buildings have been added, and the individual units now boast covered cook shelters and open-sided wooden cabins designed to look like the old tents but to stay dry during the rainy seasons. In 1965 a heavy wet snow engulfed the camp, felling trees and collapsing many of the outbuildings. A work party of volunteers tore down the shattered hutches. With mallets and hammers, we wantonly smashed everything to pieces, then stacked the broken lumber into removable piles. By summertime, the old remains were gone; permanent shelters with roofs and cement floors and raised fire circles stood in their places.

Walking around camp a third of a century later, I find these 'new' buildings tucked in the trees as if they'd always been there. The canal-side area hasn't been logged since the Robbinses sold the property, so the forest recovery is remarkable. I remember a few big trees looming here and there—that huge one we hid behind, for example—but now I see several more cedar and Douglas fir inching toward immensity. The undergrowth is thicker, too, nurse logs almost buried beneath moss and bracken and vine maple and sprouting evergreens. In 1951, two years after my first summer at camp, a bulkhead was built from the lodge to where the old dock had almost floated away. In 1953 the bulkhead was extended, and in 1957 it was enlarged again. I remember disliking the intrusion at the time. Now the bulkhead is a permanent part of the landscape, with opportunistic trees growing as if they had been planted and heavy lichen covering the rocks. The old trail above the beach, no longer necessary, has completed disappeared, swallowed by an understory of alder, salmonberry, and salal.

Near the north end of the bulkhead sits a tiny log cabin. Built in 1925, it housed the Robbins family while the men were logging nearby. Every summer for seven years, Mrs. Robbins kept house in the lean-to. Bart Robbins—whose grandfather, Daniel M. Robbins, originally bought the land in 1900, and whose father, Harry M. Robbins, ran the far-reaching logging operation—happily remembers the 1920s, when he and his brother and sisters came from Minnesota to Hood Canal to play along the beach while his parents "liquidated" their investment. Bart smiled when he said the word 'liquidated.' Thirty thousand acres; fifty million board feet per year for ten years! Then the trees were gone. He shrugged. "Dad kept only about a quarter the land, all burnt over and cut. The rest reverted to the county, and subsequently to the state. We couldn't pay the taxes."

The Robbinses moved on to Seattle, and to other timber interests. For a time, they owned a pulp mill in Bellingham but, as Bart said, "it was a touch and go living." Finally, in 1955, he and his family returned to the mouth of the Hamma Hamma River to do some salvage logging, to somehow earn money by splitting cedar shakes, shrimp fishing in the canal, and "running a little oyster operation." Listening to Bart talk about the Hama Hama Logging Company and his own Hama Hama Oyster Company—"Dad didn't want to bother writing the extra *m*, so I never used it either"—is like hearing, in miniature, a history of small-cap Olympic Peninsula logging. Boom years, followed by decades of inactivity and frustration, followed by a genuine management plan calculated to generate and sustain a cash flow from year to year.

Bart calls trees a 'crop.' Unlike most farmers, however, he won't see a harvest during his lifetime. Instead, he says, "it's a transfer of money from yourself to your grandchildren." He and his son, David, who now manages the family firm, plant new trees and log older ones every year. Bart explains that it takes an eighty year cycle to grow a cedar or a Douglas fir on the eastern slope of the Olympics. If the Robbinses cut 40 of their total 3200 acres each year, the income will be sufficient to cover their costs and "some profit." Their own acreage could sustain them in perpetuity. Inheritance complications are as prevalent in small logging operations as they are in ranching, however, so money that might be put back into additional acreage or modernized equipment is dispersed through generations of children and grandchildren.

A second complication involves environmental regulations. Bart shakes his head in disgust. "We can't add land as fast as they're taking it away from us. Can't log two hundred feet on either side of a stream now. So we'll need to get to 4000 acres to make the same living as before." Then he grins. "Sure glad we don't have spotted owls around here." In truth, both timber and oysters are fruitful hedges against inflation. When Bart began his oyster business in 1955, the shellfish sold for $3.50 a gallon. Today, oysters sell for $35 a gallon. Smoked, they're worth more than a dollar apiece. What once were weed trees—small cedar and alder and maple, for example—are now quite remunerative. Douglas fir is still the most profitable for the Robbins operation, but hemlock brings a good price as paper-making wood. Bart points to the bookcases and cabinetry lining the walls of his living room. "That's quilt maple—valuable now, and hard to find. They make musical instruments out of it." Then he tells me a story of poachers. "Jim caught them on the Girl Scout property. They were after a single tree. Worth ten or maybe twenty thousand dollars!"

I finger the fine whorls of the figured maple, look up at Bart's hand-hewn cedar ceiling. And I listen to him muse about his family's future. "If we buy 200 new acres, even with nothing growing, we can immediately increase the cut elsewhere. If we do this conservatively, proportionately, we can keep this operation going forever." Once the entire Hamma Hamma drainage was owned by only four entities—the national monument, the national forest, the state of Washington, and the Hama Hama Logging Company. Bart would like to buy back some of the land his father forfeited. He's not much interested in bidding on government timber sales, however. "I guess I was never ambitious enough," he modestly confesses. Instead, Bart is content to re-log and re-seed his own plantation. "If you don't harvest one crop, you can't grow another," he concludes.

A sign on the road up the Hamma Hamma River glosses what Bart has said.

> Hama Hama Co.
> "Custodians of the Land"
> Renewable Forest Resources
>   First Clear Cut   1923
>   Second Clear Cut 1984
>   Planted   1985
>   Weeded   1990

The trees behind the sign look healthy, though pipestem small. And the uniformity seems unnatural to me, the sameness of size and color. Yet they're thriving in this damp fecund climate, with its sixty to a hundred inches of rain each year. After talking with Bart, I try to imagine that I'm just looking at a field of corn, row after row of a single crop, Douglas fir in this instance, planted and weeded as any farmer would cultivate his acreage. But I find it almost impossible to be dispassionate. I want my trees in a high-diversity forest, not in a monoculture; I want aesthetic appeal, not homogeneity. Bart would scoff at what he would construe as a naïve tree-hugging point of view. I, on the other hand, cannot make the translation from forest primeval to amber waves of grain.

A few miles farther up the road, on state forest land, I spot a fresh cut that enables me to compare fifteen years of planting and weeding on the Robbins property with perhaps fifteen days of incipient recovery. On the new site, a bulldozer pushes slash heaps together and then distributes them in some predetermined design. Although most of the trees have already been trucked away, a few are still standing. This is New Forestry, as currently practiced in the Pacific Northwest, a small patch of a clearcut that leaves an occasional tree for nesting birds and logging debris for ground cover but removes everything else. Hamish Kimmins, in a 1997 text entitled *Balancing Act: Environmental Issues in Forestry*, admits, "Massive clearcut size is probably the single greatest mistake made in clearcutting." Kimmins is in accordance with Bart Robbins when he writes, "As long as the *renewability* of all desired ecosystem values is sustained, and as long as a mosaic of forests of different ages is maintained across the landscape, there will be a sustained supply of these resource values from the region, even though at any one location within that landscape the supply of particular resource values may be intermittent." Thus Kimmins professorially articulates the down-to-earth Robbins formula for success—forty acres a year, every year for eighty years, then repeat the cycle, over and over again.

Intermittent clearcuts are obviously more economically feasible than selective logging, and foresters rationalize that they're actually less destructive, too, arguing that an invasive logging operation only has to gut the land once every century or so, getting in and getting out with dispatch, then essentially leaving the site alone. Some foresters would even testify that the seeding and weeding process is a healthy one, and that the sequence is natural. Kimmins explains. "According to the time scale used to measure ecosystem recovery from clearcutting, the recovery can occur almost instantly (evolutionary time scale), very rapidly (ecological time scale), acceptably rapidly (forest management time scale), or unacceptably slowly (the visual alteration caused by clearcutting as perceived by a senior citizen, for example)." As I drive along this particular Hamma Hamma clearcut—the name *Hamma Hamma* may best be translated as *smelly smelly*—I feel like Kimmins's composite senior citizen. I just don't like what I see.

Farther up the road, a spate of Forest Service campgrounds has prevented further harvest. I park my truck in the shade, ready to hike up a Lena Lakes trail that will pass through a cut made more than half a century ago and will finally come to a pristine grove of ancient trees. Although the upper Hamma Hamma drainage has been heavily used for years, most of the trees around the lake were left intact. From 1927 until 1941, Lower Lena Lake was home to a Boy Scout camp, Camp Cleland. A plaque in the midst of the old-growth commemorates the

Boy Scout memory, "Where our youth learned to appreciate our outdoor HERITAGE." After the boys left, the Girl Scouts regularly backpacked to the lakes. My excursions there linger in my memory. One four-day trip when the rain never stopped. A campfire, left burning by someone else, that nearly got out of hand. Trout, caught with twine and a safety pin, then baked on hot coals. A sixty-pound pack, the heaviest I ever carried, after one camper at the end of the line became too sick to tote her own load. Tin cans, burned and buried and left behind. Campfire songs, a ukelele accompaniment, cedar smoke, the sweet smell of toasted marshmallows.

Now the twenty-nine prescribed campsites at Lower Lena Lake must be reserved in advance. A large bulletin board emphasizes that this is "a very popular backcountry camping area." *Giardia* "may be present" (we used to drink directly from any stream anywhere). A "pack it home" slogan accompanies pictures of cans, bottles, and assorted plastic bags (I'm embarrassed to recall our habits of half a century ago). The attached sign-in sheets reveals some amazing statistics, data that accounts for the rules and regulations. Hikers and campers filled in six and a half pages in the last three days. At eighteen lines per page, one group per line, that's how many hikers altogether? I give up on the math. In the twenty-first century, a lot of people enjoy this trail.

A *Visitors' Guide to Ancient Forests of Washington* justifies the popularity of the Lenas. It describes how the route begins in a valley both heavily logged and unfortunately burned, then emerges into "magnificent virgin forest." Walking up a series of sharp switchbacks that I fondly remember as one rather pleasant uphill traverse, I can't see across the valley because morning mist obscures my view. But on either side of the trail, I pass stumps with springboard cuts and lots of young Douglas fir crowding each other for sunlight. Then, as I near the lower lake, I come to the older trees. The booklet tells me to "look for Douglas fir up to 5 feet in diameter and western redcedar more than 6 feet thick." There they are, right where they must have been in the 1950s, though I didn't think about them when I was young. Now my so-called senior citizen point of view relishes their concurrent enormity and grace. I want to put my arms around a particularly old specimen that's cloaked heavily with moss. I want to lean into its bark, smell the incense of the past. I want to admire its reflection in the lake, water that also mirrors the ghost of the girl who camped here every summer so many years ago. I also want to be oblivious to the fact that a heritage of heavy logging haunts the Olympic Peninsula.

Such ancient trees once covered the Robbinswold property, too, though most of them had vanished by the time I began going to camp. A few small clusters of old-growth forest remain on the property west of Highway 101, either because the trees were of such poor quality that the loggers weren't interested or because the trees were too difficult to access. One stand in particular, called the Paul Bunyan Grove, has been highlighted by the Girl Scouts in recent years. A carefully maintained trail—ironically built on an old logging skid road—leads up the hill from main camp and meanders through the ancient trees. I believe my first backpacking trip traced that skid road up the drainage, though I can't be absolutely sure.

During my recent visit to Robbinswold, I spent many hours enjoying the Paul Bunyan trees. First with Jim and later by myself, I sat under the green canopy, looking at light shift through the needles and leaves, and listening to the forest whispers. More often than not, a faint drizzle of rain coated the maidenhair ferns. One particular Douglas fir fascinated me. Broken, perhaps by that first logging operation, it bent sideways, then stretched upright a hundred and fifty feet or more. Chain marks are still visible near its base, but it is an enormous specimen now. A survivor tree, I decided. Another fir looked as though the tree actually had twisted around inside its gnarled bark. Jim showed me where a family of flying squirrels have nested for years, high in the hollow of an old maple. These creatures seldom, if ever, venture down to earth. A flying squirrel might live a lifetime without ever touching ground, just as a human might live a lifetime without ever knowing an ancient forest. So I lay on my back and tipped my head to watch. The flying squirrels never appeared, but I liked knowing that they might.

One afternoon, I strolled through the grove in sunshine that brought out an opulent humidity. Filagreed shafts of light filtered through the branches, making Victorian patterns on the bark. Lush ground cover exposes what was missing at Lower Lena Lake. There, campers had long since decimated the small plants and powdered the soil with overuse. Here, licorice fern and curly hypnum and little hands liverwort coat the earth. Trillium, deerfoot vanillaleaf, nettles, and Oregon grape. Too many varieties of fungus to even count. A healthy ecosystem indeed. Again I lay on my back, perspiring this time, to watch traceries of club moss sway gently in the afternoon air. An epiphyte that takes no nourishment from a host tree, club moss causes no organic damage, but occasionally grows too heavy for its host. One Paul Bunyan fir fell with a crash last New Year's Day—the first day of the new millennium, Jim pointed out. "It was nearly four hundred years old." The life span of a huge maple can be abruptly finite, too—sometimes one falls in the silent springtime, victim of the weight of its own new leaves.

Jim showed me another spot, not far from the Bunyan trees, where an underground seep collapsed in on itself a few years ago. Uprooted logs sprawl topsy-turvy in a new ravine, but moss already is camouflaging the rocks and trees. Gooseberry and toadflax and the ever-present vine maple are taking hold, too. Jim described how the water had roared through camp, five feet of gravel and water and dirt rushing downstream with freight-train power. But the resilient forest is covering its own chaos. I suppose the site lends credence to Bart Robbins's assertion that there's really no such thing as a genuine ancient forest. With or without human interference, the Olympic Peninsula undergoes constant upheaval and recovery. Whether from fire or wind or heavy snowfall or an underground seep, government regulations, or just old age, these trees do die and their seedlings reproduce and persevere. Bart would say that logging is just another phase of sorts, that forest renewal will always occur.

Jim's point of view belongs in the middle of the political spectrum that at one end calls timber a cash crop and that at the other advocates a zero cut. Some stands of trees, like the Paul Bunyan Grove, should never be logged; others, for the health of a forest, should be managed, even harvested periodically. Jim, in fact, thinks the real environmental problem lies with the frequency with which trees are cut. A two-hundred-year cycle makes sense to him, though the economics of such restraint would be prohibitive for a business enterprise. Jim, however, can manage the Girl Scout property in a way consistent with his own definition of healthy forest ecology. Since 1978, when he was hired, Robbinswold has been on a biennial schedule of timber harvest and road construction. One hundred and sixty acres—the land on the canal side of the highway and the remnants of old-growth forest to the west—are sacrosanct, but the remaining two hundred and seventy acres will eventually be logged by shelterwood thinnings, even-age thinnings, or the occasional clearcutting of one to seven acres. Jim, gesturing toward some slash visible at the edge of the Bunyan grove, outlines the rationale behind his plan.

Regularly scheduled thinning and selective logging help protect the watershed, provide enhanced wildlife habitat, and sustain the forest health. Douglas fir, prone to laminated root rot, is especially susceptible to disease and, if infected, needs to be removed. I suspect the huge tree we hid behind as children was razed for this very reason. When logging takes place, Jim supervises the process carefully. On gentle slopes, loggers use only rubber-tired skidders, and only when absolutely necessary. The most recent cut was a high-lead logging operation, where cables from above kept hillside damage to a minimum and where no ground machinery was used off-road at all. Then those three acres were replanted with 1200 cedar seedlings—I could see them taking hold already. After a logging or thinning operation is completed, Jim turns the skid roads into trails, giving better access to a larger percent of the property, including Lake Armstrong, a tiny lake that sits above the immediate drainage. And he converts the logging landings to flat sites where the girls conveniently can tent overnight.

The trail to Lake Armstrong is a steep one, rising 600 feet in the first half-mile. It's no wonder I still remember my nine-year-old experience, with my sleeping bag dragging down my pack. I think we slept on a slant, too, with our feet slipping downhill all night long. Now the destination is a level established campsite, with a latrine, a cook shelter, picnic tables, and a decent fire circle. It differs as much from my primitive memory as does the modern, more functional dishwashing set-up at main camp. Even more disparate, though, are Jim's revelations about logging at Camp Robbinswold. Just as I want my forests ancient and diverse, so I want my camp untouched and certainly unharvested. I prefer innocence when, in fact, Robbinswold has never been innocent of logging. Apparently the ghosts of my own past—the trees, this very special place—have always been figments of my imagination. The reality is quite different—more dynamic than my memory had fixed in time.

Jim follows a plan that parallels real-life ecological permutations, delimiting a logging rotation that actually helps keep Robbinswold "the way it was." Tearing down the old lodge and building a new one from the ground up would have been more economical than revitalizing the original, but timber sale proceeds provided sufficient money for an historic renovation. In the twenty-two years of logging management, the Girl Scouts have netted almost $600,000. As a nonprofit agency, they must put every penny back into the property, so refurbishing the lodge was a decision easily made. Logging, which led to the existence of Robbinswold in the first place, actually sustains it today. "Without that steady influx of dollars," Jim assured me, "Robbinswold might be a very different place." Sitting by Lake Armstrong, I lean against a log and think about the irony. I always knew that Robbinswold grew from a past wholly immersed in logging, but I never considered the ramifications of that tradition. If I were to rewrite its history in "environmentally correct" ways, I would, in effect, be rewriting its present as well. Without logging, Robbinswold probably wouldn't exist.

Beside me, carpenter ants work on a never-ending task of consuming something a billion times their size. Two wood ducks paddle softly on the water. Off to one side, a pileated woodpecker attacks a snag with a great rackety-tat. I'd like to be here in the May, I think, when the massive rhododendrons are in bloom. An hour ago, I was hiking through head-high patches of huckleberry. Stopping to sample the red berries that I've always loved, I realized I was either stooping or reaching up. At mouth level, every bush had already been stripped, as if a live vacuum cleaner had swept through the undergrowth. So lush were the bushes, though, that the vacuum cleaner hadn't needed to raise or lower its head. Cruising along at mouth level, it had eaten its fill. Behind me, a gentle exhalation, a sort of "whoof, huff, whoof," suggested not so subtly that a black bear might not care to share its movable feast. As I kept hiking, the exhalations slowly receded. In more ways than one, I was pleased at the non-encounter, and at the wildness that remains an untarnished part of Robbinswold's character. Here, at least, Aldo Leopold misspoke.

For thirty years I've stayed away from the Olympic Peninsula— content to live with my memories, grateful that I never saw it loved to death, or cut to the quick. I was afraid it might resemble a Scotty's Castle, a Tucson, a Mount Rushmore, or, worse yet, a Glen Canyon buried beneath the silt. Except for the massive clearcuts in the valleys outside the Olympic National Park, however, I discovered a landscape much as I remembered it. Steeper, perhaps, the passes more distant than they seemed when I was twenty, the trails a little more vertical, the peaks a little higher. Many of the desirable campsites are overused, to be sure, but I found it's still possible to hike away from people. Wolves may not shadow the trails—though there's a plan for their reintroduction—but I might well encounter a black bear browsing for berries, hear elk bugle in the fall, or lean against the trunk of a very ancient tree.

It's possible to sit alone at Robbinswold, too, on the beach in front of the staff house, the same spot I frequented during my counselor years. I can see harbor seals floating on their backs, and a great blue heron skimming along the shore. Four girls, shouldering two canoes, carry them into the boathouse. Six more prowl the water's edge, pick tiny crabs from under the rocks. As the bell on the lodge porch rings for the hoppers to come to their tasks, I think about being twelve again. At breakfast this morning, a counselor nicknamed Oshkosh explained a sociological theory about the appeal of summer camps. Anticipatory patterns draw us back year after year. We don't need to relearn the structure, since it repeats itself in rituals as predicated as they are predictable. It's a safe place for an adolescent, a nurturing environment where children and teen-agers—and even young adults—grow toward maturity. It always remains a haven of sorts, even for a senior citizen who might wish to hug a giant cedar.

If that cedar falls, it may become what is called a rain forest collonade, which sprouts several seedlings equidistant along its fallen trunk. With the passage of time, those tiny evergreens grow straight and tall. Perhaps Robbinswold is a kind of human collonade, its rituals and its stories nursing women from generation to generation. But just as a rain forest is a continuous process of succession, so is a summer camp. Although I may anticipate and appreciate the repetitions and the patterns, I would never, ever, under any circumstances, want to be twelve or twenty again. It's good to be here today, but I happily close the photo album's pages.

A bald eagle soars off the rocky point south of camp, traces the waves and then speeds into the distance. I watch the tide cover the shingle beach, the pebbles and rocks, the starfish and barnacles, the kelp and the oysters. The water laps around and then nearly over the Barnacle Bay rock that hasn't moved in half a century. Tomorrow morning, fog will cover Hood Canal. The light will play tricks again, pretend to be a colorless rainbow, perhaps. Gradually, the sun will burn off the mists, the water will sparkle, and Robbinswold will be as I've always remembered it. I'll interpret it differently, though. I'll better understand its history of ghosts, the trees that once were here, the people who both logged and loved the land. I'll better understand *GhostWest*, too, a place where the future has always depended on the past, where stories have always intertwined, where the dynamics of place have always been truer than the stasis of memory.

Some spirits from the past have vanished completely—the American Indian bones from Nevada's playa, the mountain men of Wyoming, the Great Sioux War participants, even the vast prolific herds of buffalo. Others, like the logging and ranching Robbins and Irwin families, or like the women of the Willa Cather Pioneer Memorial, have transformed their ghosts into presences as immediate and as compelling as the past that helps define them. Still others, Cather's stories or Georgia O'Keeffe's paintings, for example, will never be ghosts at all, though they may haunt our imaginations forever. And then there are our own personal spirits—our individual experiences, our particular memories, our idiosyncratic reconstructions. Sitting alone on the Robbinswold beach, watching the mists and the tide, my own ghost haunts me still. The ancient trees shadow me more restlessly, however, a reminder of the cost at which the West was won.

SOURCES AND SUGGESTIONS
FOR FURTHER READING

GhostWest came to my imagination while I was writing *Earthtones: A Nevada Album* with photographer Stephen Trimble. When I finished the *Earthtones* chapter titled "Ghosts," I realized that my thinking about a West haunted by its histories had only begun. My reading had only begun, too. I've always devoured books about the American West, but *Earthtones* and *GhostWest* led me into other fields as well. In addition to thick novels and environmental essays, the usual favorites of this English professor, I found myself reading about geography and geology, archaeology and anthropology, biology and biography, ecology and economics, more and more history, and popular culture. To name every single book that may have influenced my thinking would be impossible, for *GhostWest* is really an assimilation of a lifetime of research and experiences. What follows is a brief discussion of the most useful direct and indirect sources for each chapter's research, plus some suggestions for further reading on each topic.

As I traveled into new territory, a great many people shared information and ideas with me. I acknowledge their contributions in the following pages. I also want to emphasize the critical roles played by my colleagues and students in the Literature and Environment Program at the University of Nevada, Reno. Without their constant stimulus, *GhostWest* might still be haunting my imagination instead of appearing in print. A number of people read drafts early and late, and made very helpful suggestions—Mike and Eryn Branch, Scott Casper, Valerie Cohen, Muriel Davis, Bob Merrill, Elizabeth Raymond, David Robertson and his University of California at Davis graduate seminar. I appreciate all the sound advice. Finally, I thank Lois Snedden once again, for listening to my embryonic musings, for reading lots of pages eventually discarded, and for sharing all the adventures.

Introduction: Shadowed Places

Originally published in 1896, James Mooney, *The Ghost-Dance Religion and the Sioux Outbreak of 1890* (Glorieta, N. Mex.: Rio Grande Press, 1973), is crucial to any interpretation of Wovoka and the Ghost Dance religion. So is Paul Bailey, *The Indian Messiah* (Los Angeles: Westernlore Press, 1957), and Michael Hittman, *Wovoka and the Ghost Dance* (Yerington, Nev.: Grace Dangberg Foundation, Inc., 1990). The latter contains the most recent research about Jack Wilson. Mooney's book contains the old "Song of the Ancient People." Among the many intriguing books about the Donner party, my favorite remains an old standby first published in 1960, George R. Stewart, *Ordeal by Hunger* (Boston: Houghton Mifflin, 1988). Two informative new publications are Donald Hardesty, *The Archaeology of the Donner Party* (Reno: Univ. of Nevada Press, 1997), and Frank Mullen, *The Donner Party Chronicles* (Reno: Nevada Humanities Committee, 1997), which reports first-hand accounts of the trek and includes a full array of photographs by Marilyn Newton. The well-marked site of the Donner tragedy and the lesser-known Ghost Dance locale are almost in my own backyard. To see the sharp contrast between history preserved and history neglected, both are worth visiting, especially in the winter when snow makes the stories seem more immediate.

Chapter 1. Montana: Battle Stations

So many books have been written about George Armstrong Custer and the Battle of the Little Bighorn that it's difficult to single out the most significant. James Welch, with Paul Stekler, *Killing Custer: The*

SOURCES

Battle of the Little Bighorn and the Fate of the Plains Indians (New York: Penguin Books, 1995), is a good place for a nonscholar to begin. Two other major influences on my thinking were Brian W. Dippie, *Custer's Last Stand: The Anatomy of an American Myth* (Lincoln: Univ. of Nebraska Press, 1976), which dissects the multiple versions of Custer's reputation, and Richard S. Slotkin, *The Fatal Environment: The Myth of the Frontier in the Age of Industrialization* (New York: Atheneum, 1985), which puts the Custer myth into a national perspective. Charles E. Rankin, ed., *Legacy: New Perspectives on the Battle of the Little Bighorn* (Helena, Mont.: Montana Historical Society, 1996), brings together the best recent scholarship. Richard Allan Fox, Jr., *Archaeology, History, and Custer's Last Battle* (Norman: Univ. of Oklahoma Press, 1993), teaches the importance of bullets and spent cartridges in reconstructing the process of the encounter.

To understand more about the battle itself, and the events surrounding it, I looked at several early recollections. For the Rosebud, I recommend John Gregory Bourke's memoirs, *Diary of John Gregory Bourke, 1872–1896* (Ann Arbor, Mich.: Univ. Microfilms International, [198–?]) and Bourke's *On the Border with Crook* (Chicago: Rio Grande Press, 1962), as well as John F. Finerty, *War-Path and Bivouac: The Big Horn and Yellowstone Expedition*, ed. Milo Milton Quaife (Chicago: Lakeside Press, 1955). For the Little Bighorn, key accounts include trooper William C. Slapper's in E. A. Brininstool, *A Trooper with Custer* (Columbus, Ohio: Hunter-Trader-Trapper Co., 1925), Frazier Hunt and Robert Hunt, *I Fought with Custer* (New York: Charles Scribner's Sons, 1947), and John M. Carroll, ed., *The Two Battles of the Little Big Horn* (New York: Liveright, 1974). American Indian recollections like Chief Two Moons' can be found in Leslie Tillott, ed., *Wind on the Buffalo Grass* (New York: Thomas Y. Crowell Co., 1976), and David Humphreys Miller, *Custer's Fall: The Native American Side of the Story* (New York: Meridian, 1992). My favorite, however, is Thomas B. Marquis's translation of Kate Bighead, *She Watched Custer's Last Battle* (Hardin, Mont.: Custer Battle Museum, 1933). Though I couldn't fit verse into my chapter, I thoroughly enjoyed scanning *Bards of the Little Big Horn*, compiled by Brian W. Dippie in collaboration with John M. Carroll (Bryan, Tex.: Guidon Press, 1978).

Neil C. Mangum, *Battle of the Rosebud: Prelude to the Little Bighorn* (El Segundo, Calif.: Upton and Sons, 1987), is the standard interpretation of that confrontation. Useful, too, is J. W. Vaughn, *With Crook at the Rosebud* (reprint, Lincoln: Univ. of Nebraska Press, 1988).

Conversations with Kitty Belle Deernose, archival curator, and John A. Doerner, chief historian at the Little Bighorn Battlefield National Monument, helped me interpret the subtleties of the battle and the subsequent myths. Moreover, Kitty shared a photocopy of Arapooish's "Crow Country." Both Kitty and John took time to read a draft of my chapter. The Park Service has published several informative pamphlets, brochures, and trail descriptions that may be obtained at the monument. I especially recommend the official park handbook, Robert M. Utley, *Little Bighorn Battlefield* (Washington, D.C.: U.S. Department of the Interior, 1988). Finally, my thanks to Wallace Stevens for "The Snow Man," a poem that has always intrigued me.

Chapter 2. Kansas: Buffalo Grounds

The quotations which begin and end this chapter came from the 1843 diary of Warren Angus Ferris, *Life in the Rocky Mountains* (Denver: Old West Publishing Co., 1983). Francis Haines, *The Buffalo* (Norman: Univ. of Oklahoma Press, 1995) gives the most definitive biological and historical information about the herds and their demise, and narrates the "true" Buffalo Bill Cody story. Most of the remaining buffalo observations can be found in the nineteenth-century eyewitness accounts quoted in Eugene D. Fleharty, *Wild Animals and Settlers on the Great Plains* (Norman: Univ. of Oklahoma Press, 1995). The National Cowboy Hall of Fame was helpful, too, with a display that cites Matt Clarkson, who hunted and hauled hides near Grinnell in 1872.

I thoroughly enjoyed two older books—Martin S. Garretson, *A Short History of the American Bison* (Freeport, N.Y.: Books for Libraries Press, 1934), which suggested that "a man might have walked across the valley on their huddled backs," and Mari Sandoz, *The Buffalo Hunters* (New York: Hastings House, 1954). A quirky 1899 biography written by Buffalo Bill's sister, Helen Cody Wetmore, *Buffalo Bill: Last of the Great Scouts* (reprint, Lincoln: Univ. of Nebraska Press, 1965), is fun to read. Finally, I want to thank Karen Tanner, who works for the Garden City Visitors Convention Authority and who so generously shared her knowledge and her time.

Chapter 3. Texas: Cowboy Country

I would guess that more people have written books about Texas than about the Battle of the Little Bighorn, so I will mention only those that had a direct bearing on this chapter. Andy Adams, *The Log of a Cowboy* (reprint, Lincoln: Univ. of Nebraska Press, 1964), first published in 1903, in my opinion remains the best composite view of nineteenth-century cattle trailing, although Frank Collinson, *Life in the Saddle*, ed. and arranged by Mary Whatley Clarke, (Norman: Univ. of Oklahoma Press, 1963), is almost as informative. Critical to understanding how Clear Fork cowboying changed to ranching is Sallie Reynolds Matthews, *Interwoven: A Pioneer Chronicle* (Austin: Univ. of Texas Press, 1936), and its prequel, Frances Mayhugh Holden, *Lambshead before Interwoven: A Texas Chronicle 1848–1878* (College Station: Texas A&M Univ. Press, 1982). A day-to-day overview of twentieth-century Clear Fork ranch life can be found in *Lambshead Legacy: The Ranch Diary of Watt R. Matthews*, ed. Janet M. Neugebauer (College Station: Texas A&M Univ. Press, 1997). Three other books give further local and historic details: *The Throckmorton County History* (Throckmorton County History Committee. Lubbock, Tex.: Craftsman Printer, Inc., 1984), the 1894 *Historical and Biographical Record of the Cattle Industry and the Cattlemen of Texas and Adjacent Territory* (New York: Antiquarian Press, 1959), and the recent DeGolyer Library reprint of the 1914 *History of the Cattlemen of Texas* (Austin: Texas State Historical Association, 1991). *Tracks along the Clear Fork: Stories from Shackelford and Throckmorton Counties*, ed. Lawrence Clayton and Joan Halford Farmer (Abilene, Tex.: McWhiney Foundation Press, 2000), preserves recent interviews, personal reminiscences, and Clear Fork stories for posterity.

The most scholarly account of the history of this part of west Texas is Ty Cashion, *A Texas Frontier: The Clear Fork Country and Fort Griffin, 1849–1887* (Norman: Univ. of Oklahoma Press, 1996). I, of course, am partial to Lawrence Clayton's more personalized studies: *Cowboys: Ranch Life along the Clear Fork of the Brazos River* (Austin, Tex.: Eakin Press, 1997), *Ranch Rodeos in West Texas* (Abilene, Tex.: Hardin-Simmons Univ. Press, 1988), and *Watkins Reynolds Matthews: A Biography* (Abilene, Tex.: Hardin-Simmons Univ. Press, 1990). I learned about cross-breeding from *Deep in the Heart of Texas: Texas Ranchers in Their Own Words*, photographed and produced by Kathleen Jo Ryan, (Berkeley, Calif.: Ten Speed Press, 1999). George A. Boeck, Jr., *Texas Livestock Auctions: A Folklife Ethnography* (New York: AMS Press, 1990) helped me translate what I saw in Ranger, Texas. Berta Hart Nance's poem, "Cattle," is cited in full in *Here's to the Vinegarroon!* ed. Barney Nelson (Alpine, Tex.: Territorial Printer, Inc., 1989). For fiction about Texas, I recommend the books of Benjamin Capps and of Elmer Kelton. The latter's 1973 novel, *The Time It Never Rained* (New York: Forge Books, 1999), certainly clarified my understanding of drought. Tongue in cheek, I also recommend *http://www.wvmcattle.com* for a direct line on video auctions.

Lou and Charles Rodenberger, old friends from the Western Literature Association, helped me get started with my Texas research, introduced me to Mary Batchler Gaggino and her husband, Gino, and arranged for my stay on the J Lazy C Ranch. Without the help of Lawrence and Sonja Clayton—their hospitality, their stories, their insights, their suggestions about the first draft of the Texas chapter—I would have floundered. Thanks, too, to Laquetta Coan of the Ranger Livestock Auction. Texas covers a lot of territory, so I appreciate the focus all these friends helped me find.

Finally, I want to dedicate this particular *GhostWest* chapter to Lawrence, who died on December 31, 2000, a victim of ALS, Lou Gehrig's Disease. Although he was ill the whole time I was writing

SOURCES

"Cowboy Country," Lawrence graciously shared his vision of both the past and the future of west Texas. He epitomizes, for me, the genuine cowboy spirit in this land of mythic and very real ghosts.

Chapter 4. Wyoming: A Rendezvous

Fred R. Gowans, *Rocky Mountain Rendezvous* (Layton, Utah: Peregrine Smith Books, 1985), which contains Joseph Meek's description of the lady missionaries, gives the best-informed overview of the sixteen gatherings. Editors James H. Maguire, Peter Wild, and Donald A. Barclay, *A Rendezvous Reader: Tall, Tangled, and True Tales of the Mountain Men 1805–1850* (Salt Lake City: Univ. of Utah Press, 1997), bring together in one volume a wide variety of tall tales and excerpted first-hand recollections, although both Ferris's *Life in the Rocky Mountains*, which was listed in the sources for Chapter 2, and Washington Irving's *The Adventures of Captain Bonneville*, ed. Robert A. Rees and Alan Sandy (Boston: Twayne Publishers, 1977), are worth perusing more thoroughly. For the best fictional version of the mountain man's heyday and demise, I recommend A. B. Guthrie, Jr., *The Big Sky* (Boston: Houghton Mifflin, 1974), first published in 1947.

Chapter 5. Colorado: Savage Basins

Without Harriet Fish Backus's *Tomboy Bride* (Boulder, Colo.: Pruett Publishing, 1977), there could be no "Savage Basins" chapter. Written in 1969, *Tomboy Bride* is one of the most teachable memoirs of western settlement. I enjoyed my telephone conversations with Mrs. Backus's grandson, Rob Walton, and I thank him for suggesting that I contact Duane Smith, a historian of Colorado mining camps, who then read a draft of my chapter. I thank Dave Rote, of Dave's Jeep Tours in Telluride, for his happy-go-lucky conversation and his memorable drive up the Tomboy Road. Richard L. Fetter and Suzanne Fetter, *Telluride: From Pick to Powder* (Caldwell, Idaho: Caxton Printer, Ltd., 1979), detail the history of Telluride's early days.

Because Leadville played such a prominent role in Colorado's mining history, there are many books about its past. The critical first-person narrative to pair with *Tomboy Bride* is Otis Archie King, *Gray Gold* (Denver: Big Mountain Press, 1959). To learn more about Horace Tabor, I suggest Duane A. Smith, *Horace Tabor: His Life and the Legend* (Boulder, Colo.: Colorado Associate Univ. Press, 1973). Crucial to interpreting Leadville's history and its sequence of mining booms are Stephen M. Voynick's two studies, *Climax: The History of Colorado's Climax Molybdenum Mine* (Missoula, Mont.: Mountain Press, 1996) and *Leadville: A Miner's Epic* (Missoula: Mountain Press, 1984). Another useful book is Stanley Dempsey and James E. Fell, Jr., *Mining the Summit: Colorado's Ten Mile District, 1860–1960* (Norman: Univ. of Oklahoma Press, 1986). I also recommend Richard B. Francaviglia, *Hard Places: Reading the Landscape of America's Historic Mining Districts* (Ames: Univ. of Iowa Press, 1991).

Chapter 6. Oregon: Sand and Sea

All of this chapter's information about historic shipwrecks comes either from Don Marshall, *Oregon Shipwrecks* (Portland, Ore.: Binford & Mort Publishing, 1984), or from one of James A. Gibbs's two books, *Pacific Graveyard* (Portland: Binford & Mort Publishing, 1950) and *Shipwrecks of the Pacific Coast* (Portland: Binford & Mort Publishing, 1957). The seamen's quotations are found in *Oregon Shipwrecks*, but all three sources describe every wreck's demise. A reader, intrigued by one of my short paragraphs, can find many more descriptive details and historic information in either Marshall or Gibbs. Gibbs's *Oregon's Seacoast Lighthouses* (Medford, Ore.: Webb Research Group, 1992) provides an interesting corollary. A broader view of history along the Columbia River can be found in William Dietrich, *Northwest Passage: The Great Columbia River* (New York: Simon & Schuster, 1995). Finally, I strongly recommend a visit to the Columbia River Maritime Museum in Astoria, Oregon, which turned out to be one of the most fascinating museums I discovered while researching *GhostWest* chapters.

Chapter 7. North Dakota: Train Time

Ian Fraser, *Great Plains* (New York: Penguin, 1990), gives an excellent introduction to the people and the scenery of the Dakotas and eastern Montana. He, too, interviewed Bill Shemorry. Another perceptive book is Jonathan Raban, *Bad Land: An American Romance* (New York: Vintage Books, 1996). Even though Raban doesn't deal with North Dakota in particular, he captures the complexities of making a living today on the high plains. Two volumes more directly related to Dakota settlement are Elaine Lindgren, *Land in Her Own Name* (Fargo: North Dakota Institute for Regional Studies, 1991), and *Plains Folk: North Dakota's Ethnic History*, edited by William C. Sherman and Playford Thorson, (Fargo: North Dakota Institute for Regional Studies, 1988). Lundgren's book includes the words of Lucy Goldthorpe. Elwyn B. Robinson, *History of North Dakota* (Lincoln: Univ. of Nebraska Press, 1966), is the standard state history. Even more specialized is *The Wonder of Williams: A History of Williams County, North Dakota*, 2 vols, Marlene Eide, coordinator (Williston, N. Dak.: Williams Country Historical Society, 1975). I recommend driving the secondary roads of Williams County armed with *The WPA Guide to 1930s North Dakota*, reprinted by the State Historical Society of North Dakota in 1990. For a more contemporary assessment, with a pictorial accompaniment, I suggest Bryan Hodgson, photographs by Annie Griffiths, "Tough Times on the Prairie," *National Geographic*, March 1987.

Mostly, though, I recommend talking with the Shemorrys. Hospitable, gracious, knowledgeable, willing to share their stories and their experiences, Glo and Bill Shemorry are wonderful to interview. After just a day or two, I felt like I was with family. Four of Bill's books were critical to my understanding of North Dakota's past: William E. Shemorry, *The Lost Tales of Old Williston* (1986), *More Lost Tales of Old Dakota* (1988), *Mud, Sweat and Oil: The Early Days of the Williston Basin* (1991), and *Williams County Centennial Memoirs* (1991). Any of these may be obtained by writing directly to Bill, at P. O. Box

33, Williston, ND, 58801. I spoke with many residents of Williams County, but Chuck Wilder of Books on Broadway, Lane Thompson of Epping's Buffalo Trails Museum, Jerry Engle of the Williston Council for the Aged, the Nelsons from Temple, John Thorson from Tioga, and Avis Kohlman of the Hanks' Pioneer Trails Museum contributed most directly to *GhostWest*. I thank them all for taking time to welcome an outsider and to share so many stories.

Chapter 8. Nevada: Buried Bones

My chapter purposely disguises the location of a very special playa in Nevada. Because I want to keep visitors away and because the Paiute people would prefer silence, I also am purposely omitting the bibliographical reference to the 1988 archaeological study that explains what took place there and that is available to credentialed researchers. Thanks, too, to the Nevada Humanities Commission, which first published this chapter as "Dust to Dust" in *Western Technological Landscapes*, edited by Stephen Tchudi (Reno: Nevada Humanities Committee, 1998): 87–90. I later incorporated "Dust to Dust" in a longer essay, "Kingdom, Phylum, Class, Order: Twentieth-Century American Nature Writer," *Western American Literature* 33 (Winter 1999): 399–402. For those interested in the overall picture of the Great Basin before historic times, one book stands out, Donald K. Grayson, *The Desert's Past: A Natural Prehistory of the Great Basin* (Washington, D.C.: Smithsonian Institution Press, 1993). My thanks, of course, to Emily Dickinson for poem 258, "There's a certain slant of light."

Chapter 9. California: Sand Castles

Early Death Valley history is fully described in Leroy and Jean Johnson, *Escape from Death Valley* (Reno: Univ. of Nevada Press, 1987), Richard E. Lingenfelter and Richard A. Dwyer, *Death Valley Lore* (Reno: Univ. of Nevada Press, 1988), and Lingenfelter, *Death Valley and the Amargosa: A Land of Illusion* (Berkeley: Univ. of California Press, 1986). More particularized information can be found in Edwin Corle,

SOURCES

Death Valley and the Creek Called Furnace, photos by Ansel Adams (Los Angeles: Ward Ritchie Press, 1962). *Death Valley*, ed. Cheri Rae (Santa Barbara, Calif.: Olympus Press, 1991), an updated version of the 1938 WPA guide, is fun to use when traveling in the valley today.

Stanley Paher, *Death Valley's Scotty's Castle* (Las Vegas, Nev.: K C Publications, 1993) outlines, as its subtitle indicates, "the story behind the scenery." It provided my quotes describing the castle and nearby surroundings. *Death Valley Scotty's Castle: As Given by the Castle Guides* (Goldfield, Nev.: Castle Publishing Co., 1941) is an intriguing insider's look at the early tourist spiels. Eleanor Jordan Houston, *Death Valley Scotty Told Me* (Palm Desert, Calif.: Desert Printers, Inc., 1954) and Hank Johnston, *Death Valley Scotty: The Fastest Con in the West* (Glendale, Calif.: Trans-Anglo Books, 1981) tell more about the man behind the myth. Donald Duke, *Fred Harvey: Civilizer of the American Southwest* (Arcadia, Calif.: Pregel Press, 1995), best traces the Fred Harvey phenomenon. Edward Abbey writes about Death Valley in *Abbey's Road* (New York: E. P. Dutton, 1979) and also in *The Journey Home* (New York: E. P. Dutton, 1977). I borrowed Michael Cohen's title phrase, *A Garden of Bristlecones* (Reno: Univ. of Nevada Press, 1998), because it so aptly characterizes the flank of Telescope Peak.

To examine the American Dream in more detail, especially in terms of its California consequences, I recommend all three of Kevin Starr's books: *Americans and the California Dream: 1850–1915* (New York: Oxford Univ. Press, 1973), *Inventing the Dream: California through the Progressive Era* (New York: Oxford Univ. Press, 1985), and *Material Dreams: Southern California through the 1920s* (New York: Oxford Univ. Press, 1990). Enlightening, too, is Philip L. Fradkin, *The Seven States of California* (New York: Henry Holt and Co., 1995).

March and April weather can be chilly in Reno, so I have spent more spring vacations in Death Valley than I can recall. This chapter blurs together approximately a dozen different trips. Because I have good friends who have worked hard on the Timbisha Shoshone negotiations, I have been able to talk with the principals several times. My thanks to Pauline Esteves and Barbara Durham for those conversations, to past tribal administrator Richard Bolland who now works for the Park Service, and to Bill Helmer who left the Park Service to work for the tribe. Finally, I appreciate the guidance of Kay Fowler of the University of Nevada, Reno, anthropology department, whose energy and incomparable scholarship are preserving the wisdom of the Shoshone in Utah, Nevada, and California.

Chapter 10. Arizona: The Old Pueblo

Two old-timers' books were especially helpful in evoking the atmosphere of the Old Pueblo: Roy P. Drachman, *From Cowtown to Desert Metropolis* (San Francisco: Whitewing Press, 1999) and C. L. Sonnichsen, *Tucson: The Life and Times of an American City* (Norman: Univ. of Oklahoma Press, 1987). John Bourke's *On the Border with Crook*, cited in Chapter 1, tells about southern Arizona, too. I gleaned even more stories of the past from *Tucson: A Short History* (Tucson: Southwestern Mission Research Center, 1986). For recent data, I used information found in *High Country News* (January 18, 1999). Judy Nolte Temple, *Open Spaces, City Places: Contemporary Writers on the Changing Southwest* (Tucson: Univ. of Arizona Press, 1994), edited a collection of essays asking provocative questions about Sunbelt settlement patterns in the late twentieth century. Robert D. Kaplan, "Travels into America's Future," *Atlantic Monthly*, July 1998, offers some particularized answers.

Chapter 11. Nebraska: Catherland

Willa Cather's own writing gives the very best access to Cather country, so I quote her extensively in this chapter. Specifically, I drew excerpts from 1913's *O Pioneers!* (New York: Vintage, 1992), 1915's *The Song of the Lark* (New York: Vintage, 1999), 1918's *My Ántonia* (New York: Vintage, 1994), 1923's *A Lost Lady* (New York: Vintage, 1990), *Collected Stories* (New York: Vintage, 1992), and *Willa Cather in Person: Interviews, Speeches, and Letters*, edited by L. Brent Bohlke (Lincoln: Univ. of Nebraska Press, 1986). Under the general editorship of Susan Rosowski, the University of Nebraska Press is currently publishing new editions of Cather's works in the Willa Cather Scholarly Edition, with careful textual editing, explanatory notes, and an accompanying historical essay for each novel. Readers interested in further background information about Cather's books should consult these scholarly editions. To date, novels that have been published in the series include *O Pioneers!* (1992), *My Ántonia* (1995), *A Lost Lady* (1997), *Obscure Destinies* (1998), *Death Comes for the Archbishop* (1999), and *The Professor's House* (2001).

Mildred Bennett's 1951 study, *The World of Willa Cather* (reprint, Lincoln: Univ. of Nebraska Press, 1989), is crucial to understanding the writer's Red Cloud history, as is Edith Lewis, *Willa Cather Living: A Personal Record* (Athens, Ohio: Ohio Univ. Press, 1989). To learn more about Cather's life in general, I particularly recommend two books by James Woodress, *Willa Cather: A Literary Life* (Lincoln: Univ. of Nebraska Press, 1987), and *Willa Cather: Her Life and Art* (Lincoln: Univ. of Nebraska Press, 1970). I found Sharon O'Brien, *Willa Cather: The Emerging Voice* (New York: Oxford Univ. Press, 1987), intriguing, and Hermione Lee, *Double Lives* (New York: Pantheon Books, 1989), quite informative, too. Because Cather scholarship has increased tenfold in recent years, literary studies of Willa Cather's works abound. I hesitate to make specific recommendations because so many of those studies are focused in particular ways.

I owe special thanks to Sue Rosowski, another long-time Western Literature Association colleague and friend, who shared that hotel room in Fort Worth where I first met Mildred Bennett, who has nurtured and guided my appreciation for Willa Cather's writing, and who critiqued an early draft of this chapter. Many other Cather scholars are WLA friends, too—Marilyn Arnold, Ron Butler, Evelyn Funda, John Murphy, and Bob Thacker all have taught me something about their muse. Mildred Bennett, who died in 1989, figured crucially in my design of this chapter and in my interpretation of Red Cloud. And finally, my thanks to Pat Phillips, who now has moved with her family to Omaha, away from Catherland.

Chapter 12. New Mexico: Land of Enchantment

As was true of Willa Cather, the best way to understand Georgia O'Keeffe is through the work of the artist herself. *Georgia O'Keeffe, A Studio Book* (New York: Viking Press, 1976), contains her words as well as reproductions of many of her best-known paintings. A display at Ghost Ranch (where O'Keeffe lived and painted for many years—now a Presbyterian conference center and retreat) highlights her possessive pronouncements about the Cerro Pedernal. Laurie Lisle, *Portrait of an Artist: A Biography of Georgia O'Keeffe* (Albuquerque: Univ. of New Mexico Press, 1986), thoroughly narrates the events of O'Keeffe's life.

Two books by Charles C. Eldredge put O'Keeffe's artistry in context: *Georgia O'Keeffe* (New York: Henry N. Abrams, 1991) and *Georgia O'Keeffe: American and Modern* (New Haven: Yale Univ. Press, 1993). A recent article by Thomas Larson, "Skull and Roses: Reflections on Enshrining Georgia O'Keeffe," *Southwest Review* (1998), offers a unique perspective on the ever-expanding O'Keeffe coterie. Leslie Poling-Kempes, *Valley of Shining Stone* (Tucson: Univ. of Arizona Press, 1997), fully describes the Ghost Ranch country of New Mexico. The Georgia O'Keeffe museum, which opened its doors in the summer of 1997, is simply breath-taking. It is not to be missed. While there, I purchased *The Georgia O'Keeffe Museum* (Santa Fe: Harry N. Abrams, 1997) and two collectors' issues: *El Palacio*, Summer–Fall 1997, and *Santa Fean*, 1997. "Land of Enchantment" was published originally in *Writing Nature* (Summer 1998): 12–14.

Chapter 13. South Dakota: Sculptured Stone

Many monographs, available at the two monuments' visitors centers, describe the sculpting processes and cite the sculptors' personal visions. For Mount Rushmore, I suggest Lincoln Borglum, *My Father's Mountain*, (Rapid City, S.Dak.: Fenwinn Press, 1997), Rose Mary Goodson, *The Rushmore Story* (Piedmont, S.Dak.: Argus Printers, 1979), T. D. Griffith, *The Four Faces of Freedom* (Rapid City, S.Dak.: Mount Rushmore National Memorial Society, 1992), and Dorothy K.

Hiliburn and Steven L. Walker, *Mount Rushmore: Monument to America's Democracy* (Scottsdale, Ariz.: Camelback/Canyonlands Venture, 1997). For Crazy Horse, I suggest Robb DeWall, *Carving a Dream* (Crazy Horse, S.Dak.: Korczk's Heritage, Inc., 1992), *Korczak: Storyteller in Stone*, ed. Robb DeWall (Crazy Horse,: Korczak's Heritage, Inc., 1996), *A Dream in Progress*, ed. Robb DeWall (Crazy Horse: Korczak's Heritage, Inc., 1998), and a booklet titled *Indian Museum of North America* (Crazy Horse: Korczak's Heritage, 1996).

Sven G. Froiland, *Natural History of the Black Hills and Badlands* (Sioux Falls, S. Dak.: Augustana College, 1990), explains the biology and the geologic features of the area. Martha Linde, *Rushmore's Golden Valley* (Keystone, S.Dak.: Permelia Publishing, 1988), describes the terrain before Gutzon Borglum began his work, while Rex Alan Smith, *The Carving of Mount Rushmore* (New York: Abbeville Press, 1985) enthusiastically narrates the sculpting process and progress. Albert Boime, *The Unveiling of the National Icons* (Cambridge: Cambridge Univ. Press, 1998), gives a very different point of view about Mt. Rushmore and about several other national shrines.

Tom Charging Eagle, *Black Hills: Sacred Hills*, (Chamberlain, S.Dak.: Tipi Press, 1992) poetically critiques the way in which the white settlers desecrated hallowed land. A more theoretical treatment of American Indians and their plight in the 1860s and '70s occurs in the pages of Charles M. Robinson, III, *A Good Year to Die* (Norman: Univ. of Oklahoma Press, 1995). Peter Blue Cloud's poem, "Crazy Horse Monument," can be found in *Unsettling America*, eds. Maria Mazziotti Gillan and Jennifer Gillan, (New York: Penguin, 1994). I also want to acknowledge the lines I borrowed from Percy Bysshe Shelley's poem "Ozymandias."

Chapter 14. Oklahoma: Shades of the Past

Along with *The Fatal Environment*, listed as a source for Chapter 1, two other books by Richard S. Slotkin heavily influenced my ruminations about violence: *Gunfighter Nation: The Myth of the Frontier in Twentieth-Century America* (New York: Atheneum, 1992), and *Regen-*

eration through Violence: The Mythology of the American Frontier, 1600–1860 (Middletown, Conn.: Wesleyan Univ. Press, 1973). The University of Oklahoma Press has recently republished all three of Slotkin's studies. Equally important to my thinking was the work of Richard Maxwell Brown: *Historical Studies of American Violence and Vigilantism* (New York: Oxford Univ. Press, 1975), *No Duty to Retreat: Violence and Values in American History and Society* (New York: Oxford Univ. Press, 1991), and "Violence," in *The Oxford History of the American West*, ed. Clyde A. Milner II, Carol A. O'Connor, and Martha A. Sandweiss (New York: Oxford Univ. Press, 1994). Not everyone agrees with an American thesis of frontier violence. A provocative scholarly dissension can be found in "How the West Got Wild: American Media and Frontier Violence," *The Western Historical Quarterly*, Autumn 2000, a roundtable discussion that disputes Slotkin's and Brown's assumptions.

The imagined first paragraphs of this chapter grew from my research for Chapter 1 and Chapter 3. The General Sheridan remark is quoted by Dee Brown in *Bury My Heart at Wounded Knee* (New York: Henry Holt, 1970). Patricia Nelson Limerick, *The Legacy of Conquest: The Unbroken Past of the American West* (New York: W. W. Norton & Co., 1987), and Richard White, *"It's Your Misfortune and None of My Own": A New History of the American West* (Norman: Univ. of Oklahoma Press, 1991), strongly influenced my overall conceptualizing, too. To fathom the contradictions of Waco, I consulted *From the Ashes: Making Sense of Waco*, ed. James R. Lewis (Boston: Rowman & Littlefield Publishers, 1994). Mark S. Hamm, *Apocalypse in Oklahoma: Waco and Ruby Ridge Revenged*, (Boston: Northeastern Univ. Press, 1997), connects the two tragedies. I finally decided to omit all mention of Waco in my chapter, but my reading raised some provocative historic questions of western antagonism toward our federal government. Any discussion could surely be extended, especially in light of the September 11, 2001 tragedy, which occured more than a year after I wrote this chapter.

Jim Ross and Paul Myers, *We Will Never Forget: Eyewitness Accounts of the Oklahoma Federal Building Bombing* (Austin, Tex.: Eakin Press, 1996), is an excruciating oral history of the Murrah event. To learn more about the Memorial, I suggest going to *http://connections. oklahoman.net/memorial*. Better yet, the Oklahoma City National Memorial and the Institute for the Prevention of Terrorism should be visited in person.

Chapter 15. Utah: Glen Canyon Reservoir

I begin by recommending two web sites, The Glen Canyon Institute's *http://glencanyon.org* and The Friends of Lake Powell's *http://www.lakepowell.org*. Both contain up-to-date information about the science, the politics, and the passion. Then, any study of the river itself must start with John Wesley Powell, *The Exploration of the Colorado River and Its Canyons* (New York: Penguin, 1963). The *Dominguez-Escalante Journal*, ed., Ted J. Warner (Provo, Utah: Brigham Young Univ. Press, 1976), gives an early glimpse of the canyon, too. C. Gregory Crampton, *Ghosts of Glen Canyon* (Salt Lake City: Tower Productions, 1998), more fully explains the human ghosts. Other books containing pre-dam pictures and descriptions include: Eliot Porter, *The Place No One Knew*, ed. David Brower (San Francisco: Sierra Club Books, 1963), and *The Colorado River through Glen Canyon before Lake Powell*, ed. Eleanor Inskip (Moab, Utah: Inskip Ink, 1995).

The history of the Glen Canyon dam is specifically addressed in Russell Martin, *A Story That Stands Like a Dam: Glen Canyon and the Struggle for the Soul of the West* (New York: Henry Holt and Co., 1989). After I drafted this chapter, Jared Farmer, *Glen Canyon Dammed: Inventing Lake Powell and the Canyon Country* (Tucson: Univ. of Arizona Press, 1999), published a book that examines the ways in which tourists have impacted this area and which also shares many quotes from voices pro and con. I recommend his extensive footnotes to those readers who want the names of additional titles. Both studies—Martin's and Farmer's—are excellent. Warren Frizell, *Spillway Tests at Glen Canyon Dam* (Denver: U.S. Department of the Interior, 1985), is properly alarming.

For descriptions of the beauty of Lake Powell, I relied heavily on *Lake Powell: Jewel of the Colorado* (Washington, D.C.: U.S. Government Printing Office, 1965). No author is named, but I've been told that Floyd Doming probably wrote most of the words. I also read Stan Jones, *Spectacular Lake Powell* (Tucson, Ariz.: Sun Country Publications, n.d.—the price on the cover is $1.95) and *Stan Jones' Ramblings by Boat and Boot in Lake Powell Country* (Page, Ariz.: Northland Press, 1983), Colin Warren, *Velvet Waters, Canyon Walls: A Lake Powell Adventure* (Flagstaff, Ariz.: Northland Press, 1983), Bob Hirsch, *First Class Adventure: Houseboating on Lake Powell* (1996), and Larry L. Meyer, "Going Home: A Lake Powell Love Affair," *Arizona Highways*, June 1987. Gary Ladd has published a fine collection of photographs, *Lake Powell* (Santa Barbara, Calif.: Companion Press, 1994). I also enjoyed a good conversation with Julia Betz, director of the John Wesley Powell Museum in Page, Arizona.

For creative writing that essentially disapproves of the dam, I recommend essays in Wallace Stegner's 1969 collection, *The Sound of Mountain Water* (New York: Penguin, 1997), Bruce Berger, *There Was a River* (Tucson: Univ. of Arizona Press, 1994) and several books by Edward Abbey: *Desert Solitaire* (New York: Ballantine Books, 1968), *Down the River* (New York: E. P. Dutton, 1982), *The Monkey Wrench Gang* (New York: Avon, 1976), and *One Life at a Time, Please* (New York: Henry Holt & Co., 1988). Eleanor Inskip's book includes excerpts by many other relevant essayists. Colin Fletcher, *River: One Man's Journey down the Colorado, Source to Sea* (New York: Vintage Books, 1997), denigrates Lake Powell quite thoroughly. My favorite indictment, however, is Katie Lee, *All My Rivers Are Gone: A Journey of Discovery through Glen Canyon* (Boulder, Colo.: Johnson Books, 1998). Vaughn Short, *Raging River, Lonely Trail* (Tucson, Ariz.: Two Horses Press, 1978) and Tess Gallagher in *Lake Powell: A Canyon Transformed*, ed. Ann Weiler Walka (Flagstaff: Museum of Northern Arizona, 1994) wrote poems about the canyon country. Steven Hannon, *Glen Canyon* (Denver: Kokopelli Books, 1997) has penned a marvelously irreverent novel. Don Fowler, professor of anthropology at the University of Nevada, Reno, regaled me with stories of graduate student days spent cataloguing the artifacts now under water. His many, many Glen Canyon photographs showed me the place I could never know.

SOURCES

Chapter 16. Idaho: Lava Land

For general and geologic information, I relied on materials readily available at the monument's visitors center: the official National Park handbook, *Craters of the Moon* (Washington D.C.: U.S. Department of the Interior, 1991), Paul Henderson, *Craters of the Moon: Around the Loop* (Arco, Idaho: Craters of the Moon Natural History Association, Inc., 1994), and David Clark, *Craters of the Moon: Idaho's Unearthly Landscape* (Arco, Idaho: Craters of the Moon Natural History Association, Inc., 1990). Most important, I read R. W. Limbert, "Among the Craters of the Moon," *The National Geographic Magazine*, January to June 1924. A more scientific look at the area can be found in Jennifer A. Blakesley and R. Gerald Wright, *A Review of Scientific Research at Craters of the Moon National Monument* (Moscow, Idaho: University of Idaho, 1988).

Chapter 17. Washington: Ancient Forests

Balanced, informative, perceptive, William Dietrich's book, *The Final Forest: The Battle for the Last Great Trees of the Pacific Northwest* (New York: Penguin Books, 1992) is the one to read first. For a contemporary forestry point of view, I consulted Hamish Kimmins's textbook, *Balancing Act: Environmental Issues in Forestry*, 2d edition (Vancouver: Univ. of British Columbia Press, 1997). Ernie Niemi and Ed Whitelaw with Elizabeth Grossman, "Bird of Doom . . . Or Was It?" *Amicus Journal*, Fall 2000, clarified what has happened in the Pacific Northwest during the past ten years. I gleaned more general information from Robert L. Wood, *Olympic Mountains Trail Guide* (Seattle: The Mountaineers, 1984), from *Visitors' Guide to Ancient Forests of Washington*, by the Dittmar Family for the Wilderness Society (Seattle: The Mountaineers, 1996), and from a reference book that's absolutely invaluable to anyone who cares about ecosystem details, *Plants of the Pacific Northwest Coast*, compiled and edited by Jim Pojar and Andy MacKinnon (Vancouver, B.C.: Lone Pine Publishing, 1994).

I began looking at the Olympic Peninsula history with Robert L.

Wood, *The Land That Slept Late: The Olympic Mountains in Legend and History* (Seattle: The Mountaineers, 1995), which contains the wonderful descriptions by Joseph P. O'Neil and James Wickersham. Larry Overland, *Early Settlement of Lake Cushman* (Belfair and Shelton, Wash.: Mason County Historical Society, 1974), was useful, too. I especially enjoyed the reportorial overview in *Voice of the Wild Olympics*, ed., Sally Warren Soest (Seattle: Olympic Parks Associates, 1988), and the creative writing in *Island of Rivers: An Anthology Celebrating Fifty Years of Olympic National Park*, ed. Nancy Beres, Mitzi Chandler, and Russell Dalton (Seattle: Pacific Northwest National Parks & Forest Association, 1988). The Aldo Leopold quote comes from *Sand County Almanac with Essays on Conservation from Round River* (New York: Ballantine Books, 1970).

I owe an enormous thank you to Jim Messmer, camp properties manager for the Totem Girl Scout Council. Not only did he spend precious days with me as I walked around Robbinswold, asking endless questions, but he shared his own perspective on the camp and on logging in the twenty-first century. Thanks also to Bart Robbins, and to his family, for their stories. Finally, thank you to all my camp friends from days past. You're still there, you know, in the Robbinswold of my imagination, an important inspiration for this book of special ghosts.

www.ingramcontent.com/pod-product-compliance
Lightning Source LLC
Chambersburg PA
CBHW020751160426
43192CB00006B/303